Is It Time to Let Meritocracy Go?

Despite meritocratic claims of equal opportunity, official statistics released by the Ministry of Education, Singapore, reveal that a large segment of the Malay population has sustained the lowest academic achievement from 1987 to 2011. This statistical representation raises the possibility of a politically induced, systemic inequality as a point of investigation.

To investigate this seeming contradiction between the rhetoric and practice of equal educational opportunity, Nadira Talib analyses education policies by drawing on a synthesis of philosophical perspectives and critical discourse analysis as a way of making explicit how the historical constitution of the learner is linked to the legitimisation of inequitable education policies that favour corporatist practices. By making explicit how the underlying assumption of the policy 'logic' that increasing expenditure on 'talents' must necessarily involve the increasing welfare of everybody is both unsubstantiated and arbitrary, the book presents a moral political problem in demonstrating how education policies are unfounded and unsupported through the idea of meritocracy.

Nadira Talib holds a Ph.D. from The University of Queensland, Australia. She focuses on developing a method of synthesising philosophical deliberations with discourse analysis in analysing social policy. In questioning the systems that separate and divide human beings one from another, her work centres on examining how adhering to the perceived demands of surrealistic political economies is imbricated within the relations of morality and ethics. Her publications are featured in *ScienceDaily* and in an editorial review of 'The Top 100 Cited Discourse Studies' in the subject area of 'linguistics and language', in the years 2015–2019.

Routledge Critical Studies in Asian Education

English Language Teacher Preparation in Asia
Policy, Research and Practice
Edited by Subhan Zein and Richmond Stroupe

Lesson Study and Schools as Learning Communities
Asian School Reform in Theory and Practice
Edited by Atsushi Tsukui and Masatsugu Murase

The Asian EFL Classroom
Issues, Challenges and Future Expectations
Edited by Soo-Ok Kwen and Bernard Spolsky

Teacher Education for English as a Lingua Franca
Perspectives from Indonesia
Edited by Subhan Zein

The Governance and Management of Universities in Asia
Global Influences and Local Responses
Chang Da Wan, Molly N.N. Lee, and Hoe Yeong Loke

Building Teacher Capacity in Vietnamese English Language Teaching
Research, Policy and Practice
Edited by Van Canh Le, Hoa Thi Mai Nguyen, Thi Thuy Minh Nguyen, Roger Barnard

Is it Time to Let Meritocracy Go?
Examining the Case of Singapore
Nadira Talib

For more information about this series, please visit: www.routledge.com/Routledge-Critical-Studies-in-Asian-Education/book-series/RCSAE

Is It Time to Let Meritocracy Go?

Examining the Case of Singapore

Nadira Talib

Routledge
Taylor & Francis Group
LONDON AND NEW YORK

The HEAD Foundation

First published 2021
by Routledge
2 Park Square, Milton Park, Abingdon, Oxon OX14 4RN

and by Routledge
52 Vanderbilt Avenue, New York, NY 10017

Routledge is an imprint of the Taylor & Francis Group, an informa business

British Library Cataloguing-in-Publication Data
A catalogue record for this book is available from the British Library

Library of Congress Cataloging-in-Publication Data
Names: Talib, Nadira, author.
Title: Is it time to let meritocracy go? : examining the case of Singapore / Nadira Talib.
Description: Abingdon, Oxon ; New York, NY : Routledge, 2020. |
Series: Routledge critical studies in Asian education |
Includes bibliographical references and index.
Identifiers: LCCN 2020006037 (print) | LCCN 2020006038 (ebook) |
ISBN 9781138320000 (hardback) | ISBN 9780367502874 (paperback) |
ISBN 9780429453625 (ebook)
Subjects: LCSH: Educational equalization--Singapore. |
Merit (Ethics)--Singapore. | Discrimination in education--Singapore. |
Academic achievement--Singapore. | Education and state--Singapore.
Classification: LCC LC213.3.S5 T35 2020 (print) |
LCC LC213.3.S5 (ebook) | DDC 379.2/6095957--dc23
LC record available at https://lccn.loc.gov/2020006037
LC ebook record available at https://lccn.loc.gov/2020006038

ISBN: 978-1-138-32000-0 (hbk)
ISBN: 978-0-429-45362-5 (ebk)

Typeset in Galliard
by Taylor & Francis Books

Contents

In order to treat people the way they are being treated we have to commodify the individual. So the individual himself or herself needs to become a commodity, which means that our value is based simply on what we produce or what we acquire, but not actually who we are. It's not based on just our very existence as human beings. A way that you attain value is to contribute, so who you are as a human being, in your very existence, is insufficient to give you value. You have to be producing something. People are desperately trying to make themselves useful totally ignoring who they are. It's the foundation of most chronic illnesses in our society because of the mind/body entity. But the very ideology that dying people are useless, or that anybody is useless, is a reflection of the capitalist idea that people are only useful when they produce.

Gabor Maté, 2012, 'What Promotes Positive Health'
(https://www.youtube.com/watch?v=rYbeyU3pQvI)

Preface

Within a multi-ethnic society that could not afford ethnic discrimination, the government of Singapore sought to enshrine meritocracy as a core value and promote advancement by merit (Rahim, 1998, p. 5). Driven by economic imperatives and efficiency, streaming was introduced as a policy in 1979 and an explicit form of structuration became widely practised in schools. While official discourse seeks to defend streaming as central to achieving success and reducing attrition rates, statistics released by the Ministry of Education reveal that a large segment of the Malay population has sustained the lowest academic achievement from 1987 to 2011 (MOE, 1997; 2012), despite meritocratic claims of equal opportunity. In order to understand how the inconsistencies between educational meritocracy and inequity have been made manifest, this monograph analyses education policies by drawing on a synthesis of philosophical perspectives and critical discourse analysis as a way of making explicit how the historical constitution of the learner is linked to the legitimisation of inequitable education policies that favour corporatist practices.

Specifically, to understand how we have been trapped in our own history (Foucault, 1982a, p. 780), where the ideology that economic growth is the (only) way forward has been taken as self-evident, and to answer questions about inequality in Singapore (Goh, 2016), this monograph focuses on *how historically*, education policies contribute to systematically engineering consent for inequality within a meritocratic system. In order to know the truth of this particular dimension, the book turns to a philosophical-analytical method to examine the conditions under which pursuing the finite-driven goal of economic growth has fuelled inequality. It is not the purpose of this monograph to trace the movement of policy discourse till the present, but rather to show that inequality has deep roots in history, through analysing the evolution of education policies between 1979 and 2019. In order to interpret the contemporary state of systematic inequality, there is a need to trace its historical and evolutionary development and construction (Garrity, 2010, p. 203). Policies of the past can influence and interfere with the proposals and propositions of future policies as long as one is not aware of this past (cf. Bohm, 2005, p. 257). This is not to say that past 'explains' or determines the present state of inequality, but in showing 'how' it may have happened, this monograph describes the chain of events of which it seemed to be a part and provides empirical guidance regarding the genesis and prevalence of structural inequality (cf. Watts, 1951, p. 126).

The analysis highlights that value judgments are continually at work in policy discourse and that despite the strong discourse of meritocracy that the Singapore education system promotes, the eternally recurring metaphors of flexibility, diversity, choice, and opportunity – as 'engines' of neo-liberal discourse – provide the necessary basis from which to rationalise unequal structural reforms as a desirable form of ethical practice to pursue economic growth. By tracing and examining these metaphors, the policy texts reveal a particular emphasis on the simultaneous processes of truth production and reproduction, supporting and supported by means and modes of value distribution, in the form of meritocratic inequality. More importantly, by making explicit how the underlying assumption of the policy 'logic' that increasing expenditure on 'talents' must necessarily involve the increasing welfare of everybody is both unsubstantiated and arbitrary, the monograph presents a moral political problem in demonstrating how education policies are unfounded and unsupported through the idea of meritocracy. If this is true, meritocracy can exist only as an idea, an idea which can never be realised in practical life. Is it time to let meritocracy go?

Acknowledgments

This monograph is derived in part from the following articles:

Talib, N. (25 June 2019). Creating the conditions for human division and structural inequality: The foundation of Singapore's education policy. *Journal of Language and Politics*, 18(5), 739–759. Available online: https://benjamins.com/catalog/jlp.18070.tal. http://doi.org/10.1075/jlp.18070.tal

Talib, N. & Fitzgerald, R. (3 January2018). Putting philosophy back to work in Critical Discourse Analysis. Special issue on ethics of critical discourse studies. *Critical Discourse Studies*, 15(2), 123–139. Available online: https://www.tandfonline.com/doi/abs/10.1080/17405904.2017.1421242?journalCode=rcds20. https://doi.org/10.1080/17405904.2017.1421242

Talib, N. & Fitzgerald, R. (17 May 2016). Micro-meso-macro movements: A multi-level critical discourse analysis framework to examine metaphors and the value of truth in policy texts. *Critical Discourse Studies*, 13(5), 531–547. Available online: https://www.tandfonline.com/doi/abs/10.1080/17405904.2016.1182932. https://doi.org/10.1080/17405904.2016.1182932

Talib, N. & Fitzgerald, R. (23 April 2015). Inequality as meritocracy: The use of the metaphor of diversity and the value of inequality within Singapore's meritocratic education system. *Critical Discourse Studies*, 12(4), 445–462. Available online: https://www.tandfonline.com/doi/abs/10.1080/17405904.2015.1034740. https://doi.org/10.1080/17405904.2015.1034740

1 Introduction

Questions and themes

Overview

While Singapore's education system claims to implement meritocratic ideals, official statistics indicate that Malay students in Singapore have been under-performing when compared to other ethnic groups (MOE, 2012). This statistical representation raises the possibility of a politically induced, systemic inequality as a point of investigation. In order to interpret the contemporary state of inequality, there is a need to trace its historical and evolutionary development and construction (Garrity, 2010, p. 203). Towards this end, this research is both an investigation into how policy discourses manage the contradictions inherent in Singapore's streaming[1] system, and at the same time it is also, fundamentally, an investigation into the practice and advancement of critical discourse analysis (CDA)[2] in examining inequality.

The focus of this research is primarily theoretical and methodological, articulated through a concern with the interface between theoretical concepts and methodological principles in interpreting empirical material. In doing so, it presents detailed methods for constructing a flexible philosophical-analytical model through which to apply the analytic principles of CDA for the interpretation of policy texts, thus developing CDA as a theory and method to enhance its capacity to tackle inequality. This philosophical-analytical framework developed through the analysis makes use of Foucault's work on archaeology, genealogy, and ethics, and Nietzsche's work on valuation.

This introductory chapter presents an overview of the history of Singapore's education system and the course of events that precipitated streaming in schools, how this policy has been supported by the media, and the outcomes and critiques of the streaming policy. The following sections will outline the research trajectory, briefly summarise the significance of the research and its contribution to the field, and, finally, provide an overview of the structure of the rest of the book that highlights the theoretical-methodological coordinates of this investigation.

Making sense of Singapore's education policies

The *Report on the Ministry of Education 1978* (MOE, 1979a) was the first to propose an explicit form of ability-based streaming which heralded the introduction of the 'New Education System' (NES) (Barr & Skrbiš, 2008, p. 114; Soon, 1988, p. 1). This major policy initiative, which has since then profoundly altered the shape of Singapore's education system, is underpinned by the '*fundamental belief*' that ability grouping is responsive to learners' diverse capacities and would 'better fulfil his (a student's) innate potential' (Ng, 2008a, n.p.). Working on the fundamental principle of meritocracy, the system is designed to promote and explicitly claims to reward those who work hard (Wong, 2000, n. p.) through a 'streaming' mechanism in which different abilities and capacities can be identified, nurtured, and appropriately allocated for the benefit of a growing Singapore populace. Subsequent policies and policy adjustments in 1987, 1991, 2002, 2003, 2006, 2008, 2012a, and 2019 have adapted and reinforced the 1979 policy based on meritocratic principles. Within this frame of meritocracy, streaming is represented as an increasingly necessary driver for securing Singapore's economic strength.

While a 'horizontal' form of diversity (Archer, 2007, p. 639) featured prominently in the 1979 and 1991 MOE reports, which recommended a range of strategies designed to address the presumable absorption capacities of 'slow' learners, subsequent policies published in 1987, 2002, 2006, and 2012a focus on a 'vertical' form of diversity (Archer, 2007, p. 639). This form of diversity provides exclusive opportunities for greater diversification in the system to nurture and prepare talents for an era of what Gopinathan (2007, pp. 61–62) refers to as 'innovation-driven growth'. Using carefully constructed arguments, the original and successive policy discourses draw upon and weave together different discursive formations that are brought forward under the rubric of meritocracy. While the discourse of meritocracy is a fundamental part of official rhetoric, the shifts in emphasis within these policies that aim to identity and groom talents contradict meritocratic principles. Indeed, it is the coexistence of these apparently contradictory strands that, in the view of this research, constitutes much of what is distinctive about current education policy and practice in Singapore. This study seeks to explore and account for this hybridity. It is particularly interested in what is seen as an attempt by policymakers to broaden opportunities for students who have 'talent' as defined by policy while at the same time claiming meritocratic ideals.

Based on a historical analysis of what might happen to Britain between 1870 and 2033, in 'The rise of meritocracy' (1958), Michael Young used the word 'meritocracy' in a pejorative sense and a term of disapprobation, arguing that the test-based system of advancement emerging in post-war Britain which appeared to provide opportunity for all was actually a coercive apparatus of the state through which a particular class maintains control and reproduces itself. Young himself was profoundly critical of the development he identified, and his futuristic satire was meant to be a warning of the folly of meritocratic life that polarises society and encourages the belief that one's advancement is a result of one's own merits (Sen, 2000, p. 7). Lacking access to schools with optimal resources, children from less privileged backgrounds consistently fared poorly in the 11-plus exam – the test given to children after sixth grade that largely predetermined their professions. As a consequence, the disadvantaged remained at the bottom of the social ladder, their underperformance used to validate the status quo. With the insistence on meritocracy, the underprivileged class masses become increasingly disfranchised and deprived by educational selection; they no longer have their own people to act in their interests and bring about specific outcomes. Young's apocalyptic vision, which ends in an imagined final revolt and countermovement against meritocracy in 2033, was credited with leading to the dissolution of the 11-plus in Britain (Fox, 2002, n.p.).

Meritocracy is a key principle of educational governance in Singapore's streaming system and is defined as 'equal opportunities for each student to learn and to achieve his or her potential' (Wong, 2000, n.p.). Through a detailed examination of recent educational policy discourses, this research seeks to explore *how* these enduring meritocratic principles and procedures are increasingly forced to coexist with broader notions of talent opportunities at the expense of ensuring equality of outcomes. The following section provides some historical context and a brief lead-up to the Goh report.

History of Singapore's education system and the Goh report

Formerly a British colony, Singapore attained full internal self-government in 1959, and became part of Malaysia until 1965 (Betts, 1975, p. 149). Since gaining independence in 1965, it has been under the purview of the People's Action Party (PAP) government. In the 1950s and 1960s, 'the Singapore educational sectors inherited from the British an ethno-linguistically divided, under-resourced system incapable of meeting the twin demands of unifying a pluralistic society (i.e. nation building) or match [sic] the evolving needs of a modern economy' (Gopinathan, 1995, 1997 as cited in Gopinathan, 2006, p. 296). Rather than abandoning colonial legal and legislative traditions, the government built upon these structures and constructed a centralised system of education to forge and articulate a Singaporean identity (Chia, 2011, p. 22) and promote social cohesion among the different ethnic communities. The system had a central focus on using both English and the Mother Tongue to produce a competent workforce through systematic skill formation strategies (Gopinathan, 2006, p. 296). More importantly, within a multi-ethnic society that could not afford ethnic discrimination, the government sought to enshrine meritocracy as a core value and promote advancement by merit (Rahim, 1998, p. 5).

After Singapore gained independence, the government started to study various aspects of education. Major weaknesses were identified in the late 1960s and 1970s (Ng, 2008b, p. 114). Of major concern were the 'problems of ineffective curriculum, low literacy levels and high resource wastage in the system' (Ng, 2008b, p. 114). Recommendations of the review of the educational system resulted in the 1979 Goh report, from which various education policies emanate, including an early streaming system in schools and vocational education (Rahim, 1998, p. 121). It was not until the introduction of streaming as a policy and as an efficient allocating mechanism in 1979 that any form of explicit student division was widely practised in schools. The 1970s and 1980s saw the development of an efficiency-driven system based on the tracking and promotion of academic or cognitive achievement (Gopinathan, 2006, p. 299).

Dr Goh Keng Swee presented the 'Goh Report' in February 1979. It was an assessment of MOE's problems, and introduced the 'New Education System' (NES) (Barr & Skrbiš, 2008, p. 114; Soon, 1988, p. 1), which used streaming to provide a curriculum that would respond to students of varied abilities and backgrounds so as to reduce 'educational wastage, low literacy and non-attainment of effective bilingualism' (MOE, 1979a, pp. 3-1, 3-4). The solution was to stream students to suit slow, average, above average and outstanding learners based on their school performance and intelligence tests (Mauzy & Milne, 2002, p. 104).

Inconsistent with meritocratic claims of 'equal opportunities' (Wong, 2000, n.p.), streaming was introduced to redress the imbalance of enrolment in academic and technical streams and to ensure that the country possessed a sufficient pool of technically skilled local workers to serve the broader goals of economic development and sustainable growth (Goh & Gopinathan, 2008, p. 27; Lee et al., 2008, pp. 3–5; Rahim, 1998, p. 124). This gap was initially emphasised in a ministerial report in 1968 and radical changes were introduced in the field of technical education from 1969 to prepare the young to take up new economic activities that were being generated by an expanding manufacturing sector in the 1970s (Lee et al., 2008, p. 3). In conjunction with the Goh report, in 1979, the Vocational and Industrial Training Board (VITB) Act came into existence to meet the growing need for technical and skilled manpower. Through this, education becomes the social engineering process for national productivity within the context of educational meritocracy to meet industrial demands. Herein lies the contradiction between the discourses of meritocracy and streaming, and the efforts of the state to manage one in conjunction with the other. Established through the amalgamation of the Industrial Training Board (ITB) and Adult Education Board (AEB), the VITB's primary purpose was to provide an alternative for adults who did not continue their education up to the GCE 'O'[3] or 'A'[4] level (Ng, 2008c, p. 54). A review in the late 1980s led to the establishment of the Institute of Technical Education (ITE) to provide post-secondary training (Gopinathan, 1999, p. 298). As Lee Yock Suan, former Minister for Education, argued in June 1994:

> Singapore will be poorer if everyone aspires to and gets only academic qualifications but nobody knows how to fix a TV set, a machine tool or a process plant. We need a world-class workforce with a wide variety of knowledge of skills to achieve a world-class standard of living.
>
> (Quoted in Goh & Gopinathan, 2008, p. 27)

Streaming then becomes an instrument for determining one's precise place in a school hierarchy, ostensibly in return for greater economic successes (Barr &

Skrbiš, 2008, p. 181). As Rahim (1998, p. 124) points out: streaming facilitates the 'channelling of students from the various educational streams eventually into the varying levels of the occupational hierarchy'. As such, in defending the cause for streaming as being in everyone's best interests, the media published statements by a succession of Ministers for Education who cited strong outcomes by international standards even for 'weaker' students and low levels of attrition up to post-secondary education (Ng, 2008a, n.p.; Shanmugaratnam, 2004, n.p.). However, the official justification for streaming in the state media continues to be grounded in customising pupils' education according to their abilities (Shanmugaratnam, 2004, n.p.). In justifying pro-national and economic interests, the concept and practice of meritocracy is then unstable. The twin principles of meritocracy as equal opportunity and the pursuit of economic interest are potentially contradictory. At one level streaming is justified in terms of economic development. At another level it is justified in terms of equality of opportunity depending on abilities, which are conceived of as inherent, and not socially or culturally shaped. The central research inquiry revolves around the understanding of how meritocracy is negotiated amidst economic imperatives.

Parallel media and official discourse on the 1979 MOE report

Education policies are justified through both education policies and the media. Specifically, justifications for streaming in reducing educational wastage, catering to different abilities of students, and minimising failures and damage to self-esteem are three key elements of the 1979 MOE report that have been extended to and expressed in media discourse. In particular, how failures are constructed is discursively aligned with, and mirrors, the 1979 report. Given that official justifications in the media are drawn from the policy, this extension establishes the importance of examining *how* policy discourse legitimises streaming. Within a state-controlled media system, the media in Singapore can be taken to 'reproduce' the state discourse, as the role of the press is to support rather than to challenge government policies (Holaday & Kuo, 1993 as cited in Hao, 1996, p. 112).

In reviewing the primary school streaming system, Members of Parliament called on then Education Minister Teo Chee Hean to rethink some of the policies. His response to their concerns was published in the *Straits Times*, in an article titled, 'Education System Caters to All Abilities' on 22 May 2002. Meritocracy and appropriate opportunities for all codifies the defence for streaming by Rear-Admiral Teo, who places the institutional practice at the centre of educational reform by arguing that catering to the ability of the child is imperative (Teo, 2002a, n.p.) He argues that a standard, albeit relatively 'more-demanding', curriculum could potentially cause students who consistently fail to suffer from low self-esteem. Going by the philosophy that children learn differently, he maintains that streaming is 'the correct approach', as it helps each child to meet his or her potential through *customised* programmes made to ensure their academic success and consequently, a high possibility of employment (Teo, 2002a, n.p., italics added).

In a subsequent article 'Meeting Different Needs' published on 26 November 2002 in the *Straits Times*, Teo continues his defence of a more diversified education system, explaining the changes recommended by the review committee on upper secondary and junior college education. Teo's defence highlights two guiding principles: 'meritocracy' and 'the need for students who have benefited from the best the system had to offer to recognise their obligation to the country' (Teo, 2002b, n.p.). These two key forms of rhetoric within the official discourse are used to bolt together conflicting and contrasting motivations and interests. This rhetoric had a self-contradictory proposition: while meritocracy dictates equality of access for everyone, it does in fact recognise that a particular section of the student population receives privileged access to specialised programmes (Teo, 2002b, n.p). This official prescription that subscribes to curriculum customisation is in fundamental conflict with the meritocratic dictum which purports 'equal opportunities'. The rhetoric of meritocracy has a strong flavour of favouritism that privileges the stance of inegalitarianism.[5]

It could hence be argued that meritocracy, as that which constitutes 'equal opportunities' does not entail equal outcomes. As Mr Heng Sweet Keat, then Minister for Education, points out, schools in Singapore are not meant to achieve 'identical outcomes' (Heng, 2014, n.p). In addition, he emphasises in an earlier speech:

> We cannot guarantee *equality of outcome*, but we seek to provide *equal opportunity* for every student. We thus:
>
> - Ensure that no child is deprived of educational opportunities because of their financial situation;
> - Leverage on our school system to provide more support for families from poorer backgrounds;
> - Invest in pre-school education targeted at children from families with poorer backgrounds; and
> - Invest in levelling-up programs in primary schools that attempt to level up academically weaker students in both English and Mathematics, so as to improve their foundations for future learning.
>
> (Heng, 2012, n.p.)

This claim seems to suggest that the aim of the education policies is not to elide the production of unequal outcomes, but rather, to rationalise them. Drawing on Lee Yock Suan's (quoted in Goh & Gopinathan, 2008, p. 27) argument in the previous section, it may seem that the education system aims to deliberately (re)produce inequality in order to produce better economic outcomes for society. Further, in spite of this rhetoric and its defence of streaming 'to cater to different abilities of students for the good of all' (Teo, 2002b, n.p.), statistical trends have indicated that streaming has sustained systematically low academic achievement for a particular ethnic group.

Outcomes and critiques of the streaming policy: a moral political problem

While official discourse seeks to defend streaming as central to achieving academic success, ethnic-based results released by the MOE from 1987 to 2011 indicate that Malay students in Singapore have been underperforming when compared to other ethnic groups in core subjects like English, Mathematics, and Science (MOE, 2012c, n.p.; 1997, n.p.) for 25 years. Consequently, they are over-represented in the Normal (Academic) and Normal (Technical) streams in secondary schools[6] (Barr & Skrbiš, 2008, p. 163; Rahim, 1998, pp. 121, 127; Sharpe & Gopinathan, 2002, p. 158). Paradoxically, while the education system claims to implement meritocratic ideals, streaming appears to systematically reproduce Malay underachievement. As a large segment of the Malay population has continuously been channelled into the lower streams, this statistical representation not only serves as an indicator that an entire ethnic group is 'less academically inclined'[7] than the rest of the ethnic groups, but more importantly, raises the possibility of a politically induced, systemic inequality as a point of investigation. That is, instead of accepting this unequal representation as an empirical given, this paper questions or brackets this presupposition, taking it as a provisional base for the possibility of systemic discrimination. Exposing the assumptions underpinning structural proposals and propositions in policy discourse can lend weight to this presumption.

Persistent underachievement would then serve as an apparent indicator of the systemic meritocratic inequality of the NES; that is, systematic inequality is inbuilt into the system, and gaps between the *more* and *less* 'academically inclined' would persist, despite claims of equal opportunities. Indeed, former prime minister Lee Kuan Yew 'asserted that the Malays would never close the gap in educational attainment with the Indians and Chinese *because as they improve, the others also improve*' (Lee, 2011 quoted in Lim, 2013, p. 4, emphasis included). If this argument is correct, then streaming can be seen as a sorting mechanism which serves to systemise and, more importantly, legitimise *unequal access to knowledge* according to whether a student is *more* or *less* 'academically inclined', and consequently, systematic inequality.

The common presumption about academic underachievement is that it resides primarily in those students with inadequate capacity to benefit from what the education system has to offer. Particularly, there has been a heavy reliance on the cultural deficit thesis[8] to explain the educational marginality of the Malays (Rahim, 1998, p. 185). Exploring the historical, ethnic, and class-related factors to explain and address the Malay educational malaise is not the focus of this study. This would relegate and deflect attention from its central concern in examining how structural inequality is built-in to the system. There is a need to explore policies and their implications for structural reforms, as part of the problem. Rather than viewing learners as the locus of the problem, which entails deficit thinking[9] (Valencia, 2010), the analysis in this monograph points to the conditions under which unequal access to knowledge may occur.

In relation to systematic inequality, previous research reveals that the concept of an egalitarian meritocracy is unstable, as its constituent ideas, particular in relation to streaming within the education system, are potentially contradictory. Gopinathan (1996, p. 82) points out that by adopting streaming, Singapore abandoned the British practice of comprehensive schooling designed to equalise opportunities. Soon (1988, p. 19), in reviewing the public's reaction to streaming, advances the argument that pupils channelled to a lower course would have reduced access to higher education. As such, it is debatable whether attempts by the Ministry for *equal opportunity* (see previous section) characterised by levelling up academically weaker students (Heng, 2012, n.p.) have succeeded.

Cogently, Rahim (1998, pp. 120–124) argues that the PAP leadership's educational philosophy is driven by eugenics notions which influenced the belief that the innately 'talented' minority should be invested with a disproportionate amount of the state's public resources in order to lead and inspire the nation to succeed. Hence, various elite programmes for the educationally 'talented', as defined by policy, were institutionalised. The underlying assumption of this logic is that the more 'talented' students would generate economic growth for the nation in the long run. In his speech entitled 'Core Principles of Government', Deputy Prime Minister Lee Hsien Loong (1992, p. 22, quoted in Rahim 1998, p. 131) emphasises that, 'Because we have invested more in the more able, all Singaporeans have progressed faster'.

In relation to this, Tan (2008, pp. 7–10) points out that Singapore's concept of meritocracy that focuses on talent allocation, competition, and reward can obscure how an education system that emphasises efficiency systematically excludes particular groups of people based on race and class from the mainstream society, economy, and politics. He argues that a merit-based selection that focuses on the principle of non-discrimination may serve to both ignore and conceal the advantages and disadvantages of an unequal society. This practice perpetuates rather than levels inequality: those who are rewarded based on merit may already have a starting point of positional advantage. Further, compounded by policies such as the SAP[10] (Special Assistance Plan) schools which favour the Chinese, Singapore's choice of meritocratic action strategy has continued to keep ethnic groups apart (Rahim, 1998, pp. 121, 127; Sharpe & Gopinathan 2002, p. 158). Due to the privileging of differential access, these studies highlight that the pursuit of securing equality of opportunity is conceptually untenable and will be severely underestimated within streaming policy and practice, even if the official justification was constructed as catering to the ability of the learner (see Teo, 2002a, n.p.).

Whilst researchers (Rahim, 1998, pp. 117–118; Sharpe & Gopinathan, 2002, p. 151; Soon, 1988, p. 19; Tan, 2008, p. 10) highlight the weaknesses of the education system and its role in sustaining academic or ethnic inequality, it is particularly instructive that such linkages between the system and the reproduction of inequality, particularly through education policy documents, remains unclear. That is, it is not clear *how* ability-based streaming is used as a mechanism through which inequality of educational opportunities is established, transmitted, and maintained. This is an especially important area of research given that educational and social consequences arising from underachievement can be severe, such as increasing income inequality (Sharpe & Gopinathan, 2002, p. 158). Although inequality has been defended by the government as an inevitable consequence of globalisation, critics have pointed to the inadequacies of the education and training system (Sharpe & Gopinathan, 2002, p. 158).

To add to the complexity of the issue, the field of Singapore's education policy analysis (see Rahim, 1998, pp. 123–124; Sharpe & Gopinathan, 2002, pp. 155–156) has been dominated by commentary and critique rather than empirical research. The lack of research using critical qualitative approaches that have the potential to challenge the 'ideological' premises of government policies is not surprising because of the political constraints on academic research in Singapore (Rahim, 1998, p. 8). The culture of self-censorship and lack of serious intellectual critique, particularly by researchers employed by Singapore's tertiary institutions, is likely to have been reinforced by the dismissal of the Deputy Secretary General of the Singapore Democratic Party, Chee Soon Juan, in 1992, from the Psychology and Social Work Department of the National University of Singapore on minor charges (Rahim, 1998, p. 8). Researchers tend to avoid investigating sensitive issues involving government policies such as the early streaming system (Gopinathan & Gremli, 1988 as cited in Rahim, 1998, p. 8). To exacerbate matters, this self-control is also exercised by expatriate academics based on the experience of those 'who have been detained for questioning and sued for defamation or have not had their contracts renewed for publishing articles critical of the PAP government' (Asiawatch, 1990, as cited in Rahim, 1998, p. 8). These substantive constraints against Singaporean scholars' overt critique of the state are real and, without a thorough examination, will likely encourage a disturbing trend of speculative research about the effects of policies.

Policies have direct material force in Singapore society. In *The Public Policy-Making Process in Singapore*, Jon S. T. Quah (1984) points out that public policies are formulated by the cabinet, which is the 'supreme policy-making body of the government' (p. 113). The PAP government as the directive authority then ensures the successful implementation of policies to achieve the desired objectives by providing the 'necessary manpower, legislation, financial resources and equipment to the relevant implementing agencies' (p. 119). He highlights that the PAP government is 'not very tolerant of independent critics' who criticise government policies (p. 117). Furthermore, the inability of opposition parties to provide intelligent alternatives and to point out the flaws in policies has resulted in little or no public resistance (p. 119).

Within these factors, the rhetoric of meritocracy seems to be holding back the education system as it first allows a certain group to be systematically disadvantaged, and second, it does not allow incisive critique or the questioning of prevailing notions and prior assumptions within the system by which to improve it – because of the *belief* in the system as being fair on the basis that it is meritocratic and that every child has the *same* opportunity to succeed, thus resisting evidence of incoherence which leads to problems of inequality (see Bohm, 1994, p. 28). The notion of 'meritocracy' as conceptualised by official policy discourse as necessary needs to be examined – that is, how has this concept been made necessary to the extent that 'it cannot be otherwise', which in effect is saying 'It has got to be this way. We have to keep it this way' (Bohm, 1994, p. 89). Employing CDA can uncover underlying assumptions in policy discourse that produce and sustain 'what subsequently counts as being self-evident, universal, *necessary*' (Foucault, 1991c, p. 87). The critical analysis employed here involves ideological deconstruction, which helps to discover underlying implicit assumptions of (absolute) necessity.

The central thrust here is thus concerned with *how* the ideological notion of 'meritocracy' is conceptualised through discursive processes in policy documents, rather than how it is theorised. The purpose here is not present what may be seen as a traditional literature review in the sense of summarising a series of mainstream perspectives on critical terms, but rather seeks to *problematise the construction* and use of this term in the first place. This is at the heart of this book's theoretical position. As such, to include the diverse theoretical groundings, which would constitute an ideal of what should be, or what has been stated of 'meritocracy' would be to undermine the conceptual integrity of the work. This analytical process which takes the problematisation of truth as a point of departure to examine *what is Here and Now* actually taking place within the policy data, rather than drawing on the historical, social, and political contexts to understand the object under investigation, provides a practical anchorage to the normative dimension of ideological critique. Here, the purpose is to examine how the idea of meritocracy works not as an abstraction, not as an idea, but in actuality. Further, a comparison with the situation in other countries in relation to meritocracy and education policy would not be of significant interest. It is not clear what is the basis or need for this comparison, or how differences could contribute to making up a coherent subject matter in trying to learn about Singapore's education system and its problems. To make sense of things against some background of previous or existing expectations or situations may hamper the observation of *what is*, what is *Here and Now* actually taking place within the policy data, although it may seem as though they were helping that observation by providing possibilities of *what should be* or *what has been*.

Data-driven analysis

Without evidence to prove and give clarity as to *how* ability-based streaming is a major mechanism through which inequality of educational opportunities is transmitted and maintained, assumptions by researchers exist about the perceived harmful effects of educational inequality under the rubric of meritocracy in policies. As such, the current position of streaming cannot be questioned or systematically distilled unless the language use in policy documents supporting this reality is fundamentally challenged (Liasidou, 2008, p. 485). In a fair and just society, it is the public's prerogative and responsibility to actively and continuously identify and question assumptions underlying the truths of policy proposals and propositions. Doing so can contribute to the progressive development of social policy for the future.

The aim here is to make transparent the conditions under which streaming practices are producing inequality. As the legitimation of structural reforms is contingent on the assumptions that are operating, exposing the implicit assumptions embedded in policy proposals and propositions is a necessary, critical step to tackle structural inequality. The assumptions underlying policy proposals and propositions are not self-justifying and should not be taken as self-evident. Their legitimacy has to be demonstrated, failing which the structures that were built through these policies should be dismantled and reconstructed from below (Chomsky, 2013, p. 110). Given this possibility, this research focuses on *how* historically, education policies contribute to engineering consent for inequality *within a meritocratic system*. This is an area that has not been seriously examined in scholarly literature to date. Specifically, policy documents which are central to understanding how the system has been operationalised have not been explored and analysed in relation to this issue. This is clearly an area that needs investigation.

Research trajectory

Statistical trends and previous research raise the question of whether it is possible that a whole ethnic group is somehow less academically inclined.[11] More importantly, it also raises the question of whether *being more* or 'less academically inclined' is inbuilt into the streaming system. In order to understand how the inconsistencies between educational meritocracy and inequity have been made manifest, this research aims to examine the actual policies where these initiatives were originally proposed, described, and ultimately implemented, using CDA. In tracing *discursive shifts*, which imply a 'complex, shifting field of relations' (Fraser, 1981, p. 283) between elements that legitimise social practices, policies can be used as important evidence in making explicit the implicit and opaque relationship between language and inequality so as to go beyond conjectural considerations (Taylor, 2004, p. 436). The observation of systematic formations that texts index and construct (Luke, 2002, p. 100) is then a vehicle through which to understand how the policies discursively construct the workings of the education system. Here CDA assumes policy language has social effects (Graham, 2001a, p. 765).

Given that these policy documents were commissioned by the Ministry of Education, the political nature of the policy and a principled and rigorous approach to issues of educational equity make it necessary to use a methodology that is capable of addressing political discourses. CDA is adopted as a powerful methodology to examine the discursive work of politically-based policy processes and formation. CDA provides a particular nuance to understand the subtle and intricate relationships of language to other social processes, and of how language works within power relations (Taylor, 2004, p. 436). In addition, CDA demands a rigorous systematic approach to provide a capacity for transparency through language analysis. More importantly, the methodology enables the examination of discursive processes as they unfold.

By tracing a historical sequence that has gone unbroken for 40 years – from the initiation of streaming in 1979 to 2019 – this study situates the construction of meritocratic inequality as a historically established fact. An analysis of the initial 1979 policy document and subsequent policies can provide a rich source of discursive evidence for the implicit relationship between language and social inequality (Taylor, 2004, p. 436). The use of the methodological approach of CDA to education policies can help to understand and uncover the conditions of this inequality (van Dijk, 1993, p. 369), by examining how policy texts manage the practice of systemic inequality discursively. The purpose is not one of finding mechanical patterns of causality, but to examine how a series of discursive practices make sense of or conceptualise systematic educational 'underachievement' within a meritocratic system. This would consequently provide a stronger ground for claims of discriminatory practices. Towards this end, this research is just as focused on the development of a more broadly applicable analytical CDA framework for the analysis of policies in general, especially those that are driven by neo-liberal economic agendas.

The positioning of subjects is central to legitimising the streaming policy. As previously discussed in the section 'Parallel media and official discourse on the 1979 MOE report' above, the three key elements that justify streaming in media and official discourse – to reduce educational wastage, to cater to different abilities of students for the good of all, and to minimise failures and damage to self-esteem – are discursively aligned with the 1979 report. Hence, this research examines how the identities of learners are discursively constructed in education policies. This investigation could potentially play a significant role in providing a preliminary understanding of how differential access to knowledge is legitimised.

Towards this end, this research develops a form of critical discourse analysis (CDA) to examine Singapore's Ministry of Education (MOE) policies on streaming in two stages. The first stage examines the original 1979 MOE report that proposed a streaming policy for Singapore. Foucault's archaeological method is used in combination with an amalgamation of CDA approaches to investigate how policy works to recognise, define, and classify learners through binary categorisations. This methodology critically examines the 'regime of truth' that makes possible capability-based identity constructs. This section of the study brings together Foucault's perspective on power-knowledge-truth, which provides insights into how learner identities are constructed within 'truth' claims, and CDA to describe, interpret, and explain the ways in which identities are constructed within policy discourse. By problematising truth – that is, making transparent the assumptions that underpin the truths in policy discourse, the analysis makes explicit the necessary conditions (of possibility) for the disclosure of what is pervasive and recurring, which in the case of this analysis, is the objectification of learners.

In order to grasp the changes in the conditions for the objectification of learners in successive policy texts, this approach is then developed in the subsequent genealogical-analytical stage of the research, which traces the *historical* and discursive construction of learner identities in policy texts from 1979 to 2019 and how they are constituted in various moral discourses. The genealogical method provided a basis from which to trace the regulatory forces and events that shape these discursive practices into a recursive network of power relations over time. This stage builds on the methodological and theoretical work of the first to formulate and employ a *micro-meso-macro* CDA framework to examine metaphors and the value of truth in policy texts. This framework draws upon a relationship between language analysis, the philosophical study of valuation, and political economy to analyse how changes associated with new modes of value determination serve to legitimise inequality within a frame of meritocracy. The concerns and questions of how social categories and practices are shaped by discourse that arises out of policy analysis found parallels in Foucault's and Nietzsche's theoretical and philosophical orientations. Together, this central mode of inquiry and philosophical orientations works in a critical analysis of policy discourse to understand how inequality can exist within a frame of meritocracy. This stage involves, simultaneously, the development of Foucault's work on the truth formulation of subjects by synthesising his philosophical perspective with the work of Nietzsche. Nietzsche's work is critical in mobilising an understanding of power, will, and truth by bringing the concept of valuation to centre stage in exposing the underlying assumptions that guide institutional practices for differentiated learners. The synthesis of these philosophical concepts with CDA is useful in critically analysing the formulation of truths that constitutes the focus of policymaking.

As revealed through this second stage of analysis, policy-oriented moralities are the principal means of fashioning men and women according to the pleasure of a creative and profound will, which has prevailed over time through multiform conditions of possibility that can change quite drastically (cf. Nietzsche, 1967a, p. 501). This will to power as 'being' is expounded in the form of values and valuation,[12] revaluation and transvaluation (Nietzsche, 1967a). The production and gaining of knowledge breeds and is bred by these fragmented forms of valuation that relate value judgments to the ideology of economic growth. These valuations are hence an exercise of power that brings particular truths into being. To make concrete this philosophical dimension, this analytical stage synthesises the multiple layers of intersections between methods that have been developed by critical discourse analysts for analysing evaluations. In doing so, this study is concerned with the unfolding of the will to power, and simultaneously, the production of *being* [13] of ideology of economic growth as that of the objective desire (cf. Heidegger, 2003c, p. 141). The problematisation and critique of economic growth as the only way forward requires exposing and challenging the assumptions underlying this ideological logic. Within the context of this research, those assumptions allude to modes of e/valuation.

The analytical chapters reveal that whilst the initial discursive formations of policy texts were focused on catering to the constructed needs of learners with lower abilities, subsequent policy discourses revealed conflicted discourses and reworked policies towards the institutional practice of providing greater educational access for individuals with higher capabilities in relation to meeting the needs of changing political economies. This phenomenon of inequality of access can be explained by analysing how recursive metaphors of flexibility, diversity, choice, and opportunity as time-travellers and as engines of neo-liberal discourse interact with one another. These metaphors operate as a *fluid* movement in and through the texts to provide the *necessary* foundation from which to hold unequal structural reforms as a justifiable, *desirable* form of ethical practice. The analysis concludes that objectification is a fundamental part of the valorisation process. Forms of objectification through identity categorisation increase the relative value of subjects through upskilling and modes of valuation within the perceived demands arising from the living *movement* and changing material conditions of surrealistic political economies.

Significance of the research and its contribution to the field

Even though previous research points to the weaknesses of streaming and its role in sustaining inequality, it is not clear *how* streaming is used as a mechanism through which inequality of educational opportunities is established, transmitted, and maintained. This problem is compounded by the political constraints on academic research in Singapore. Taking the reproduction of inequality as an observable fact, the assumption that policies play a critical role in reproducing inequality is central to this research. Towards this end, CDA is employed to analyse policy texts in order to make explicit and provide critical evidence as to *how* inequality is inbuilt into the education system. To begin the analysis with 'how' is to suggest that systemic inequality (re)produced through policies as such *does not exist* until it has been made explicit *under or in what conditions* this is so (cf. Foucault, 1982a, pp. 778, 785–786). 'How' in this sense, as Foucault argues, is the *discursive* means in which inequality is re(produced) in policy discourse (cf. Foucault, 1982a, p. 786). The analysis in this monograph illustrates *how* forms of valuations perpetuated by and through policy discourse are the motivational locus of meaning making *insofar* as they strongly inform the moral force driving the overarching ideological narrative of economic growth. To build this larger 'content' using typical sociological sources or socio-historical contexts would be incompatible with the carefully developed theoretical-methodological approach. The monograph's analysis and focus are explicitly directed at the internal reasoning within the texts and where the evolving state of other aspects of linguistic representations, along with any other institutional or political or public sphere, is irrelevant to the text unless it is brought to bear within the texts in some discursive capacity.

The contribution this study makes to the field is twofold. First, the analysis of Singapore's education policies makes explicit how streaming is a major mechanism through which unequal opportunities are transferred and sustained. Second, it makes a contribution to policy analysis more broadly, contributing to a new political front in education, one that puts philosophy to work – in terms of the integration and application of suitable, multiple CDA approaches in analysing policies – in those paradigms in which education policies are conceptualised, theorised, and researched. That is, it adds to scholarship on not just educational policy in general, but more specifically to scholarship around issues of equality and the construction of learner identities. In constructing a working methodology for policy analysis, it aims to strengthen discourse analytical work by bringing the tools and perspectives of the philosophical study of valuation to bear on concrete problems that arise in addressing issues of education policy and practice.

Organisation of the monograph

This section provides an outline of the book, describing the ways in which each chapter sets out the research. Chapter 2, 'Creating the Conditions for Division and Structural Inequality: The Human Being as a Historical Construct', provides a preliminary, archaeological investigation into how policy works to recognise, define, and classify learners through binary categorisations. The purpose of the analysis is to examine how learners are represented in the original 1979 MOE report that introduced streaming. As an initial conceptual framework for analysing that report, this chapter primarily discusses Foucault's interweaving concepts of power-knowledge-truth, which explore the relations between subject and truth. Foucault uses the term 'power/knowledge' to signify that power is constituted through accepted forms of knowledge and 'truth'.

Through this, the chapter discusses Foucault's archaeological method and its suitability for a philosophically grounded, interdisciplinary piece of linguistic research in examining the objectification of subject. By detailing the source of the various approaches to CDA, the chapter presents a 'multidisciplinary' approach to discourse analysis. The analysis of the 1979 MOE report makes explicit the conditions necessary for identifying particular types of learners and how this is related to structural reforms. Three conditions emerge from this preliminary analysis: 'capabilities as social change', 'inequality as justice', and 'ethics: or *philosophy of desirability*'. They provide a basis for the genealogical research trajectory of the rest of the analysis of this research.

Out of the three, the third condition, the employment of 'ethics: or *philosophy of desirability*' (Nietzsche, 1967a, p. 181) in policy discourse is central to the analysis. An examination of ethical practices in policy discourses repeatedly reflects first the utilisation of specific metaphors. Second, the analysis demonstrates that a value system that is produced and reproduced in the theme of ethics is profoundly enmeshed in the impetus for social change and the conceptualisation of justice. Hence, an investigation of the theme of ethics would mean an investigation of the other two themes.

Chapter 3, 'Using Genealogy and Ethics to Investigate the Conditioning of Human Beings into Moral Subjects Who Desire More', unpacks the term 'genealogy' and the relationship that it bears to archaeology discussed in Chapter 2. The aim of the chapter is to examine how historical qualitative textual analysis might be located within the philosophical interstices of archaeology, genealogy, and CDA (cf. Anais, 2013, p. 125). This includes a treatise on a *genealogy of ethics* which entails the study of the modes according to which the subject is inserted as an object in the games of truth – alluding to the Truth of economic growth. For the purposes of this research, modes are conceptualised as (historical) conditions of possibility for differential learner treatment to exist in the analysis of economic growth and neo-liberalism for labour appropriation (Foucault, 1982a, p. 777). The chapter further outlines a synthesis of relevant CDA approaches, designed to operationalise Foucault's and Nietzsche's philosophical orientations on schemas of valuation in order to understand how human beings have been conditioned as moral subjects in relation to value-forming labour appropriation who desire economic growth.

Chapter 4, 'Micro-Meso-Macro Movements: A Multi-Level Critical Discourse Analysis Framework to Examine the Value of Truth', aims to model how CDA and Foucault's philosophical concepts, combined with Nietzsche's concept of truth, can be usefully synthesised to analyse schemas of valuation in education policies that have identifiable material force in structural inequality. The aim is to convert their philosophical concepts into an analytical framework capable of addressing empirical data. That is, it explores how evaluative semantic categories can be linked to sociological theories in order to bring out their relevance for the purpose of CDA. In doing so, the philosophical-analytical framework aims to make analytically observable how changes associated with new modes of value determination serve to legitimise inequality. Their philosophical perspectives are determined by the poles of valuation and truth. By drawing on these philosophical themes, arguments, and ideas, the analysis lays bare relations of power through valuations. The research argues that the abstract convergence of truth and valuation has quite specific and concrete structural implications in relation to differed structural access to knowledge.

In examining how specific values and outcomes are made desirable, Chapters 5 to 7 adopt a genealogical analytic approach that emphasises the importance of recursive discourses of the original 1979 MOE report and subsequent 1979–2019 policies. In doing so, it reveals the *pervasiveness* (Foucault, 1972, p. 221) of policy metaphors of flexibility, diversity, choice, and opportunity. Three themes emerged from the analysis of the preliminary theme of 'Ethics: or *Philosophy of Desirability*'. The first theme, 'Metaphorical Realism', illustrates *how* metaphors do *ideologising* work to varying degrees, in the service of contributing to and sustaining systemic educational inequality through micro-macro valuations.

Chapter 5, 'Theme 1: Metaphorical Realism', the first of the three themes, proposes and employs the notion of 'metaphorical realism'. The notion entails a focus on how the metaphors of flexibility, choice, diversity, and opportunity appear to contribute and sustain systemic educational *inequality* through both micro and macro valuations. As such, they serve as a critical principle of institutional differentiation. In its philosophical dimension, 'metaphorical realism' proposes that these metaphors are treated as apparatuses of power, where power includes forms of valuation that serve to turn idealised and politically induced images of the system into multiple organisations of truths that support inequality. These truths shape and retain competing economic imaginaries; that is, they construct illusions of desirable realities. This chapter presents the overarching, interacting, and intersecting constructions of macro-neo-liberal values of competitiveness, de/regulation, and market economies. It sets up the frame that these macro-neo-liberal values are both conditional upon and being conditioned by micro valuations of what is interpreted as important or/and necessary to generate desirable outcomes.[14] Both macro and micro valuations are analysed in the next two themes.

Chapter 6, 'Theme 2: De/regulation', builds on the analysis in Chapter 5 to examine how the metaphor of flexibility performs *ideologising* work that obscures the agent or agency involved in generating desirable outcomes. Specifically, it examines how the metaphor of flexibility appears to do *ideologising* work to obscure the agent or agency involved in generating desirable outcomes. The chapter explores how the lack of agency can serve to obfuscate state responsibility with respect to policy trajectories. More importantly, this chapter examines how the lack of (state) agency in discourse underplays the potential of active agents. It proposes how devolution to educators and transformation to a flexible system in no way entails relinquishing state control by illustrating the centripetal movement of power in educational governance. The analysis illustrates how policies are presumably oriented to a general depoliticisation of responsibilities in relation to decentralisation.

Chapter 7, 'Theme 3: Political Economies of Surrealism', examines how metaphors appear to be *ideologising* work to bring together realities that appear to have limited logical relationship or rational link, to produce conditions of emerging political economies that permit new knowledge and new truths (cf. Adonis, 2005, p. 41). Specifically, this chapter calls the 'real' notion of reality into question through the notion of 'surrealism'. This chapter ties previous analyses into a wider reflection on how metaphors sustain the ideology of economic growth as the only way forward. Throughout the three movements, the texts reveal a set of correlations through the play of positive significations that it ascribes to the idealised images. These correlations exist between the metaphors of flexibility, diversity, choice, and opportunity, social-economic life, and an indivisible whole system of differential valuations. Further, these metaphors are used to advance capitalist-corporatist imperatives (cf. Graham & Luke, 2011, p. 106; cf. Foucault, 1997, pp. 90–91). By alluding to macro-neo-liberal values of competitiveness, de/regulation, and market economies, these three movements argue that inequality is desirable. The organisation of values is thus at the same time a 'mechanism of selection and exclusion' (Foucault, 2001, p. 173).

Chapter 8 is titled 'Inequality as Meritocracy'. The discussion in this chapter relates the material presented in previous chapters to the theoretical and operational objectives of the study. That is, it outlines the specific aims of the research and its theoretical and methodological contributions to the field of critical discourse analysis scholarship. The research draws on a theoretical framing from Foucault augmented by Nietzsche's views on valuation to develop a multi-level CDA framework for policy analysis and to make analytically observable how changes associated with new modes of value determination serve to legitimise educational inequality within a meritocratic education system. Overall, the research argues that metaphors are central to recontextualising, disseminating, and legitimating dominant political imaginaries that construct and sustain structural inequality for economic growth. It then presents a critique of the philosophical-analytical concerns of the study. More importantly, in demonstrating how education policies are unfounded and unsupported by the idea of meritocracy, the chapter proposes an opportunity for the emergence of a 'Singapore model' to lead education policies for advanced economies.

Summary

Driven by economic imperatives and efficiency, streaming was introduced as a policy in 1979 and an explicit form of structuration became widely practised in schools. While official discourse seeks to defend streaming as central to achieving success and reducing attrition rates, statistics released by the MOE indicate that Malays have been underperforming since 1987. In order to understand how the inconsistencies between educational meritocracy and inequity have been made manifest, this research aims to analyse education policies from 1979 to 2019. Policy texts can be used as important evidence in making explicit the opaque relationship between language and inequality. This process is necessary so as to go beyond speculation and demonstrate how policy texts work in order to provide empirical support for previous claims of discriminatory practices through which structural inequality of educational opportunities is established, transmitted, and maintained. In using CDA to expose underlying assumptions in policy discourse, it is possible to make visible how policy discourses justify, legitimise, and sustain unequal opportunities for knowledge access and differentiated treatments within a meritocratic system.

The next chapter moves on to an analysis of the 1979 MOE report. This preliminary analysis will provide an initial understanding of *how* inequality of access is inbuilt and sustained within the system through dichotomous conceptions of learner identities that are a product of power-knowledge-truth relationships inherent in policy discourses (Foucault, 1969, 1972, 1979, 1981 as cited in Rogers et al., 2005, p. 370). More importantly, this initial analysis is a necessary, preliminary step in providing an analytical-genealogical trajectory for further investigation.

Notes

1 'Streaming is underpinned by the fundamental belief that students had varying learning ability, and would therefore be better off being grouped together to learn at their appropriate pace. Put simply, streaming allows each child to better fulfil his inherent potential' (Ng, 2008a, n.p.).
2 Where CDA is concerned with analysing language 'as one element of the social process dialectically interconnected with others', in order to demonstrate the ways 'socio-economic systems are built upon the domination, exploitation, and dehumanization of people by people, and to show how contradictions within these systems constitute a potential for transforming them in progressive and emancipatory directions' (Fairclough & Graham, 2002, p. 5).
3 Students in the Express course at the end of Secondary 4 typically offer six to eight subjects at the Singapore-Cambridge General Certificate of Education (Ordinary Level) examination. Those with exceptional academic ability may offer a ninth subject (MOE, 2012b, p. 6).

4 A pre-university course leading to the Singapore-Cambridge General Certificate of Education (Advanced Level) Examination prepares students for further education by equipping them with the essential skills and knowledge required for tertiary education (MOE, 2012b, p. 8).

5 The characteristics of how the term 'egalitarianism' is mobilised and made sense of in the context of Singapore's education policy will be explicated in the section 'Egalitarian-excellence educational philosophies' of Chapter 2.

6 Generally, at the end of four years, students who are placed in the Express stream sit for the Singapore-Cambridge General Certificate of Education Ordinary Level (GCE O-Level) examination. Students who are placed in the Normal (Academic) stream sit for the Singapore-Cambridge General Certificate of Education Normal (Academic) Level (GCE N(A)-Level) examination, then one additional year to prepare for the GCE O-Level examination. Students who are placed in the Normal (Technical) stream sit for the Singapore-Cambridge General Certificate of Education Normal (Technical) Level (GCE N(T)-Level) examination to gain entry into the Institute of Technical Education (ITE), which offers a technical-vocational education (Normal course curriculum, n.d., n.p.).

7 This term was used by the Minister for Education, Ong Ye Kung, at the Schools Work Plan Seminar on 28 September 2018 in relation to the current school curriculum which 'caters to students of different learning paces and learning needs'.

8 The cultural deficit thesis, which suggests that academic achievement is culturally based and so the problem lies primarily within the Malay community (Rahim, 1998, p. 186), can be linked to Bernstein's and Bourdieu's competence models of language and human development within class-based societies (see Collins, 2000). Their research programmes, which focus on social and educational reproduction, draw on mechanisms of socialisation and subjectivity (Collins, 2000, pp. 65–66).

9 Valencia argues that deficit thinking operates on an unsubstantiated assumption that inherent abnormalities such as limited intellectual ability, low motivation, and linguistic shortcomings are the source of academic failure among low socioeconomic-class students. Rather than relying on this 'blaming the victim' thesis to explain educational malaise, Valencia observes that systemic factors, such as inequities in basic school resources, have a strong relationship to the academic failure of low-SES students (Garcia-Perez, 2012, pp. 278–279).

10 The SAP scheme was introduced in 1979 to preserve the best traditions and ethos of the old Chinese medium schools, and to nurture a core group of students who are proficient in both English and Chinese. Currently, there are 11 SAP secondary schools and 15 SAP primary schools (MOE, 2008b, n.p.).

11 This term was used by the Minister for Education, Ong Ye Kung, at the Schools Work Plan Seminar on 28 September 2018.

12 Valuation here as 'I believe that this and that is so' as the *essence* of '*truth*' (Nietzsche, 1967a, p. 275, italics included). The term here denotes the desirability of certain acts.

13 The disclosure of this 'being' is understood in 'terms of the conditions of their possibility' (Heidegger, 2003c, p. 238). Through the analysis in this research, 'being' is conceptualised as a fluid, continual flux of discursive formations to bring the ideology of economic growth into immanent existence, and the constant anticipatory state of potential becoming of *surrealistic* economies.

14 *Desirable* outcomes are conceptualised in this study as those which increase economic growth through appropriation of labour for irrealis industrial economies. See the section 'The desiring-desirable subject, hyperrealist structures, and schemas of valuation as elements of ethical relations within the 'games of truth'' of Chapter 3.

2 Creating the conditions for division and structural inequality

The human being as a historical construct

Overview

To investigate the apparent contradiction between the rhetoric and practice of equal educational opportunity, this chapter conducts a preliminary analysis of the 1979 policy report which legitimised streaming based on recognising different capabilities of learners. In examining this policy development, the analysis is situated in a combination of Foucault's perspective and critical discourse analysis (CDA) as a way of understanding the 'regime of truth' (Foucault, 1980, p. 131) that made possible capability-based identity constructs in the original policy.

In doing so, this chapter provides a preliminary archaeological investigation into how policy works to recognise, define, and classify learners through binary categorisations. The analysis makes explicit the conditions necessary for identifying particular types of learners and how this is related to systemic changes. Three conditions emerge from this preliminary archaeological policy analysis: 'capabilities as social change', 'inequality as justice', and 'ethics: or *philosophy of desirability*'. They provide a basis for the genealogical research trajectory of the rest of the analysis of this research.

The 1979 Ministry of Education report (Goh Report)

In his speech at the Committee of Supply Debate on 5 March 2018, Minister for Education Ong Ye Kung proposes that the education system 'must build' on the 'solid foundation' originally set by Goh Keng Swee in 1979 of 'allowing students to study at different paces that suited them' because 'the uniform curriculum did not cater for students' varied pace of learning'. Contrary to the meritocratic principle of 'equal opportunities' (Wong, 2000, n.p.), the Goh report asserts that a school system informed by a commitment to egalitarianism negates the fundamental tenet 'that different children have different capacities to acquire knowledge' (MOE, 1979a, pp. 1–5). As the official justification for streaming continues to be underpinned by the 'fundamental *belief* that students had varying learning ability, and would therefore be *better off being grouped together* to learn at their appropriate pace' (Ng, 2008, n.p., italics added) the analysis of this report provides crucial evidence in understanding by what discursive processes and under what conditions learners become categorically objectified in language, in the ultimately dichotomous objectifying terms 'slow' and 'fast' learners (MOE, 1979a, pp. 1–3).

In August 1978, then Deputy Prime Minister Goh Keng Swee was tasked to lead a study team of systems engineers to identify problems in Singapore's education system and propose solutions for reform (Raman, 1978, p. 1). They had to streamline and align the education system and make it more sensitive to the rapidly changing social and economic needs of the country (Goh and his team get down to the task, 1978, p. 1; Soon, 1988, p. 1). A key aim of the exercise was to consider how education policies and their implementation could be made more flexible to enable each child to learn at a pace suited to their ability (Raman, 1978, p. 1).

Submitted on 9 February 1979, the *Report on the Ministry of Education 1978*, known as the Goh Report, was endorsed by Parliament on 30 March 1979, and identified three main shortcomings in the education system, namely, high education wastage, low levels of literacy, and ineffective bilingualism (MOE, 1979a, p. 4-1). Having identified the problems in education and their underlying causes, the study team made several recommendations that became the basis of the New Education System (NES) (Soon, 1988, p. 1).

The Goh Report was the first of a series of educational reforms of the NES, and it was not until the introduction of early streaming as a policy in 1979 that any explicit form of structuration was widely practised in schools (Rahim, 1998, p. 123). Among the major changes brought about by the Goh Report was the streaming of pupils into different courses at the upper primary and secondary levels depending on their language proficiencies and academic abilities at Primary 3 and Primary 6 (MOE, 1979a, pp. 6-1, 6-4). More importantly, 'the report recommends different streams of education to suit the slow, average, above average and outstanding learners' (Dr Goh pinpoints the three real causes of trouble in the system, 1979, p. 8). The Goh Report was endorsed by Parliament on 30 March 1979 (Fong, 1979, p. 1).

The report consists of 113 pages. It has an opening address to the Prime Minister by the review committee and an address to the Deputy Prime Minister and Minister of Education by the Prime Minister. There are six chapters in the report. Chapter 1: An overview of the problem; Chapter 2: History of the education system in Singapore; Chapter 3: Existing problems in the education system; Chapter 4: Education policies – Contributing factors to the existing problems in the education system; Chapter 5: Contributing factors – Systems and procedures; and Chapter 6: Recommendations, annexes and references. The following recommendations ensue from the report (MOE, 1979a, p. 6-1, italics added):

- Those pupils who cannot cope with two languages would be better off being literate in one language than attempting to learn two languages and being literate in neither.
- The academic and intellectual abilities of children vary. The pace which is suitable for the *bright pupils* would be inappropriate for *slow learners*. There should be provisions for *slow learners* to proceed at a pace more relaxed than that for the *bright pupils*.

- There should also be provisions for late developers to join the *brighter pupils* when they (the late developers) can cope with the faster pace.
- Pupils who do not succeed in academic studies could succeed in technical or commercial training.(MOE, 1979a, 6-1, italics added).

The 1979 report names categories of predetermined, divisive capability identities (bright pupils and slow learners) with their 'appropriate' forms of knowledge access (faster pace for brighter pupils) but without giving reference to any substantive evidence. These assertions argue for change to be driven exclusively by distinctive capability identities as a simple and certain way forward. In order to understand how these arbitrary propositions and the notion of an *identified* being (Bohm, 1994, p. 222) are able to hold themselves as true and taken as 'an end in itself ' (Medina & Wood 2005, p. 9), the analysis of the 1979 MOE report examines the underlying conditions of truth that constituted what was acceptable and necessary for the appearance and transformation of *subject positions* – a central concern in Foucault's work (1982a, p. 777). This would provide initial evidence of how the objectification of subjects makes possible divergences in curriculum and opportunities that arose from policy discourse. Here, 'arbitrary', in the sense of 'no rational explanation' refers to the binary logic underlying categorical designations of learners that necessarily frames the basis for structural changes. By making 'transparent' discursive policy processes, it is possible to trace how a national educational policy text strategically positions, defines, and classifies learners through dichotomous constructs, that is, what the report termed as 'bright pupils' and 'slow learners' (MOE, 1979a, p. 6-1). In doing so, the analysis makes transparent the discursive construction of identities, and how this relates to structural access.

In order to understand how a differentiated structural reform catering to different abilities has been given legitimacy, this chapter first examines *how* this historical policy works to recognise, define, and classify learners through binary categorisations, that is, what the report termed as 'fast' and 'slow' learners (MOE, 1979a, p. 1-3). In this sense, the *truth* of subjects is circumscribed into distinct opposites. In doing this the analysis provides an initial understanding of how discursive processes function to produce and locate 'slow learners' as requiring institutional segregation while the discursive strategies employed subsequently build the case for streaming which in turn make explicit the *conditions* necessary for identifying particular types of learners.

Combining CDA with the philosophical discussion of truth can be a bridge between questions concerning identity and structural inequality. To develop a theoretical-analytical framework suitable for revealing the historically situated construction of unequal learner identities, this chapter explores Foucault's work that can be synthesised with critical discourse analysis (CDA) approaches. More particularly, the research examines by what discursive processes did particular identities emerge, and how these identities were made 'manifest, nameable, and describable' (Foucault, 1972, p. 41). In particular, the aim of this stage of analysis is to examine the naming process and discover precisely *how* unequal learner identities are constructed to legitimise streaming. Oriented towards these foci, Foucault's archaeological method is used in combination with an amalgamation of CDA approaches to make explicit how power works through methods and techniques or historical conditions that regulate discursive policy formations of learner capability identities.

The theoretical-philosophical framework underpinning the analysis draws on Foucault's perspectives because his insights provide the initial opportunity to understand how the historical constitution of subject is linked to the legitimisation of unequal practices. In order to understand how the problem is not with the subject but with institutions, Foucault's engagement with historical work enables him to examine how the human subject is placed in complex relations of institutional power through modes of objectification in discourse (1982a, pp. 777–778). More importantly, in relation to this research, without a historical focus that examines a chronology of policy discourses, how unequal educational practices for different categories of learners are produced, sustained, and legitimised throughout the years within a frame of meritocracy could not be adequately addressed. In order to scaffold the research's central analytical examination on the relations between the notion of truth and the formation of subjects, the following section outlines archaeology as an analytical method.

Archaeological method: how power is constituted through knowledge and 'truth'

The concept of 'power/knowledge' spans Foucault's work in its entirety, from his 'archaeological' and 'genealogical' works to his 'ethical'[1] works (Feder, 2011, p. 55). Foucault uses the term 'power/knowledge' to signify that power is constituted through accepted forms of knowledge and 'truth' (Gaventa, 2003, n.p.) rather than 'imposed on the subject from the outside according to a necessary causality or structural determination' (Foucault, 1984b, n.p.). As such it is important not to assume a prior objectification and constitution of subjects as an exercise of power relations but rather, to explore *how* the objectivising of subjects is conceptualised through discursive formation (Fairclough, 1992, p. 64; Foucault, 1972, p. 205; 1982a, p. 778). A discursive formation is formed by a 'group of statements' (Brown & Cousins, 1986, p. 33). To begin the analysis with 'how' is to suggest that linear power as such does not exist (Foucault, 1982a, p. 786).

The philosophical theory[2] presented within this data-driven research hence does not assume a prior objectification of power. Furthermore, a framework that presupposes the existence of power undermines the complexity of relationships between language and social practice, as it requires the researcher to negotiate the process of interpretation within stipulated boundaries. Thus, the point of departure of this research's analysis, the access to the phenomenon of identity, the passage through changing policy discourses must secure their own reflexive method if it is to have any prospect of examining the phenomenon and the conditions of possibility of inequality (cf. Heidegger, 2003a, pp. 66–67). It is thus not a matter of 'examining "power" with regards to its origins, its principles, or its legitimate limits but of studying the methods and techniques' (Foucault, 1984b, n.p.) used in policy documents to modify subjects (Foucault, 1982a, p. 777).

Foucault calls the initial axis of his analyses 'archaeology' (Davidson, 1986). Of particular importance in Foucault's archaeological method is the observation that 'discursive formations *produce* the object about which they speak' (Dreyfus & Rabinow, 1983, p. 61). In exploring how policy discourse imputes forms of divisive identity to individuals, it is not institutional power but the objectification of the subject, as those who are shaped through discursive formations of 'truth' claims, which is the general theme of this research. This objectification, formed through discursive practices in policy documents, provides an opportunity to produce *widely dispersed* 'new' knowledge (Feder, 2011, pp. 60–62). Citing Foucault, Rouse (2005, p. 110) argues that this 'new' knowledge produces a new sense of far-reaching relationships of power; it produces new 'understandings', new 'truths', not only about particular learners, but about other learners who would be identified under the *pervasive*, albeit less conspicuous standards and conditions that structure, define, induce, and extend this new identity. As Foucault (1986, p. 74) argues:

> 'Truth' is linked in a circular relation with systems of power which produce and sustain it, and to effects of power which it induces and which extends it. A 'regime' of truth.

In relation to economic growth, this regime is not merely ideological; it is a *condition* of the formation and development of neo-liberalism that builds and sustains inequality (Foucault, 1986, p. 74). Further, Foucault (1991b, p. 57) terms these new evolving 'truths' as 'mutations' which 'simultaneously affect several discursive formations'. These 'new' truths are *elementary* conditions of possibility – in the sense of their productive appropriation for both learner identities and the legitimation of streaming as an institutional practice. The premise being that these new 'truths', constructed within the workings of the marriage between power–knowledge–truth, demonstrate the legitimacy of streaming and how it has been made necessary.

The first stage of the analysis examines the relationship of 'truth' claims about particular learners and systematic inequality. By tracing the continuous reconstruction of 'new' but unequal forms of representation of different learners, it is possible to make visible how policy discourses justify, legitimise, and sustain unequal opportunities for knowledge access and differentiated treatments within a meritocratic system.To understand this relationship, the research draws on Foucault's (1982a, p. 792) arguments on how the power–knowledge–truth nexus is the condition as well as the result of a 'system of differentiation'. These concepts will be made explicit by employing CDA in the analysis of the 1979 policy report. Drawing on Foucault's (1972) archaeological work, the examination of truth in the first stage of analysis requires the consideration of two domains: first, how truth is implicated in the *identity* construction of learners within the workings of the institutional processes, and second, the *pervasiveness* of this construction within various iterations of the policy document. As an initial attempt to isolate the level of discursive practices and formulate the (historical) rules of production and transformation for 'truth' claims in relation to learner identities, this archaeological level is an indispensable and distinct primary level of analysis (Davidson, 1986, p. 227), providing a much more complex focus on the subject depicted. The focus is on developing the principles for the analysis taken up in later chapters.

The concept '*regime* of truth' in Foucault's writings progressively evolves, with increasing emphasis, into the '*games* of truth' as mechanisms of power. While the initial analysis in Chapter 2 focuses on what the subject must be in order to become a legitimate subject of this or that type of knowledge through the 'regime' of truth, subsequent philosophical deliberations and analyses in Chapters 3 to 7 examine the conditions under which the subject is formed, transformed, and constituted as an object in the 'games' of truth – alluding to the Truth of economic growth (Foucault, 1984b, n.p.). In his most mature writings, Foucault (1984b, n.p.) developed the power/knowledge concept to refer to 'relations between the subject and truth ... the study of the modes according to which the subject was able to be inserted as an object in the games of truth'. As Foucault (1984a, p. 127) argues:

> when I say 'game' I mean ensemble of rules for the production of truth ... it is an ensemble of procedures which lead to a certain result, which can be considered in function of its *principles* and its *rules of procedures* as valid or not, as winner or loser.

What Foucault offers is the basis for a discourse-analytic investigation of relations between systems of classification through a 'streaming' mechanism and privileges to knowledge access (Fairclough, 1992, pp. 47, 64). However, while Foucault provides an intensive insight and conceptual understanding of how certain types of identities are encoded in policy discourse through a classificatory grid, he does not present the means by which his perspectives can be empirically situated; and conceptualisations of such identities remain retrospective. Policies have deposited constructed truths through discourse that can be unearthed only by employing close textual analysis techniques such as CDA. In the discussion below, the focus is on identifying and consolidating CDA approaches that are compatible with the theoretical and epistemological tenets of archaeology. His perspectives *constitute* and *are constituted by* these various analytical approaches.

Analysing the 1979 MOE report: designing a multidisciplinary CDA to explicate the truth-value of statements

This section outlines a synthesis of relevant CDA approaches, designed to operationalise the field of power-knowledge-truth as the guiding principle for the discursive construction of subjects. This study adopts a multidisciplinary CDA approach rather than relying on preformulated frameworks which may lead to an overdetermination of how a discursive phenomenon is implicated in social and structural inequality, imposed prior to any analysis taking place. In adopting a CDA perspective, the research is located in exposing forms of 'power', of how power works through methods or techniques, or conditions, and the discourses it permeates in order to reach individual modes of subjectivity.

The first analytical stage focuses on formulating a multi-layered approach and issue-oriented framework (van Dijk, 1993, p. 279) that draws from the intersection of Foucault's (1982a; 1984b) power-knowledge-truth concept and CDA's approaches developed by Fairclough (2001) in *Language and Power* and van Dijk (1993) in *Principles of Critical Discourse Analysis*. Individually, these approaches are useful in elucidating the discursive processes involved in constructing the 'regime of truth' about learner identities through policy texts. Together they form a cluster of studies whose themes and conceptual-analytical points on subject representation are quite adjacent.

For the preliminary analysis of the 1979 MOE report, Foucault's argument is used to ground the conceptual scope while using Fairclough's approach for the initial analytic data focus. Fairclough's perspectives on the intersection of experiential, relational, and expressive value of words in understanding the discursive practices of social representations correspond significantly to Foucault's central concept of the truth-value of statements. That is, Fairclough's analytical approach makes explicit the conditions by which certain statements are sanctioned and how they work to construct a 'regime of truth' about particular subjects in policy texts. The close alignment between Fairclough's and Foucault's understandings of discourse means that a rapport can be readily established between Foucault's critical purpose and Fairclough's analytical methods: the domain of inquiry is the same. In this instance, Fairclough's work provides a much needed entrance and platform from which added engagement using other approaches can yield new areas of investigation and debate. While the preliminary analysis of the 1979 MOE report draws on Fairclough's types of values, the second stage of analysis traces the discursive formations and transformations between and across chronological texts from 1979 to 2019 through drawing on several other CDA approaches to make explicit the phenomenon of evaluative propagation. This is an extension of the historical examination of how 'techniques and procedures' of institutional practices are 'accorded value in the acquisition of truth' (Foucault, 1980, p. 131) of economic growth as the (only) way forward in policy discourse.

In *Language and Power*, Fairclough (2001) distinguishes between three types of value that are simultaneously inherent in any textual element: experiential, relational, and expressive value. Experiential value relates to the 'text producer's experience of the natural or social world' (p. 93), broadly corresponding with the contents of the text, knowledge, and beliefs. Relational value is concerned with relations and social relationships enacted by and through the text. Last, and central to the purpose of this analysis, expressive value is associated with subjects and social identities. By exploring all three values, the analysis aims to show how the texts encode beliefs about particular learners, as well as how they construct the intra-discursive relationships and social identities of the learners concerned. These different aspects of value – the experiential, relational, and expressive values – happen at once in any given instance of meaning making, and are best seen as interdependent conveniences for analysis. Fairclough's approach on the social function of the expressive values of words is then further extended through van Dijk's approach.

Van Dijk's (1993, p. 257) *Principles of Critical Discourse Analysis* complements Fairclough's perspective on the social function of the expressive values of words. Van Dijk argues that discourse control is a form of social action control: it implies the conditions of control over the minds (the social cognition) of other people. This control plays a prominent role in the management of social representations, particularly that of learners. His work examines how controversial decisions in managing social representations are rationally defended through discursive strategies. Further, his analysis demonstrates how such acts are justified and legitimised through the manipulation of public opinion (1993, p. 267).

Since none of these frameworks are blueprints, they need to be drawn on selectively for the particular research at hand and if needed combined with other forms of social analysis (Taylor, 2004, p. 436). The analysis in the first preliminary analytical stage combines Fairclough's and van Dijk's approaches with those of other researchers who build on and extend their work to enhance the understanding of syntactic and linguistic processes. This initial work renders visible the discursive processes of policy practices that permit policy statements to emerge and to be legitimated as knowledge about learners (Marshall, 1996, p. 121).

The approaches developed by Fairclough and van Dijk have influenced the way in which researchers examine questions of language and society. Graham (2011), Peters (2007), Scheurich (1997), and Walshaw (2007) have drawn on the Foucauldian approach. Furthermore, Hamilton and Pitt (2011), Mulderrig (2012), and Trew (1979) have drawn on a Faircloughian version of CDA, while Mautner's (2009) approach to CDA draws on a combination of both Fairclough's and van Dijk's approaches. The preliminary analysis also refers to Fraser's (1995) study, which examines the circumstances in which a politics of recognition supports a politics of redistribution. Her approach provides further analytical interpretations of the processes involved in the objectification of learners. These seemingly eclectic but actually interrelated approaches provide the initial means to explore how unequal learner identities are designed and made apparent through discursive practices. The preliminary analysis, which presents and synthesises these methods, is explorative, indicating significant patterns without claiming to be exhaustive.

This sensitivity to discursive practices, coupled with a strong focus on the objectification of the 'subject', leads to an issue-oriented approach (van Dijk, 1993, p. 279) that is appreciative of the complexity of the ways in which the linguistic predilections of the document are implicated in the power-knowledge-truth grids. The analysis focuses on the following broad question: What are the conditions necessary for identifying particular types of learners? In this instance, the study uses what Foucault (1972, p. 221) terms as 'the circumstances of repetition' of discourse that make possible not only the 'reappearance' but the *pervasiveness* of identity construction. The focus is not on dichotomous learner identities as a pre-existing phenomenon, but on the conditions that make this binary construction possible.

The first analytical stage of this research is the domain in which the identity of learners is constituted through objectification: that is, learners become objectified in language through arbitrary assignments that are transposed into conventional designations heavily predicated on the categorically conditioned duality, 'slow' and 'fast' (MOE, 1979a, p. 1-3). As an extension of Fairclough's (2001) work on the values of words, the second analytical stage, presented in Chapters 5, 6, and 7, marks the point at which the research orientation moves from a concern with objectification and the logic of policy language towards a perspective more grounded in the problems of the values of policy language, and conceptions of value within the context of value-forming labour.

The following three sections outline the three themes that emerge from the preliminary analysis of the 1979 MOE report, which situate the conditions by which learner identities are categorised through examining the appearance of subject positions as they become discursively constructed. These themes then provide the basis for the subsequent analysis of policy extracts in the rest of this research study. They serve as starting points for the current investigation of the conditions by which learner identities were historically situated. This exploratory analysis forms the basis upon which further research will investigate the evolution of discursive change.

Theme 1: capability recognition as social change

The first theme explores the ways in which the text constructs the subjectivities of school pupils as learners: how the text positions and defines pupils as learners and what specific claims have been made in relation to these positions (Walshaw, 2007, p. 46). Extract 1 below provides an illustration of the discursive strategies deployed to make the objectification of pupils possible. While the following subsection focuses on how a certain segment of the student population, constructed as 'failures' is associated with the inability to perform within the prescribed educational system, the subsection that follows focuses on how this identity is sustained.

The 'failures'

In Extract 1, students 'who do not make the grade' (line 3), are repeatedly associated with an inability to perform within the prescribed educational system with the words 'do not make the grade' (line 3) and 'suffer repeated failures' (lines 3–4), Further, when they are 'exposed to competition from brighter children' (line 7), they suffer from a loss of 'self-confidence, self-esteem' (lines 4–5) and develop 'a host of character defects produced by feelings of inadequacy' (lines 5–6). The proliferation of terms focusing on one group of participants can be seen as 'over-lexicalisation' (Fairclough, 2001, p. 96) where the descriptions differ only slightly in meaning. Moreover, the lexical classifications are embedded in and express a system of discourse about different forms of under-intelligence presented as manifestations of the inherent nature of these students. Each term

Extract 1: MOE, 1979a, 'An overview of the problem', '*Fast and slow learners*'

Extract
Educationists and others who oppose streaming of children according to their ability to absorb instruction often forget that the final result could be even more cruel to the children who do not make the grade and suffer repeated failures. The end product would have lost self-confidence, self-esteem and developed a host of character defects produced by feelings of inadequacy. It is far better that these children leave school literate in one language. Since they are not exposed to competition from brighter children in classes, there is less danger of loss of self-esteem.

Source: MOE, 1979a, p. 1-4.

within the discourse lends itself to a shift in educational practices in the direction of more control through tracking practices to measure these students' educational attainments, and seeks to block any request for a reconsideration of the policy. Coming all at once in one short text, they resonate with Trew's (1979, p. 136) view of 'an incantation and have a kind of axiomatic, tautological effect that forecloses all discussions'. The overall effect is one that constitutes the primary categorisation of these students as possessing all these undesirable traits. Through this discursive strategy, policymakers are not just giving their views about 'children who do not make the grade' (line 3) – they are formulating and constructing the very nature of these children through personalisation.

In line with Fairclough's (2001, p. 81) argument on ideology and meaning, this suggests a conflation of acts by children who do not make the grade with undesirable personalities and social traits which simultaneously indicate an inherent character defect on the part of 'these children' (line 6), construed as convincing evidence of their intrinsic deficiency. In returning to the concordance output related to *failure* and its coordinated adjectives, drawing on Mautner's (2009, p. 128) review of examining concordances, negative emotions (i.e. *loss of self-confidence, self-esteem* and a *host of character defects* [lines 4–5]) are also linked to 'these children' (line 6). The collocational profile thus points to the twin nature of academic failure as a social phenomenon with a manifestly psychological impact on individuals. Further, this kind of discourse not only interpellates and constitutes a subject; it also outlines the specific and technical expertise required to deal with that particular perception of the subject (Graham, 2011, p. 670). Following Graham's Foucauldian approach to the construction of categories as objects of scrutiny, then, it is possible to argue that the cultural description of a child's behaviour as 'loss of self-confidence, self-esteem' (lines 4–5) and 'a host of character defects' (line 5) builds the case for a system through which the child is properly classified and can be referred to the 'appropriate' stream. Specialised treatment to avoid 'feelings of inadequacy' (lines 5–6) may then begin.

In this way, despite in some sense appearing to reinstate a concern for the learner, this discursive strategy locates the causes of failure primarily within individuals and their personal deficits, and aggregates those individuals into generalised, and pathologised, social groupings. Paradoxically, the failure of the individual, and not the operationalisation of the system, is thus constructed as the crux of the problem. Moreover, this preferred discourse of streaming seeks to overturn 'educationists and others' (line 1) who oppose streaming. Based on the behaviour-modification speculations of 'these children' (line 6), the discourse emphasises the importance of the streaming exercise for the well-being of students. Hence, criticisms of the system based on its 'cruel' influence on 'children who do not make the grade' (line 3) would appear more justifiable. In doing so, the 'inadequate character-defective slow learner' message is reinforced textually, marks slow learners as deficient and leads to a blanket inference about group differences. To the degree that these problems exist, the proposed solution is institutional segregation. The apparent sympathy that characterises such discourse paradoxically lends weight to the acceptability of biased opinions about 'these children' (line 6) that cause or confirm social inequality (van Dijk, 1993, pp. 267–268).

This remedy of subordinating students 'along one axis of social division' that is required to redress the injustice insistently calls attention to a proposition for explicit capability recognition as opposed to capability equality (Fraser, 1995, p. 92). By combining ability and curriculum together too tightly, the proposition reinforces and relies on group distinctions, proliferating ideologies of intellectual inferiority to justify differentiation. Significantly, this strategy treats the complexities of low learning capacity as effectively reducible to the need for a tailored curriculum.

How the identity of failures is sustained

In identifying how the text constructs the learner identity 'failures', the focus now is on how this identity is made solid and persistent. In Extract 1, the text revealed the way a deficit view of students as failures was constructed. The presumably collective[3] fear of 'these children' (line 6) is assuaged and segregation from other children is reconstructed as a necessary treatment to avoid exposing them to 'competition from brighter children' (line 7). The focus is on children's presumed deficiencies and an attempt to discursively construe a distinct group of students gauged against an arbitrary notion of normality.[4] These discursive formations 'objectify and subjugate the individual who is perceived as a problem' (Scheurich, 1997, p. 107).

The concept of streaming in the ensuing discourse introduces a 'mild' form of justified exclusion by pointing to the *necessity* for differentiated instruction. This necessity is formulated through claims of deficiency. By 'juxtaposing the positive with the negative in a way that highlights the deficit' (Hamilton & Pitt, 2011, p. 600), the claim, '*Since* they are not exposed to competition from brighter children in classes, there is less danger of loss of self-esteem' (lines 7–8), reduces complex social and educational inequalities to a lack of innate learning capacity and poor sense of self. That is, the 'deficiencies' of these children would be accentuated should they be educated alongside the brighter children.

This reductive common-sense discourse presents policymakers with the dilemma of how to match the daily classroom realities with inequalities in the 'ability to absorb instruction' (line 2) experienced by this class of learner. The policy proposes that streaming is necessary because it helps less able children to cope and allows able children to excel. This suggests that the policy text implicitly assumes deficiencies within 'these children' (line 6) and presents 'prescriptive remedies and packaged answers' to alleviate these deficiencies (Walshaw, 2007, p. 56). The text, by fixing 'these children' (line 6) within a 'system of differentiations' (Foucault, 1982a, p. 792), regulates them and exercises power over them, by imbuing them (Walshaw, 2007, p. 56) with esteem issues.[5] By the same token, they are projected as possessing low reasoning capacities and easily influenced to the point of developing 'a *host* of character defects' (line 5).

Here, then, the analysis reveals implicit assumptions about the nature of 'the children who do not make the grade' (line 3) and about the relationship between them and successful children. It is assumed that the learner category 'failure' is a homogeneous, predictable group imbued with vulnerable attributes, and would easily develop a host of 'character defects' (line 5) as a result of persistent failure. Since they are susceptible to failure when exposed to the binary opposite learner category of successful children and cannot sustain the clarity of objectives for themselves, it falls to the policymakers to intervene on their behalf for their own realistic educational horizons and personal psychological health – to ensure that 'these children leave school literate in one language' (lines 6–7). It is assumed that the economic or psychological stability of 'these children' is dependent on the institutional division of them from 'brighter children' (line 7).

At this juncture, it is necessary to draw on the theme that underlies Foucault's *The Subject and Power* (1982a). The theme highlights the relationship between power and knowledge, and how the former is used to control and define the latter. The use of the terms, 'these children' and 'brighter children' is a means of social control through what Foucault (1982a, pp. 777–778) calls 'dividing practices' – a process that objectivises subjects. This process constructs each of these groups as a collective, homogenised whole and negates any expression of individuality. The effects of institutional power are linked with knowledge, definitions of competence, and qualification: conflicting discourses on the privileges of knowledge are correlated with who has access. But they are also a demonstration of static representations imposed on people (Foucault, 1982a, p. 781). As Foucault (1982a, p. 781) points out:

> This form of power applies itself to immediate everyday life which categorises the individual, marks him [sic] by his own individuality, attaches him to his own identity, imposes a law of truth on him which he must recognise and which others have to recognise in him.

Thus, in imposing a state-sanctioned definition of competence and qualification there is a movement away from paternalistic discourse in the sense that it is not about protecting 'these children' as much as protecting the wider society and generating the best outcomes economically. That is, 'the children who do not make the grade' are vulnerable to being presented as a kind of 'risk' to the state and the economy.

In understanding the processes that work to sustain the categorisation of these pupils, the next section examines how this is intimately tied to the conceptualisation of social structure and the notion of justice. This second theme, inequality as justice, involves certain fundamental ideas on equality and justice in relation to a sustainable educational philosophy. The theme includes a proposal for more 'target-appropriate', as opposed to equitable, practices through a differentiated curriculum. Significantly, it aims at critiquing and transforming an existing educational organisation premised on 'an egalitarian philosophy' (MOE, 1979a, p. 1-5, line 2).

Theme 2: inequality as justice

The second theme explores the ways in which the notion of inequality as justice is constructed. The analysis of Extract 2 illustrates how the notion is built through the juxtaposition of educational philosophies. The analysis of Extract 3 focuses on how justification of a differentiated system is made possible by highlighting the support given by school principals.

Egalitarian-excellence educational philosophies

In Extract 2, certain fundamental ideas about learner capacities are explicitly provided and explicitly recognise that learners have different learning developments and rates of progress. More importantly, by juxtaposing 'egalitarian' versus 'excellence' educational philosophies, it provides an understanding of how sustainable educational trajectories for 'different children', premised on certain sanctioned categorical descriptions of learners, can be thought about and rationalised, through a divergence regime. Similar to Extract 1 above, the notion of 'diversity' here is constructed within the context of inclusive practices.

In the above extract, the term 'egalitarian' (line 2) becomes the focus of the ideological struggle as the discourse argues against the Western belief that egalitarianism should be exercised in the interests of the majority in education. More specifically, this ideological struggle draws upon pre-existing classification schemes which are in part already established *systems of evaluation* (Fairclough, 2001, pp. 96–98). One is a scheme in which the educational development of different students may be constrained in the absence of streaming: 'This philosophy partly rests on a prejudice against pursuit of excellence' (lines 3–4). This scheme is constructed on the belief that different children have different capacities to acquire knowledge. Another scheme is for ways of evaluating egalitarianism, a common philosophy used in 'other countries' (line 10) within the Singapore context; it is

Extract 2: MOE, 1979a, 'An overview of the problem', '*Problems of streaming*'

Lines	*Extract*
	Much of the prejudice against streaming of school children derives from an **egalitarian** philosophy fashionable in the Western World after World War II. This philosophy partly rests on a prejudice against pursuit of excellence. We do not want to enter into a controversy against those egalitarian ideas. Perhaps this is just what Western societies need. But in Singapore, many of the problems in the present school system would not have arisen if those concerned had earlier accepted the logical consequences of the fact that different children have different capacities to acquire knowledge. Further when this knowledge is imparted in languages which most of them do not speak at home, following what other countries do will not help much. The system has been structured such that only the brightest 12% to 15% of school children can cope. To subject the less able students to the same regime has been the chief defect of our educational system in the past.

Source: MOE, 1979a, p. 1-5.

implicit in the collocations 'many of the problems' (line 6), 'the logical consequences' (lines 7–8), 'different children have different capacities to acquire knowledge' (lines 8–9), 'knowledge is imparted in languages which most of them do not speak at home' (lines 9–10), and 'following what other countries do will not help much' (lines 10–11). Here, the policy challenges the general acceptance that a 'standard' discourse of egalitarian-based system serves as a universal educational philosophy and a guiding principle. More importantly, an egalitarian-based system is constructed as having the reactionary effect of failing to engage with diverse student needs.

Egalitarianism is rated in terms of educational efficiency, social impact, and efficacy within the local context and is negatively evaluated in classification schemes associated with education. The text points to a way the classification scheme constitutes a particular way of projecting some aspect of social and educational realities. These realities are built upon a particular representation of egalitarianism. If a diagnosis of a perfect equal arrangement is inherently problematic, then the entire strategy of egalitarianism is deeply impaired, even if every conceivable alternative in the world were available. What follows from this argument is that a non-egalitarian education system, and from this a non-egalitarian society, is necessary for the pursuit of excellence.

Here, then, the discourse argues that in conceptualising the nature of educational problems present in the school system, policymakers need to subscribe to the argument that a school system informed by a commitment to egalitarianism negates the fundamental tenet 'that different children have different capacities to acquire knowledge' (lines 8–9). Egalitarianism thus, does not accept the value of group differentiation, whereas policymakers tend rather to promote it. Indeed, this conception of a Western egalitarian philosophy, which advocates standardised, fair institutional norms through equitable practice, though 'fashionable' (line 2), is constructed as both socioeconomically and culturally unjust as it systematically disadvantages some groups of people.

Thus, maintaining the 'same regime' (line 13) of egalitarianism characterises the very culture of ideologies and practices with which the 'less able students' (lines 12–13) are unable to 'cope' (line 12). Hence, sustaining a 'regime' of equal educational standards for all is constructed as inappropriate and ineffective in meeting the diverse needs of Singaporean students and society.

The text then goes on to formulate the educational dilemma in a form that focuses on distinctions between Western egalitarian philosophy and a local reality that is more amenable and attractive to the proposed resolution. Through this juxtaposition, the text reveals a clash of perspectives that reflect the educational heteroglossia – 'We do not want to enter into a controversy against *those* egalitarian ideas' (lines 4–5). This also suggests ongoing contestations of the Western educational philosophy against the needs of the Singapore society. The statement, 'This philosophy partly rests on a prejudice against pursuit of excellence' (lines 3–4), is an evaluative critique of the Western philosophy and a rebuttal to those who would keep in place an egalitarian philosophy where the 'pursuit of excellence' (lines 3–4) is relegated. Here, then, in order to clarify these competing dilemmas, the 'Western' notion of egalitarianism is constructed as undermining rather than supporting the 'pursuit of excellence' (lines 3–4). This conceptualisation enters one crucial preliminary caveat. In proposing to assess egalitarianism from the standpoint of social equality, the text constructs the fundamental tenet of egalitarianism that proposes a purely idealistic notion of equal access to knowledge regardless of capability, as failing to respect the rights of individuals to excel. Thus, egalitarianism is *unacceptable* as it does not recognise that educational opportunities need to be mobilised around capability needs.

Support of school leaders for a differentiated system

The following analysis of Extract 3 demonstrates that there can be serious differences between competing principles of educational philosophy that claims to serve students' interest. Obviously, controversial decisions must be rationally defended. While focusing on the justification of a differentiated system, the following analysis emphasises the positive properties of a revised system, which are embraced by school principals.

Paradoxically, within the justification for differentiation, those who espouse the cause of educational equality are themselves surrounded and influenced by a climate which generates academic inequality. The word 'convince' (line 9) suggests that the Director of Education, who carries the social and moral authority of the education community, has responded positively – despite the initial concern about 'streaming children according to ability' (lines 4–6) – to the ideological position of the policymakers and the notion

Extract 3: MOE, 1979a, 'An overview of the problem', '*Problems of streaming*'

Lines	*Extract*
1	This system of having three sub-systems of education, each of which is
2	adjusted to the rate at which children can absorb instruction, means that
3	children have to be streamed at some stage in their school career. The
4	subject of streaming children according to ability evokes strong emotional
5	response, especially among professionals in the Ministry of Education,
6	and the Institute of Education. However, we find that school principals
7	who face the problem of slow learners have come to the conclusion that
8	one system cannot do justice to all children, and they support our
9	proposals. Eventually, we managed to convince the Director of Education
10	that teaching children of different levels of ability under special
11	circumstances of Singapore, cannot be conducted in the same way as used
12	by more homogeneous societies, where the language of instruction is the
13	language spoken at home.

Source: MOE, 1979a, pp. 1-4, 1-5.

of ability differences. Further, it suggests that those who are truly committed to the pursuit of education for 'slow learners' (line 7) should accept the concept of streaming in its entirety. This consensus is brought about by the use of the verb 'support' (line 8). The verb suggests that the principals are orchestrating or managing in some way the actions (Mulderrig, 2012, p. 713) of the government, instead of the reverse. There tends to be, however, more resistance to accepting this policy by 'professionals in the Ministry of Education, and the Institute of Education' (lines 5–6). By categorising students as 'slow learners' (line 7), and by conceiving them as a 'problem' (line 7), policy decision-makers detail how, in their opinion, a way to address this 'problem' would be by reconstructing the system because 'one system cannot do justice to all children' (line 8). This framing of a singular mode of instruction as unjust renders those who resist streaming unintelligible or morally reprehensible. Streaming is then positioned as a key requirement for a heterogeneous student population to meet its diverse needs (Archer, 2007, p. 649). The point to note here is that accepting that rationality demands curriculum inequality, so that justice is served to 'all children' (line 8). To further understand how curriculum inequality is conceptualised as just, the following theme examines the way in which policy discourse constructs limited access to knowledge for the 'less capable pupils' as ethical.

Theme 3: ethics: or *philosophy of desirability*

Finally, in proposing segregation, the report appeals to morality and ethics to provide the *necessary* foundation from which to hold unequal structural reforms as a justifiable, *desirable* form of educational practice. It is important to emphasise that foregrounding ethics in determining learners' learning experiences is a form of regulatory power aimed at governance (Walshaw, 2007, pp. 54–56). The analysis of Extract 4 highlights the way the learner category of 'less capable pupils' is to be subjected to knowledge exclusion. The excerpt also illustrates the effectiveness of metaphors in structuring reality in a particular way. Of particular significance is the use of the metaphors to justify unequal resource distribution in relation to how learners are represented.

This section of the analysis draws on notions of ability, curriculum, and opportunity to examine the operationalised discursive positioning of less capable pupils, configured through a discourse of 'difference' (Walshaw, 2007, p. 55), positioned in relation to the ethical aspects of education policy. Several steps are needed to make sense of the text's argument in providing reduced educational opportunities (i.e. 'a pace slower' [line 2]) for 'less capable pupils' (line 3).

First, in order to coherently link the recommendation of 'giving half a loaf when a whole loaf would choke' (lines 10–11) as a practical solution, it must be assumed that giving half a loaf *is* practical. Second, the word 'instead' (line 10) in

Extract 4: MOE, 1979a, 'Recommendations', '*A suggested education system: Reduction of the attrition rate*'

Lines	*Extract*
1	The suggested education system provides an opportunity for the less
2	capable pupils to develop at a pace slower than that for the more capable
3	pupils. However, a more relaxed pace for the less capable pupils is only
4	one of the important factors influencing the attrition rate. It must be
5	complemented by a properly-organised implementation programme; a
6	realistic curriculum, competent teachers, sufficient teaching materials and
7	facilities and a healthy social environment. The system also recognises
8	that not everyone is academically inclined. It does not force bilingualism,
9	the PSLE[6] or the GCE 'O' Level course on those who cannot cope with
10	them. Instead, it tries to seek ways of giving half a loaf when a whole loaf
11	would choke. A child who could not cope with two languages is given one
12	language. A child who is not meant for academic endeavours is given
13	literacy and numeracy to prepare him for training in a skill. A child who
14	cannot handle the GCE 'O' Level course in four years is given five years.
15	Hence, reducing the attrition rate is secondary to offering a child the most
16	appropriate opportunity.

Source: MOE, 1979a, p. 6-4.

this sentence is the cue for an assumption necessary to connect the problems with the solutions and make them cohere. This coherence is based on the implicit assumption that 'giving a whole loaf would choke' (lines 10–11), a metaphorical representation of the problem with the current system. On the other hand, the suggested system also recognises 'that not everyone is academically inclined' (line 8), 'it does not force bilingualism' (line 8), 'the PSLE or the GCE "O" Level course on those who cannot cope with them' (lines 9–10). To make a coherent link between the problems and the solution that precede it, the assumption here is that an ethical solution to these problems lies in 'giving half a loaf' (line 10) to the child. This discursive strategy serves to typify changes peculiar to unequal resource redistributions (Foucault, 1991b, p. 57) – for, in this case, different learners.

Metaphorical transfer from one domain to another

The mobilisation and movement of metaphors for particular persuasive ends, here arguing for structural reforms, is particularly interesting where the metaphor is put to work in ideologically contrastive classification schemes. Different metaphors have different ideological attachments (Fairclough, 2001, pp. 95, 99–100; 1992, p. 195) and this is clearly illustrated by the metaphor used to characterise the intentions of a streaming policy: 'it tries to seek ways of giving half a loaf when a whole loaf would choke' (lines 10–11). This metaphor suggests that streaming will attend to the needs of both 'more capable' (line 2) and 'less capable' (lines 1–2) students and abilities. Further, it explicitly states the intended processes and ideological attachments of different opportunities: the more capable deserve a whole loaf whereas the less capable *should* be satisfied with half a loaf. That is, this metaphorical construction implies that first, 'A child who could not cope with two languages is given one language' (lines 11–12), second, 'A child who is not meant for academic endeavours is given literacy and numeracy to prepare him for training in a skill' (lines 12–13), and third, 'A child who cannot handle the GCE "O" Level course in four years is given five years' (lines 13–14). These recommendations, which are based on common-sense assumptions, give coherence (Fairclough, 2001, p. 68) and social meaning to the metaphorical representation and suggest the systematic redistribution of opportunity so that it is 'the most appropriate' (lines 15–16) for the child. According to Peters (2007, p. 102), the adjective 'appropriate' used to describe education for 'less academically inclined' students has been utilised 'to justify special and segregated educational provisions'. This metaphorical representation constructs contradictory opportunities: there is a focus on meeting capability needs and, yet, access to knowledge is valorised.

The affordances of constructed identities in policy discourse

This section outlines the implications of the analysis of the 1979 MOE report for the research, and sets the trajectory for the next three analytical chapters.

Research findings and implications

The preliminary analysis of the 1979 MOE report indicates how, within the policy discourse, 'three sub-systems of education' (MOE, 1979a, p. 4-5) are closely linked with and used to signify 'justice' and the 'ethical' aspects of policy inception and practice in the context of catering to specific interests and inclinations. These two formations interlink, to the extent that a diversity of just-and-ethically-driven provision is integral to offering a learner 'the most appropriate opportunity' (MOE, 1979a, p. 6-4). The analysis highlights a fundamental and irreconcilable tension within the streaming policy's dual commitment to both 'customisation' and 'opportunity' agendas. Whilst policy discourse proposes to provide the learner with 'the most appropriate opportunity' (MOE, 1979a, p. 6-4), this preliminary analysis has made transparent the linguistic entrapments in the official policy document, which far from working towards providing the meritocratic principle of 'equal opportunities' (Wong, 2000, n.p.), are actually the agent of the subjugating effects of discourse. This tension generates a paradox within a meritocratic educational policy discourse that actually threatens to undermine the very opportunistic mentality that it (purportedly) seeks to promote through the principle of educational meritocracy.

Taking the reproduction of inequality as an observable fact, the assumption that policy plays a critical role in reproducing inequality is central to this research. Combining CDA with the philosophical discussion of truth can be a bridge between questions concerning identity and structural inequality. While Foucault's work provides an understanding of how the objectivising of subjects is conceptualised through discursive formation, this abstract philosophical concept takes its concrete form by employing CDA in policy analysis. The use of this archaeological-methodological framework demonstrates *how* inequality of access is inbuilt and made possible under three distinguishable conditions – 'capability identification for social change', 'inequality as justice', and 'ethics: or *philosophy of desirability*'.

The analysis strongly suggests that being 'less academically inclined' is built into the system. The report anticipates and encourages the proliferation of preferred norms of subjectivity, by presuming capability inferiority and psychological instability. Through exposing the assumptions underpinning claims to truth, the analysis revealed how blame for inherent abnormality is apportioned to 'slow learners' (MOE, 1979a, p. 6-1), as a way of reinforcing justificatory judgments and propositions for policy prescriptions that rejects calls for greater equality of educational opportunity. Specifically, the analysis demonstrates how these texts implicitly presume deficiencies within particular learners, and present prescriptive remedies and packaged solutions to alleviate these constructed deficiencies (Walshaw, 2007, p. 56). The proposed revisions of inequitable curriculum, which comply with the text's categories for the learner, are hence read as normal development, and therefore are institutionally sanctioned (Walshaw, 2007, p. 60). Fundamentally, that these assertions or causal link of factors to the performance of 'slow learners' are assumed rather than supported by empirical evidence, makes the education system vulnerable to arbitrary rule.

Although causality is not something discursive analyses can empirically establish, and should not even be considered within this discourse-analytic approach, looking at *how* patterns of relationships that relate to these three themes develop in consecutive policies can help in explaining how systematic inequality has been historically situated. Rather than supporting the causalistic logic of systemic discrimination, the analysis of the 1979 MOE report points to the specific conditions under which inequality may occur. The purpose here is not one of finding patterns of causality between the workings of the system and ethnic disadvantage as this acts a barrier to systemic analysis, but in examining how a series of discursive practices legitimise inequality within a meritocratic system. In setting out to explore this concern, the analysis highlighted how the *arbitrary positioning of subjects* is the central thrust in legitimising unequal access to knowledge. While any attempt to generalise from the data from this initial analysis would be premature, the themes, which constitute the 'capability–justice–ethics' paradigm, may prove useful in providing an analytical-genealogical trajectory to trace evolving conceptualisations of learner identities in education policies over time, and how they possibly relate to legitimising asymmetrical forms of structural access. Regarding the last theme on ethics, of particular interest is the mobilisation of metaphors for specific persuasive ends leading to structural reforms in the next analytical stage. In particular, that they allude to, and support ideologically contrastive classification schemes for learners.

The next stage of the research

In the next stage of the project, a historical analysis of changes affecting the 1979 streaming policy is examined using eight major educational policy documents, spanning primary to tertiary education, published by the Ministry of Education in the years 1979 (two reports), 1987, 1991 (two reports), 2002, 2006, 2008a, 2012a and four policy-oriented speeches – 2003, 2006[7], and 2019 (two speeches) Addressing compulsory primary education first, most notably with the 1979 MOE report, the government then moved on to secondary education, pre-tertiary, and university education, a selection of which is the subject of the policies examined in this research (refer to the Appendix for a brief description of each report). In selecting empirical material with which to explore how inequality is inbuilt, the object of critique is a large body of discourse. That is to say, the data is a complex body of discourse consisting of different parts (i.e. policy documents, but also policy speeches, and an integration of these data as part of the whole) in diverse relationships (Fairclough, 2014, pp. 6–7). Drawing on the different bodies of text is partly a matter of intertextuality, that is, 'how texts draw upon, incorporate, recontextualise and dialogue with other texts' (Fairclough, 2003, p. 17). The analysis focuses on the relationship between discourse configurations and socially situated learner identities as it can be understood through domains of discursive practice (cf. Rogers, 2004b, p. 68). It focuses on the subtle nuances that are anchored in close analysis of particular texts which are not selected based on a predetermined conceptual understanding of power relations. For practical purposes, the term 'extracts' refers to physical artefacts (often also referred to as 'documents' or 'speeches') (Saarinen, 2008, p. 722), whereas 'discourse' is used when texts are discussed as a form of social practice (Fairclough, 1992, p. 28). Thus, discourses are seen as being socially formative, or 'practices which form the objects of which they speak' (Foucault, 1972, p. 49).

Given the amount of data, the focus is limited to selecting texts in relation to the 'capability–justice–ethics' thematic paradigm. As a preliminary to the next stage of the research, texts from 1979 to 2019 relating to each of these three themes were systematically selected, grouped, and a second-stage preliminary analysis was conducted, according to each theme. Several policy texts were found to allude to all three themes, which serves to indicate the inextricable and interconnected nature of the themes. These preliminary themes provide a starting point for organising data, but do not constitute a sustainable pattern to explain how inequality is built into the system; this will require further elaboration with rigorous analytical examination of historical texts and philosophical principles. This historical and systematic approach in selecting a population of data based on themes that emerged from a preliminary and subsequent analysis, provides a framework for exploring the genealogy of systematic inequality and how this practice has been given legitimacy within a meritocratic framework.

Tracing discursive pathways and the theme of 'ethics: or philosophy of desirability'

In the process of analysing overlapping policy extracts that allude to the 'capability–justice–ethics' paradigm, while being aware of subject objectification, a cursory examination of ethical practices in policy discourses repeatedly reflects: first, the consistent utilisation of the metaphors of flexibility, choice, diversity, and opportunity; and second, a value system that is profoundly enmeshed in all three themes. The analysis demonstrates that a value system that is produced and reproduced in the theme of ethics is profoundly enmeshed in the impetus for social change and the conceptualisation of justice. Hence, an investigation of the theme of ethics would mean an investigation of the other two themes. This marks the point at which the research orientation moves from a concern with developing the trajectories of all three themes to the development of the theme of 'ethics: or *philosophy of desirability*' (Nietzsche, 1967a, p. 181). To develop a genealogical-analytical framework suitable for revealing the historically situated construction of unequal learner identities, the next chapter explores Foucault's works in moral philosophy and ethics that can be synthesised with critical discourse analysis (CDA) approaches.

Notes

1 The concepts of genealogy and ethics are elucidated in Chapter 3.
2 The philosophical perspectives drawn on for this research are elucidated in Chapters 2, 3, and 4.
3 An alternative reading could include a kind of paternalism here; that is, 'we' should 'care' for these children and not let them be unduly harmed by a competitive education system.

4 It is beyond the scope of this study, but it may be useful to look at how pupils are valued based on categories, that is, 'bright' students are more *desirable* for the nation at large. The notion of 'desirability' is then subsumed under the notion of normality. However, as explicated in Chapters 5, 6, and 7, this research focuses on desirability in terms of desirable outcomes within the future-oriented logic of policy discourse.

5 It might be argued that, rather than imbuing them with esteem issues, a paternalistic point of view implicit in this text seeks to protect them from acquiring esteem issues, that is, to prevent them from becoming particular kinds of subjects that would be inevitable in a competitive system. It is possible for the discourse to be read as both – as offering a kind of paternal care while at the same time categorising them as having deficits.

6 The PSLE, or Primary School Leaving Examination, is conducted in Singapore annually. It is a national examination which pupils sit at the end of their final year of primary school education (General information, 2015, n.p.)

7 Recommendations for a primary school subject-based banding policy and the Teach Less Learn More (TLLM) policy, and the rationale for both, were communicated by former Minister of Education Tharman Shanmugaratnam at the 2006 and 2005 Work Plan Seminars respectively rather than reports by committees.

3 Using genealogy and ethics to investigate the conditioning of human beings into moral subjects who desire more

Overview

This chapter unpacks the term 'genealogy' and the relationship that it bears to archaeology discussed in Chapter 2. In particular, it discusses Foucault's analytical methods on genealogy and ethics and their suitability for a philosophically grounded interdisciplinary piece of linguistic research in examining the objectification of the subject. Specifically, his concept of a *genealogy of ethics* provides a methodological treatise to study the moral codes through which the subject is able to be inserted as an object in the games of truth. The chapter further outlines a synthesis of relevant CDA approaches, designed to operationalise Foucault's and Nietzsche's philosophical orientations on schemas of valuation in order to understand how human beings have been constituted and objectified as moral subjects in relation to value-forming labour appropriation who desire economic growth.

Genealogical method

The coordination between archaeology and genealogy is neither uniform nor constant (Anais, 2013, p. 126). Without claiming absolute distinctions between their interests, archaeology directly relates to the *history* of the rules or conditions that regulate policy formations of learner identities (Alvesson & Karreman, 2000, p. 1128; Gale, 2001, p. 379), while genealogy looks at the regulatory forces and events that shape these discursive practices into a recursive network of power relations over time. The archaeological method, which is the focus of the first stage of analysis in Chapter 2, is thus placed in a wider, longitudinal framework through an emphasis on the genealogical method in the second stage – Chapters 5, 6, and 7.

The initial analysis outlined in Chapter 2 is used to construct a 'working' archaeological approach that synthesises various CDA approaches in combination with Foucault's perspectives to critically examine the 'regime of truth' (Foucault, 1980, p. 131) that made possible a preliminary study of capability-based identity constructs. This presents a novel amalgamation of analytical approaches. The combination of these approaches is necessary in order to understand the discursive construction of identities. They are then developed upon by drawing on other approaches in the subsequent genealogical research trajectory to trace the historical and discursive construction of identities. In this, genealogy entails a 'patience and knowledge of details, and it depends on the vast accumulation of source materials' to examine and trace the historical conditions of possibility for the objectification of subjects through truth production (Foucault, 1977, p. 140).

The discussion below focuses particularly on the reflexive importance of the 'critical' in CDA as both the approach to data and the analysis. After first arguing for the importance of placing data at the centre of any analysis as a way of generating forms of methodology for analysis, the discussion moves on to examine how data-driven analysis and philosophical inquiry are inexplicably entwined, with each informing the other within the critical analysis of Singapore's education policy.

Data-driven analysis as the basis of genealogical method

Central to CDA is the notion that textual analysis should be informed by the socio-political context within which a text is located and produced. The discourse-historical approach, for instance, seeks to investigate the historical, organisational, and political topics and text through integrating what is known about the historical sources and the social and political settings in which discursive 'events' emerged (Wodak, 2001, p. 65). This approach does not operate through a conception of discourse that is commensurate with Foucault's genealogical method (Anais, 2013, p. 127). That is, it does not 'undertake historical investigations of the emergence of certain epistemological structures and their associated discourses, as well as how *knowledge, power*, and claims to *truth* interact both to form cascades of practice and to reinforce the discourses that they emanate from' (Anais, 2013, p. 125). Instead, it tends to assume that texts are produced within the known, unchallenged, parameters of historical political and social settings. This is in contrast with the principal tenet of Foucault's analysis, which considers history to be fragmented and discontinuous by taking the problematisation of truth as a point of departure (Anais, 2013, pp. 127–128) rather than succumbing to the traditional linear successivity of historical development. That is, the analysis here pays detailed and careful attention to the historical progression of education policies from 1979 to 2019, showing in detail how particular ideas are developed, not by focusing on evolving 'contexts' but by taking the problematisation of truth in policy discourse as a point of departure.

While the discourse-historical approach may express faith in existing studies, and the assumptions on which they are based, the genealogical approach actively examines and challenges the underlying assumptions of these studies (cf. Sandberg & Alvesson, 2011, p. 40). Without actively identifying and challenging the assumptions that underlie existing literature, they are likely to have 'truth-creating effects' (Sandberg & Alvesson, 2011, pp. 23–32). And further, positioning and orienting policy text analysis within established literature are likely to preserve and reproduce those assumptions (Sandberg & Alvesson, 2011, p. 35). By this, it is argued that giving primacy to theories may hamper the observation of *what is*, what is *Here and Now* actually taking place within the data, although it may seem as though they were helping that observation by providing possibilities of *what should be* or *what has been*.

Context-dependence as a form of unexamined conditioning

Hence, the focus of the monograph is not to trace the evolving historical and formal contexts, as the 'circumstances surrounding their production' are conjectures as to what may have influenced the text. Further, although the logic is that these texts are produced in a context that informs the production of texts, it is not clear why texts should have this context-dependence (cf. Bohm, 1987, p. 85). In order to address this potential issue of preformed context, and to go beyond the limits of what is already known, it is imperative to start with the data. A data-oriented approach allows the possibility of reframing the conditions in which historical contexts emerge, and examining the texts in themselves, with an awareness of the local political and social contexts. That is, grounding the analysis in the data and developing the methods of analysis from the data keeps in view the broad question of *how*, for example, inequality exists while allowing the possibility of a genealogical analytic sense to uncover the strategies and techniques that produce and sustain 'what subsequently counts as being self-evident, universal, *necessary*' (Foucault, 1991c, p. 87).

Employing CDA in analysing policy texts enables the examination of discursive processes as they unfold, which is far from being deterministic. That is, the analysis does not seek to 'historicise' policy texts by 'explaining their motivation, influences, conditions of production, or their formal and stylistic characteristics' except by following the progression of the documents. That is, by tracing the problematisation of (moral) truths as the policies unfold rather than relying on speculative, external, 'contextual' influences. In examining the discursive processes as they unfold, CDA demands a rigorous systematic approach with analytic transparency while not falling into the potential trap of speculating on their wider social 'meaning' or production. With the problematisation of truth as a point of departure, a focus on the analysis of *what is* – on 'being' (Heidegger, 2005, p. 247) – the research undertaken here is aligned with Foucault's (1981b, p. 9) conceptualisation of a genealogical approach: an 'endeavour to know how and to what extent it might be possible to think differently, instead of legitimating what is already known'. A genealogical approach provides a means to actively identify and challenge assumptions underlying the (historical) truths of policy proposals and propositions. This problematisation of truth, rather than working from a theoretical, context-informed framework, is a key element in not only enabling points of departure for *theory development* (Sandberg & Alvesson, 2011, p. 33, italics included) but in minimising the disposition toward ideological construction.

Analysing the genealogy of truth by tracing a movable host of metaphors

A combination of CDA with a genealogical ethos enables a sustained, critical analysis of how the interaction and relation between these recursive, key metaphors as engines of a neo-liberal discourse, drive and sustain inequality by justifying differentiated treatments for different learners. The genealogical process is an allusion to the doctrine of eternal recurrence, which, in this research, is premised in enduring and regularly recurring policy metaphors (Foucault, 1972, p. 60; cf. Nietzsche, 1967a, pp. 296–298; cf. Nietzsche, 1974, pp. 168, 273–274). The analysis in Chapters 5, 6, and 7 makes explicit the conditions that make possible the *pervasiveness* (Foucault, 1972, p. 221) of the policy metaphors of flexibility, diversity, choice, and opportunity[1] throughout the years, specifically their relations with truth production.

Nietzsche's (1979, p. 84) argument that truth is 'a movable host of metaphors' provides a lens through which to view inequality as driven by the production of truth through metaphors. This abstract philosophical concept takes its concrete form by employing CDA in policy analysis. That is, the analysis makes explicit how metaphors do *ideologising* work in the service of contributing to and sustaining systemic educational inequality by hardening and congealing the Truth that 'economic growth is the (only) way forward'. This approach is necessary in order to understand how we have been trapped in our own history (Foucault, 1982a, p. 780), where the ideology that economic growth is the (only) way forward has been taken as self-evident. This is ideologising work because the metaphors could have been used to connect other things but it is these discursive links alluding to this Truth that the metaphors construct. These metaphors make links, establish more concrete links, and connect concepts that contribute to (re)producing and sustaining inequality. The genealogical approach hence adds a crucial historical dimension to the positionality and development of policy discourses as conditional upon these metaphors. In particular, examining the role of metaphorical relations in discourse will illuminate their role in contributing to the transformative dimension of the neo-liberal economic order, and subsequently provide a possible philosophical understanding of how the world is being organised and how we should live in it. These philosophical interpretations explain how and why order exists in general, that is, how and why this particular order of inequality has been established and not some other (Foucault, 1973, pp. xx). Drawing on this philosophical dimension provides the understanding of how discourse works to conceal the other possibilities within which these metaphors could be associated.

Whilst the conceptual framework for the analysis in Chapter 2 examines how interactions between power–knowledge–truth relate to dividing practices within the context of learner representation, Chapters 5, 6, and 7 draw on a genealogical approach to examine how these concepts expand in increasing emphasis toward neo-liberal economic discourse. The analysis will show how, historically, (human) agency fades and is replaced by the *hyperrealism* of a global social structure sustained through value orientations. At the heart of these accounts is the notion of global representation or what is referred to here as 'hyperrealism', and this representation was found to be implicated in the domain of ethics. In order to understand this relationship, some philosophical-methodological considerations of Foucault's work on ethics need to be established.

On the genealogy of ethics and truth

Genealogy critically converges with archaeology within Foucault's original field of interest, the human subject, where his research aims to 'study the modes according to which the subject was able to be inserted as an object in the games of truth' (Foucault, 1984b, n.p.; cf. Foucault, 1986, p. 351). Foucault's work on ethics advances his genealogical approach, which takes the problematisation of truth as a point of departure, by examining forms of moral problematisation through schemas of valuation (1981c, p. 3). That is, his work provides a philosophical dimension to understand the relations between the *value* of truth and the formation of subjects.

The domain of Foucault's ethics relates to duties to oneself, and is conceived interdependently of the structure of the moral code produced through objectification (Davidson, 2005, p. 118). The combination of a genealogical approach with an ethical ethos (Foucault, 1980, pp. 83–86; cf. Nietzsche, 1967b, p. 62) provides a methodological treatise to examine how policies that allude to the need for economic growth appeal to metaphorical notions and their relations with morality and ethics as the conceptual foundation of inequitable practices. That is, drawing on Foucault's work is useful to understand how policies form the *necessary* links between principles of 'ethics', (hyperrealist) economic structures, and the aesthetics, or conditions, of our (separate) existence as objectified humans (Foucault, 1994, p. 350).

For the second analytical stage, a preliminary examination of ethical practices in policy texts from 1979 to 2019 alludes to the theme of 'ethics: or *philosophy of desirability*' (Nietzsche, 1967a, p. 181). The standpoint of *desirability* here refers to desirable outcomes which are made true through policy propositions and proposals. These propositions and proposals point to how 'things *ought* to be different' and 'things *shall* be different' (Nietzsche, 1967a, p. 181, italics included). That is, policies focus on *what should be* instead of *what is*. This focal point of attention creates the constant moving illusions of desirable realities on one hand and forms the basis of ethics on the other – 'that the structure of the world should correspond with our human well-being' (Nietzsche, 1967a, p. 182). Therefore, policy propositions are also moral propositions because projections of *what should be* are made on the basis of moral 'truths' and the moral ideal of attaining (infinite) economic growth. The notion of desirability is the driving force that unites propositions and proposals and holds the entire structure of the irrealis[2] future (cf. Nietzsche, 1967a, pp. 180–181). In this vein, the second analytical stage traces the genealogy of desire as an ethical problem (Foucault, 1994, p. 356).

Foucault's work on ethics in *The History of Sexuality* (1981a, 1981b, 1981c) provides a possible explication of an ethical programme associated with policy-making. At least two questions are addressed through drawing on his analysis. What kinds of ethical frameworks underpin policy discourse and what kinds of ethical positionings do policies take in order to enact their economic ends? The following subsection first provides the impetus to examine how, by drawing on the truth of hyperrealist-surrealist structural frameworks, policy discourse works to construct and constitute the desiring-desirable subject within an ethical-moral prescriptive conduct that supports economic imperatives. The three subsections that follow this examine how moral obligations – as forms of ethical positionings – are constructed through valuations in policy texts and serve to constitute the ethical basis for differentiated learner treatment in the pursuit of economic interests. It is argued that schemas of (moral) e/valuations are a central mode in which the subject is inserted in the games of truth. These philosophical concepts will be extended in Chapter 4, which argues for the combination of critical discourse analysis with Foucault's and Nietzsche's perspectives. The strength of CDA is that it not only makes transparent the relations between discourses of truth, but also makes possible the synthesis of the *games of truth* and *valuations* that create and support inequality within the system.

Through the philosophical-analytical framework generated in this research, the investigation of the criteria for evaluating policy propositions and proposals concerns 'the way in which people are invited or incited to recognise their moral obligations' (Foucault, 1986, p. 353). This obligation deals with practices of certain forms of structurally-based prescription for conduct that is a necessary condition for producing economic growth (cf. Bevir, 1999, p. 75). As such, this research is an examination of the historical conditions of the contingent constraints that are imposed on subjects through both the 'care of the self' and in meeting the *perceived* demands of hyperrealist structures. As elucidated in the final part of this section, within a heterogeneous network, 'the care of the self is ethical in itself; but it implies complex relationships with others' (Foucault, 1997, p. 287) through contractual discourse. The next section sets the stage to understand how the individual has been brought to recognise themselves as a subject of desire in generating economic growth.

The desiring-desirable subject, hyperrealist structures, and schemas of valuation as elements of ethical relations within the 'games of truth'

In line with Foucault's (1981b, pp. 5–6) analysis of the modes according to which individuals are given to recognise themselves as objects, one could not very well analyse the formation and development of value-forming labour within the *perceived* demands of political economies without doing a historical and critical study dealing with desire and the desiring-desirable subject (that is, without undertaking a 'genealogy'). Specifically, a *genealogy of ethics* entails the study of the moral codes according to which the subject was able to be inserted as an object in the games of truth – alluding, here, to the Truth of the desirability for economic growth by drawing on hyperrealist structures.

The analysis in Chapters 5 to 7 makes explicit how policy discourse circumscribes, extends, and limits the way metaphors are (re)conceptualised and constantly and successively imbued with particular, narrowed positive valuations in creating distinctive visions of economic realities – what this study refers to as 'hyperrealism'. Hyperrealism is a term that is primarily applied to an independent movement of changing, potential, material conditions. To borrow Heidegger's (2003c, p. 124) words, it is 'a part of the essence of the will to power' that does not 'permit the reality which it has power over to appear in *that* reality in which it itself exists'. The term 'reality' hence indicates an unknown and unknowable, undefinable totality of ever-flowing flux that is the ground of the indivisibility of all discursive processes, including all metaphorical movements (cf. Bohm, 1980, pp. 75–76). Because of this nature of fragmentation in policy discourse, hyperrealism is founded on schemas of valuation to provide coherence (cf. Lemke, 1998, p. 43). Political economies which are found to be grounded on schemas of valuation through policy analysis in this study are thus conceptualised in this research as hyperrealist structures.

Hyperrealism, as an assertion of the power to manipulate the appearance of value and reality, is embedded in political economy as the process through which 'values of all kinds are produced, distributed, exchanged, and exercised politically' (Graham & Luke, 2011, p. 105). The perceived demands of hyperrealist structures or political economies are strategically detailed to create the illusion of a reality. That is to say that these political economies are surreal, as the illusion is a convincing depiction of simulated reality. The concept of hyperrealism helps elucidate the process through which metaphors function as apparatuses of power in policy discourse: that is, the process through which they articulate together hyperrealist or surrealist realities that have no rational explanation or links. That is to say, in order to fulfil its hortatory function (Graham, 2001a, p. 765), policy discourse draws on metaphors to produce reality. The construction of this reality is important in providing a legitimate basis for ethical conduct, that is, norms of regulatory behaviour for the pursuit of economic growth.

In order to understand how the value-forming individual could experience themselves as a subject of 'labour appropriation' and accept such position as appointed them in the state, it is essential first to determine how historically, the individual has been brought to recognise themselves as a subject of desire in generating economic growth within surrealistic economies. Within this process is the effort to isolate the elements that might be useful for a history of truth. This requires an analysis of the 'games of truth', the problematisations of truths – that is, to make explicit the assumptions that underpin the truths in policy discourse. This history is a matter of analysing the games of truth through which the being of the ideology of economic growth offers itself as necessary, and the discursive practices on the basis of which these games are formed (cf. Foucault, 1981b, p. 11). As discussed earlier, while the archaeological dimension of the analysis will make it possible to examine the initial practices of objectification of subjects, its genealogical dimension will enable the analysis of the modifications of this objectification in relation to political economies and the interaction of these relations with economic growth. Within this context, the analysis argues that political economies emerge from the field of moral philosophy of 'care of the self' (Foucault, 1997, p. 287; cf. Graham, 2005, p. 118). In the next subsection the discussion moves to examine the interaction of these relations and how, linked to the 'care of the self', can be made explicit by examining schemas of valuation in prescriptive texts such as policies. It is argued that schemas of (moral) e/valuations are a central mode in which the subject is inserted in these 'games of truth' through surrealism[3] working to shape and transform the policy formulation of ethics and practice.

Movements of valuations determine moral codes for the desired and desiring subject

In his work on ethics and moral codes, Foucault analyses historical 'prescriptive' texts in order to trace the development of schemas of rules and valuation through a movement of desire (cf. Foucault, 1981a, p. 3; Foucault, 1981b, pp. 12, 27–29). For Foucault, morality consists of the more or less explicitly formulated set of values and rules of action that are recommended to individuals through the intermediary of actions of various 'prescriptive agencies' or 'prescriptive texts', in this case, education policies (Foucault, 1981b, pp. 12, 25). Policies, especially speeches,[4] thus serve as functional devices that condition the ethical subject (Foucault, 1981b, p. 13). In relation to morality, these impositions are forms of moral subjectivation.

The prescriptions embedded within this value system are imbricated in the objectification of the subject through modes of moral subjectivation (cf. Foucault, 1981b, pp. 28–29). This process functions within a field of moral conditioning (cf. Krishnamurti, 1978b, p. 94). This concerns 'the way in which the individual has to constitute themselves as the prime material of their moral conduct' (Foucault, 1981b, p. 27): that is, how the individual should establish themselves in relation to the rules and how they are positioned through policy discourse to recognise themselves as obliged to not only comply but to put these values and rules into practice. This process is explicated primarily in the analyses of extracts from Shanmugaratnam's 2003 (Chapter 5, in the section 'Micro-meso movement: Contractual-ethical discourse for talent investment') and 2006 (Chapter 7, in the section, 'Micro-meso movement: Ability-driven system for innovation economy') speeches.

Analysing the formation and development of these valuations requires an historical and critical study dealing with desire and the desiring subject (cf. Foucault, 1981b, p. 5). Consistent with the study of the problematisation of truth, these forms of moral subjectivation intersect with and translate into the games of truth by which subjects are constituted as desiring individuals (Foucault, 1981b, p. 7). That is, in relation to forms of moral subjectivation, subjects are constituted as ones who desire for and are constituted as necessary for economic growth in education policies. Within this focus, and under the analytical theme of 'ethics: or *philosophy of desirability*', policies, especially policy-oriented speeches, are seen to create and condition the desiring subject; that is, policies create the *illusion* of desire (Foucault, 1981b, p. 13). The nature of illusion within Singapore's education policy texts is born of a desire for economic growth. The subject's 'natural' pursuit of economic growth is not due merely to the preconceived consequences that one can derive from its realisation; its naturalness is already declared by the existence of the original predilection imposed by these prescriptive texts, which establishes it as a desirable objective (cf. Foucault, 1981c, p. 153). Policy texts establish economic growth as a desirable objective through conditioning the individual as a subject desiring such growth.

Consistent with the study of rules and values – the codes of behaviour and forms of subjectivation that comprise morality (Foucault, 1981b, p. 29) – the primary focus of Foucault's (1981c)[5] ethics is how the concept, 'the care of the self' is essentially about schemas of valuation. The care of the self is the ethical transformation of the self, that is, the practice of self in light of this truth based on these valuations as its prescription (cf. Foucault, 1981c, p. 143). Next follows a discussion of how the construction of hyperrealist structures contributes to the emergence of moral valuations.

Dreams, philosophical realism, and valuation

This research is not in any sense a treatise on morality, which would be primarily concerned with formulating judgments about institutional practices. It is only indirectly, through analysis, that one can discern the valuations brought to bear on policy proposals and propositions that are taken as formulations of preconceived exigencies. It is precisely on this account that they form part of a surrealistic, dream-like but prophetic state of multiple economic landscapes. The ethical principles are not affirmed for their own sake; one can only recognise them through the actual progression of the analysis, by exposing the implicit assumptions and valuations embedded in submerged policy proposals and propositions that demand explicit action (cf. Graham, 2002, pp. 241–242). This approach aligns neatly with the hortatory function of policies: they are designed to promote imperatives for social action and are therefore always future-oriented (Muntigl, 2000, as cited in Graham, 2001a, p. 765). That is, to get people to do things is to 'prophetically create perceptions of value for new, unexplored and unknowable spaces that exist at a time-distance from the here and now – that is, to create *value* for some imagined future place *and* time' (Bernier, 1992, as cited in Graham, 2001a, p. 765, italics included). In this respect, the *perceived* demands of irrealis political economies in policy discourse essentially constitute an identity economy.[6]

The analytical framework developed in this research identifies two levels of consubstantiality between two domains: first, the elements of policy discourse, that is, the policy propositions and proposals that are taken up as materials for the analysis of their moral values; and second, the (neo-liberal) principle that make it possible to attribute a meaning (a predictive 'value') to propositions and proposals (cf. Foucault, 1981c, p. 28). A predictive value is assigned by the policy discourse based on how certain propositions and proposals are considered important or/and necessary in relation to pre-existing economic landscapes. The principle of a correlation between the moral and predictive values can be made explicit by employing what Foucault (1972, p. 221) terms as 'the circumstances of repetition' of discourse and CDA. The analysis in Chapters 5, 6, and 7 illustrates the manner in which this predictive value conditions and is being conditioned by the moral value; both are threaded through discourses oriented towards meeting the *perceived* demands of political economies. The schemas of valuation in policy discourse are made explicit below.

Schemas of valuation in policy discourse

This research argues that economic growth and the specific macro-neo-liberal[7] values of competitiveness, de/regulation, and market economies underpin the discourse of valuation articulated in Singapore's education policy discourse. These macro-neo-liberal values are both conditional upon and being conditioned by micro valuations of what is interpreted as important or/and necessary to generate desirable outcomes. Both micro and macro values are diffused, interwoven, and at the same time repetitive (cf. Foucault, 1980, pp. 78, 142). They are integral constituents of the general mechanism of the exercise of power in policy discourse, supporting, and being supported by types of truths, thus establishing certain relationships between heterogeneous elements.

Herein lies the argument that desirability is a conditioning-conditioned attribution that requires significant amounts of institutional inculcation of other 'types' of macro-micro values (cf. Graham, 2002, p. 228). That this (subjection to) '*necessity* is not a fact but an *interpretation*' (Nietzsche, 1967a, p. 297) delineates these values as constitutive of truth games. The e/valuation of policy proposals and propositions as necessary is contradicted by inconsistent forms of valuation when set against meritocratic ideals. The analysis demonstrates that since contradictory values – opportunity versus equity, for instance – have been held accountable for contradictory policy drives, it is not possible to have explicit policy reference to the conceptualisation of 'value' (Nietzsche, 1967a, pp. 149–150). Rather than maintaining a particular and concrete relationship to policy drives, values are positioned as a modulating category, based on temporal relationships that define the conditions for the emergence of changing forms of political economies. This shifting of e/valuations highlights the fact that values are not static; rather, they change, and this occurs systematically over the course of policy texts. Values and policy drives are constantly modified in relation to each other and thus modify the field of experience in which the subject is constituted under certain simultaneous conditions (cf. Foucault, 1984b, n.p.). Value then has to be viewed as an *abstract* (albeit relational) concept that 'transforms every product of labour into a social hieroglyph' of subjective value (Marx, 1976, p. 167). That is, the subjective value of an individual is determined through their acquisition of commodifiable knowledge in relation to these economies.

The pluralistic approach to making sense of morality assembled in through the analysis illustrates that in order to legitimise structural-educational reforms, emergent forms of political economies are concerned with the production, distribution, and propagation of values through *perceived* desirability, necessity, and importance

(Marx, 1973 as cited in Graham, 2001a, p. 764). In other words, the interrelated ethical e/valuations for desirability, necessity, and importance are 'propagated for and from' within the main value system 'upon which the authors intertextually draw when they construe action and its outcomes' (Graham, 2002, p. 231). Conversely, this value system reproduces precisely these schemas of ethical valuation through the utilisation of policy metaphors. That is, the analytical focus as explicated in Chapters 5, 6, and 7, is to examine the way the policy metaphors of flexibility, diversity, choice, and opportunity provide a moral basis for inequality in Singapore's meritocratic education system. The main value, as a principle of e/valuation, thus appears at the intersection of all these games of truth. By means of explication through CDA, the fundamental constitution of this system determines every mode of e/valuation. Further, structural changes are motivated by the prevailing modes of e/valuation. The allusion to this system, which is simultaneously being produced and reproduced throughout the policies, is not an explicit part of the texts, even though it provides much of their coherence (Graham, 2002, pp. 231–232). Therefore, it is important to understand how modes of e/valuation attain coherence, as discussed in the following subsection.

Ethics, schemas of valuation, and the value system of meritocracy as conceptualised through data analysis

By analysing schemas of valuation, the analysis of Singapore's education policy illustrates that the master narrative holds that incumbency in economy growth means inequality of knowledge access through this *contractual relationship* (cf. Nietzsche, 1967b, p. 64). The development of the 'care of the self' produces its effect not in the strengthening of that which can thwart the desire for self-interest, but in certain modifications relating to the formative elements of ethical subjectivity (cf. Foucault, 1981c, p. 67). Specifically, the notion of the 'care of the self'[8] is threaded throughout the analysis and embedded implicitly in a value system that suggests it is in 'our' interests that 'talents' should get privileged access to knowledge because that is how 'they' create more jobs for the rest of 'us'. Hence, within this value system is the embedded assumption that national economic growth translates into individual economic growth through increased avenues of access to employability. This promise lies in the 'simultaneous and proportional growth of individuals to one another' (Foucault, 1997, p. 317) and thus concerns 'the manner in which one ought to form oneself as an ethical subject in the entire sphere of social, political, and civic activities' (Foucault, 1981c, p. 94). This is where ethics is linked to the games of truth (Foucault, 1997, pp. 285–287) and where the relationship of power in which one wishes to direct the conduct of another exists (Foucault, 1997, p. 292). As Foucault (1997, p. 287) argues: 'The care of the self is ethical in itself; but it implies complex relationships with others insofar as the ethos of freedom is also a way of caring for others'. And as the analysis in Chapters 5 to 7 will illustrate, this form of relationship is characteristic of and is rooted in a contractual implication as a condition of economic growth and expansion of opportunity for all. By this, the essentially hortatory nature of policy discourse is not simply a matter of translating a political activity into an ethics of withdrawal, that is, in accepting that privileged knowledge access is given to some but withdrawn from oneself. By proposing a shift of cultures that privileges forms of excellence amidst global demands and political economies, the policy illustrates how it is, rather, a matter of elaborating an ethics that enables the constitution of the self as an ethical subject with respect to a complex field of institutional practices (Foucault, 1981c, p. 94). The conditions of the enhancement of culture through making possible a selection of a privilege at the expense of the mass are the conditions of economic growth (cf. Nietzsche, 1967a, pp. 81–82).

This 'for the common good' complex reveals a paradox that situates morality as problematic. Specifically, the analysis makes explicit how morality is a strategy of moralising the non-talented or those without access to state investment (cf. Foucault, 1980, p. 203). Philosophical research through a rigorous and transparent analysis is necessary to problematise this morality when juxtaposed against the 'equal opportunity' principle of meritocracy. Conversely, the policy situates the principle of meritocracy as problematic.

Together, Chapters 5 to 7 explore how metaphors have been mobilised. As such, they explore the multifarious dimensions of these metaphors in order to make sense of the ethics and ethical practices *necessary* for the production of the moral phenomena that make possible the ideology of economic growth. In doing so, these chapters undertake a critique of moral evaluations themselves, and thus demand a critique of morality by problematising desirable outcomes (Nietzsche, 1967a, p. 215). It is through these foci that the research is able to demonstrate how inequality is built in to the education system and through this contextualise the genealogy of political morality within Singapore's official discourse on meritocracy as grounded in this value system (Foucault, 1998, p. 263; Ifversen, 1997 as cited in Anderson, 2003, p. 13).

The underlying assumption of this approach, which draws on e/valuations, is that the objects (outcomes for self and nation) of desire can change and vary but desire is constant. In this movement of desire, there is endless struggle and the conflict of conditioning–conditional opposites: economic rationalism and meritocracy (a discourse of 'equal opportunity') are two conflicting yet supporting discourses. Metaphors are used to bridge, connect, and smooth over those tensions, to translate one for the other and provide the appearance of logical cohesion. It is in these metaphors that the work of policy is most perspicuous; it is metaphors that thus constitute the focus of the analysis undertaken in this research. The will to power-knowledge-truth that is cultivated through valuations in policy discourse is the cultivation of desire. In all essentials, this critique is a question of how morality *governs* statements, and the way in which these statements *govern* each other (cf. Foucault, 1980, p. 112) so as to constitute a set of propositions which give rise to a taken-for-granted moral phenomenon and consequently how this is implicated in relation to economic growth as normal.

Analysing MOE policies from 1979 to 2019

This section explicates the components involved in the second analytical stage, consisting of Chapters 5, 6, and 7. This section concludes by introducing some of the ways that Foucault's archaeological and genealogical methods and CDA might complement one another in the analysis of historical policy texts. This synthesis between Foucault's perspectives and CDA is also designed to eventually contribute to the process of putting the philosophical study of valuation to work in developing critical discourse analysis as a theory and method to enhance its capacity to address inequality.[9] In doing so, the analysis reflects the con-text (conceptualised in this research as connections between co-texts through the principle of thematic condensation)[10] that continuously *interacts* with the policy texts, that is, the conditions in which texts are (re)produced and in which they (re)produce the context. Through analysis, this research argues that the context in which policy texts are interacting with is: neo-liberalism as a system of principles of valuation and evaluation. It is important to highlight here that in order to overcome the limitations associated with a reliance on a pre-ideological, theory-informed position, the monograph does not present what may be seen as a traditional literature review in the sense of summarising a series of mainstream perspectives on critical terms, but rather seeks to *problematise* the construction and use of these terms in the first place. That is, the monograph is about how the discourses of political economy and neo-liberalism are situated and mobilised within the policy reports and speeches, rather than a treatise on these theories.

Hence, drawing on Foucault's conceptualisation of 'liberalism' in *The Birth of Biopolitics* (2003, pp. 202–203), it is possible to analyse neo-liberalism in policy discourse as a discursive governmental practice rather than a theory or ideology. Here, neo-liberalism is a 'way of doing things' that is oriented towards regulating itself by means of sustained forms of valuations to manage subjects and govern their behaviour. Neo-liberalism is to be analysed, then, as a regulative 'principle and a method of rationalising the exercise of government, a rationalisation that obeys – and this is its specificity – the internal rule of maximum economy' (Foucault, 2003, p. 202). This involves an analysis that aims to make visible the formation of value through examining the connections between the objectification of the subject through policy discourse and presuppositions underlying the growth of collective wealth (cf. Foucault, 2003, pp. 204–205).

The relationship between the objectification of learners, valuation, and political economies

Having established objectification of subjects as the analytical foci in Chapter 2, the next analytical stage of the research, presented in Chapters 5, 6, and 7, makes explicit how this objectification of learners through discourse comes from being a product of a valorising system. That is, the analysis makes explicit how these learners are being subsumed under the sphere of labour appropriation to generate *desirable* economic outcomes (Graham, 1999, pp. 488–489). Consequently, this determines the kinds of skills that differentiated groups of learners should acquire which could then be translated into commodities. Considering the division of identities that preliminary analysis entails, subsequent analyses demonstrate clear linkages between objectification as part of the valorisation process of increasing the relative value of subjects through upskilling and modes of valuation and evaluation. This valorisation process takes place in relation to the *perceived* demands arising from the changing material conditions of surrealistic political economies. E/valuations shape and legitimise institutional structures. This is a central assumption of the argument that is presented here: the underpinning assumption is that the valorisation process in policy discourse is the transference of value from skills to industries which in turn produces economic growth. In this respect, political economies essentially constitute an 'identity economy'. That is because knowledge of the world is identical to how subjects are constituted according to an understanding of the perceived needs of that world, and consequently, the relation of value-creation identities to the acquisition of skills. Furthermore, the assumption underpinning the initial and primary analysis of objectification in Chapter 2 is that in order for a world of the true, of being, to be invented, subjects of varied categories would first have to be created. Chapters 5 to 7 explore how, historically, the objectification of the subject advances the theoretical formulation of identity construction to what may be termed an 'identity economy' by problematising the desiring subject. The central assumption of this problematisation is that the transference of skills acquired by subjects to industries produces economic growth.

Examining the phenomenon of evaluative propagation

The epistemological and theoretical underpinnings of Foucault's archaeological and genealogical methods inform this research's engagement with CDA approaches that seek to examine e/valuations in historical texts. In order to sufficiently bring the mode of valuation as a necessary area of examination into view, a concrete development of critical discourse approaches that examines e/valuations – in which hyperrealism, surrealism, and ethics converge – is necessary as the point of departure for the analysis proper.

Adopting a genealogical approach requires compiling a data set that is open ended, living, fluid, organic, and growing in the sense that it is accumulated by tracing the problematisation of (moral) truths as the data unfolds (Anais, 2013, pp. 130–131). More cogently, through empirically grounded historical analysis, a genealogical approach would enable a process that closely intertwines CDA with theory formation and problem formulation. A 'systematic' approach to collecting and organising data sets based on initial and subsequent analytic themes can make genealogy more manageable (Anais, 2013, p. 131). However, this should not be the overriding imperative of the analysis.

The analytical framework developed in this research takes the considerations in relation to the methodological issues raised seriously, by first avoiding the assumption that power is embedded in language by examining what Foucault (1972, p. 221) terms as 'the circumstances of repetition', the infinite *reappearance* of certain elements in policy discourse through the genealogical approach. Second, it draws on and synthesises philosophical principles to encourage a reflexive approach to analysis, and to tease out and examine connections between elements beyond established, specialised frames of analysis (Fairclough et al., 2004, p. 3). The approach to CDA here works abductively: recursively moving through and within philosophical perspectives and numerous textual instances; in looking for patterns that connect and repeat at multiple levels through recurring elements and themes (Graham & Luke, 2011, p. 105). The 'critical' part of this research's analysis is a concern with exploring the relations of power textured in the data, through the *games of truth* (Foucault, 1984a, p. 127) and how these truths derive their value (Nietzsche, 1967a, p. 275) discursively. E/valuation is hence of central concern as it is the essence of truth.

In developing a methodological orientation in which the objectification of learners, e/valuation, and political economies converge in the second analytical stage of the research, this section is concerned with developing suitable tools and categories for analysing the evaluative dimension of language, or more specifically, the value-assumptions that are embedded in them. The approaches employed are subject to constant adaptation as the analysis progresses to decide which ones are relevant to the discourse at hand (Kincheloe, 2001, pp. 686–688). That is, in analysing the complexity of discursive strategies that are employed in policy discourse, the approaches drawn upon have to remain fluid to illustrate what such an analysis can reveal through tracing and examining the discourse of Singapore's education policy between 1979 and 2019.

To explore how micro and macro values are made manifest, Fairclough's[11] works on the relationship between discourse and political economy, on how macro-neo-liberal economic discourse is recontextualised within the micro-individual level in the field of education, are a useful starting point. In terms of educational-political economic analysis, Fairclough's approach provides a theoretically compatible mode of analysis to describe the relations between the exercise of power and the construction of 'ethics'. His analytical approaches to language and globalisation, are, for all practical purposes, the lynch-pin for the analysis undertaken in this research. However, the analysis eschews reliance upon pre-formulated methodologies and instead uses whatever methodological apparatus or combination that affords analytic access for a particular discursive change. Applying a pre-formulated methodological framework that directs a focus on what a particular discourse analyst is attempting to demonstrate may lead to other analytical aspects being ignored or not deemed important. This does not deny the utility of established approaches, as the following analysis makes use of various approaches, but that the approach and analysis should be grounded in the data; that is, the data should lead the method and theory, and not be led by them.

Underpinning this approach was the principle that CDA can be employed in any combination but needed to remain fluid and critically reflexive both internally to itself and in relation to the data in order to be able to engage with constantly changing and emerging forms of discourses. The synthesis of these approaches is more demonstrative of methodological affinities between ostensibly diverse analytical tools than it is definitive of the research project. Moreover, the emergent synthesis between philosophical perspectives and multidisciplinary approaches to CDA is also designed to contribute to the process of putting the philosophical study of valuation to work in developing CDA as a theory and method to enhance its capacity to address the ideological veil of inequality and to explicate general trends in policy discourse. The strength of this approach is that it provides an embedded interpretation of Foucault's and Nietzsche's philosophical perspectives that perhaps mitigates against more ideological interpretations and opens up alternative possibilities of defining identity. While ideological interpretations operate on the basis of prior decisions and predicted thematic outcomes, an embedded interpretation of texts asserts an evolving, *ongoing* conceptualisation of themes as the analytical work proceeds. As such, an embedded interpretation explores *how* inequality is (re)produced through policies rather than demonstrate its existence (Pennycook, 2001, p. 93).

In adopting multidisciplinary approaches that synthesise both philosophical perspectives and CDA methods that are sensitive and responsive to the data, the analysis reveals that these findings relate to the mode of governance and the ethics of labour appropriation, as illustrated by employing Mulderrig's approach (2003; 2007; 2008; 2009; 2011a; 2011b; 2012; 2014) in which responsibility (towards self and others) becomes central to economic growth. In order to make sense of the need for structural changes and the constitution of commodifiable knowledge, the analysis also draws on Fairclough's (2003), Graham's (2001a; 2001b; 2002; 2005; 2011), Halliday's (1994), Lemke's (1995; 1998), Mulderrig's (2009), and van Leeuwen's (1995; 1996; 2008) approaches for analysing broad evaluative or semantic dimensions or value-orientation based relations among metaphors that are deployed to evaluate policy propositions and proposals and their roles in shaping and reshaping political economies. In synthesising philosophical perspectives with the analysis of the empirical data, which will be further discussed in Chapter 4, employing multiple CDA approaches will push the methodological and interpretive envelopes (cf. Kincheloe, 2001, p. 688). The bridge to CDA using Graham's and Lemke's work on metaphor and evaluative attributes of propositions and proposals is crucial in making the link with the theoretical framing via Foucault, and the augmentation of Nietzsche's views on valuation, and to bring out their relevance for the purpose of CDA.

Further, the analysis presented in Chapters 5, 6, and 7 demonstrate how policy discourse argues for change to be driven exclusively by changing political economies as a simple and certain way forward by drawing primarily on a synthesis of both Graham's and Fairclough's approaches. The analysis employs Graham's methods to make explicit how values are propagated at multidimensional, dynamic, levels of abstraction and the production and distribution processes by which evaluative patterns are *globally* inculcated (in which contentious and imagined 'global' configurations are continuously renegotiated) (2002, p. 263). Fairclough's work is necessary to explore the production and distribution of neoliberal discourse as self-evident. Together, they provide an understanding of specific forms and gradations of axiological configurations in different policy texts that privilege economic growth. As the analysis demonstrates, the notion of ethics or 'ethical-political' choice made from amongst many possibilities in relation to educational practices is subordinated to permeable, and malleable, imagined futures. In consideration of the analytical approach to be adopted for Chapters 5, 6, and 7, the next section discusses a synthesis of methods suitable for analysing e/valuations.

Methods for analysing e/valuations

The following synthesises the multiple layers of intersections between methods that have been developed by critical discourse analysts for analysing e/valuations. Graham's (2001a; 2002; 2005) works drew on methods developed by Lemke's (1995; 1998) and Halliday's (1994) works. The analysis draws most directly on methods developed by Graham's (2001a; 2001b; 2002; 2005) investigation into the relationship between language and social perceptions of value in his entire 'hypercapitalism' series of works which makes the point that desirability is key in evaluative meaning but it is *mutually* mediated by the evaluative dimension(s) of importance or/and necessity. Each facet of the synthesis in Graham's work, and the development thereof, is a proposition from which to view 'social change from specific functional perspectives: from the perspective of mediation systems; from the perspective of *value-production* systems; and from the perspective of *language systems*' (Graham, 2001a, p. 765, italics included).[12]

The perspective of language systems is drawn from Lemke's (1998) resources for attitudinal meaning and evaluative orientations in text semantics. This work discusses the feasibility of drawing on lexicogrammatical resources to facilitate the construction of attitudinal stances toward the ideational content of propositions and proposals. His critical model is organised around the broad 'evaluative dimensions' that are employed to evaluate propositions and proposals (Graham, 2002, p. 227). His earlier work (1995) on textual politics is about the construction of meaning through words and the symbolic values of every object and action in policy discourse. Further, it explores the relationship between discourse and the notions of power and ideology made explicit through the use of technical language in policy arguments.

Lemke's work on meaning was drawn from Halliday's (1994) work, which explains the principles of systemic functional grammar: the relation between grammar, meaning, and discourse. Specifically, Halliday identifies six broad intersecting categories of processes: material, mental, relational, behavioural, verbal, and existential (Halliday, 1994, as cited in Graham, 2001a, p. 767). Of particular importance for this research is the use of *process metaphor* such as 'opens up' which can act concurrently throughout these processes (Graham, 2001a, pp. 767–768). Graham's (2001a) work foregrounds the functional feature of process metaphor to illustrate how aspects of human experience are shaped for mass commodification by mediating between *realis* (actual) and *irrealis* (potential) spaces. His (2002) work demonstrates a synthesis of the methods developed by Lemke (1998) and Martin (2000) for analysing evaluations in English (p. 227). Graham's (2005) work on analysing policy values in a knowledge economy points out how policy is produced to support and operationalise particular neo-liberal values such as competition (pp. 125–126).

Bourdieu (1998, as cited in Fairclough, 2003, p. 4) argues that 'Neo-liberalism is a political project for facilitating the re-structuring and re-scaling of social relations in accordance with the demands of an unrestrained global capitalism.' In one of his more recent works, Graham, together with Luke (Graham & Luke, 2011), uses CDA to analyse material shifts in the political economy of communications. Their approach is a resource for examining the relationships between corporation, discourse, and political economy. They suggest that changes in political economy are associated with a political-economic shift from traditional concepts of 'capitalism' to a new 'corporatism' in which the connections between public and private, state and individual interests are reformulated and made implicit through new discourse strategies.

This redefinition of relationships can be explicated through Mulderrig's (2009) work, which was developed from van Leeuwen's (1996) framework. Mulderrig's work explores the interactions between policy, rhetoric, and the often conflicting demands of economy and society. In particular, by developing a computer-aided method of analysis, she systematically applies this method to a large body of historical data to examine the textual dynamics of evolving forms of educational governance, and critically studies the tensions and inequalities intrinsic to the processes involved in shaping a knowledge-based, learning society. This research also adopts her approach in explicating the increasing use of a personalised, inclusive, style of political rhetoric to legitimise contentious policy claims. Her approach to the analysis of the increasing language of 'managerialism' in contemporary governance, in relation to the discourse of competitiveness and the discourse of skills as part of neo-liberal values, is also considered for the investigation of Singapore's policies.

Van Leeuwen's (1995) framework for CDA elucidates the transformations which social actions can assume through discourse. These include objectivation, de-agentialisation, generalisation, abstraction, and overdetermination. As an extension of this earlier work, his (1996) work presents a sociosemantic framework for how social actors can be characterised in discourse. Building on this, his (2008) work presents methods for analysing the representation of social action and social actors as well as methods for analysing the construction of purposes, legitimations, and moral evaluations of social practices in discourse.

Fairclough's (2003) work is an extension of his earlier work on a more detailed linguistic analysis of texts. By synthesising systemic functional linguistics (SFL) with social theoretical themes presented by critical theorists like Bourdieu and Habermas, his work presents a detailed framework of linguistic analysis that links and shunts between the 'micro' analysis language of texts and the 'macro' analysis of social relations/social theoretical issues (pp. 15–16). In particular, the analysis in this research draws on his approach in analysing both modality and evaluation that 'are seen in terms of what authors *commit* themselves to, with respect to *what is* true and *what is* necessary (modality), and with respect to *what is* desirable or undesirable, good or bad (evaluation)' (p. 164).

Within these works, how metaphors are used as resources for packaging meaning has been instrumental in examining the phenomenon of evaluative propagation. In forging a multiple approach to CDA, the analysis draws most heavily on Graham's methods for analysing policy values and evaluative meanings, and the propagation of evaluative semantics (2002; 2005). The way the analysis engages with CDA is mainly influenced by Graham's method for analysing evaluative meanings in technology policy, and shares with it a research interest in investigating how forms of e/valuations are foregrounded over the course of a text, and more pertinently how they provide coherence for the text (Lemke, 1998, as cited in Graham, 2002, p. 230).

Significantly, there is a considerable diversity of discursive means for evaluations employed in these approaches. In recognising their individual usefulness and complementarity in understanding the semantic phenomena surrounding evaluative meanings, the analysis in this research deploys an eclectic amalgamation of these approaches in different extracts to analyse policy evaluations. Nevertheless, the analysis does not attempt to present either a fully systematic or exhaustive account of evaluative meaning resources. From this it is suggested that, rather than these methods being seen as a modification of conventional approaches, they can be considered as common resources drawn upon to make clear the (moral and discursive) phenomena of *what is*.

It is with a sensitivity to these various data-led approaches that the data can be repeatedly be subjected to a layered analysis. This process would yield an appreciation of the complex discursive strategies used, deployed, manipulated, worked upon, evident within, and embedded within policy discourse. Furthermore, it is with this appreciation of discursive orientations and the eschewing of any pre-formulated approach that a working methodology which is both adaptable and sensitive to discursive changes can be conceptualised and operationalised. As such, the analysis of data does not end with the discovery or explication of a particular analytical method that would yield definitive, testable predictions. These resources are employed to explore the phenomenon of evaluative propagation that gives rise to a 'value' system of regularity. The notion of 'system of regularity' that is developed through the analysis refers to a regulative and organising principle that serves as a mechanism for a system of differentiation – a master system which holds together conflicting policy proposals and propositions. That is, this value system means a set of mutually interdependent, connected parts. In doing so, the analysis explores the *rules of formation* or *conditions of existence* for e/valuation that brings this system into *being* (cf. Foucault, 2002, p. 42).

Summary

The philosophical theory presented within this data-driven research does not assume a prior objectification of power. Further, as argued, the theory should not be asserted as a basis for analytical work but should be an evolving, *ongoing* conceptualisation as the analytical work proceeds (Foucault, 1982a, p. 778). Hence it is fundamental to this research's approach to avoid an artificial separation of theory and method, principally so during the analytical processes.

To overcome the limitations associated with a reliance on a pre-ideological, theory-informed position, the problematisation of truth in policy discourse is taken as a point of departure through employing Foucault's approaches. This provides a means to identify and challenge assumptions underlying policy propositions and proposals that form the fundamental basis for constructing 'truths' about learners to legitimise structural inequality. In addition, the chapter has laid out a working methodology that proposes the integration of multiple approaches for the analysis in this research. By adopting a reflexive, philosophical-analytical approach, the policy analysis in this research seeks to offer explicit accounts of the connections between the theoretical narratives of policy and the data used to present them.

Within the broader examination of the ideological Truth that economic growth is the (only) way forward as the basis for inequality, the next chapter aims to model how CDA and Foucault's philosophical concepts, combined with Nietzsche's concept of truth, can be usefully synthesised to analyse schemas of valuation in education policies that have identifiable material force in structural inequality. The aim is to convert their philosophical concepts into analytical frameworks capable of addressing empirical materials. That is, to formulate a grid of intelligibility for desire of economic growth as an ethical problem.

Notes

1 These metaphors appear pervasively in Chapters 5 to 7 from the analysis of the third theme of 'ethics: or *philosophy of desirability*' that emerged from Chapter 2.
2 While realis spaces refer to states that exist in the here-and-now, irrealis spaces portray future and imagined states (Graham, 2001a, p. 767).
3 The concept of surrealism is further elucidated in Chapter 7.
4 Policy speeches embed coding senses of 'we' – inclusive *we*, exclusive *we*, and ambivalent *we* – that constitutes inclusion and shared responsibility. This makes the genre particularly hortatory (see Mulderrig 2011b, pp. 568–569). Through this process, speeches engage the people to behave in certain desired ways (see section 'Micro-meso movement: Contractual-ethical discourse for talent investment' of Chapter 5).
5 See Foucault (1981c): Part One, 'Dreaming of One's Pleasure' in *The Care of the Self* (*The History of Sexuality Volume 3*).
6 This term is explicated in the section, 'The relationship between the objectification of learners, valuation, and political economies' of Chapter 3.
7 Neo-liberalism as a system of principles of valuation and evaluation is explicated in the section, 'Neo-liberalism as a system of principles of valuation and evaluation' of Chapter 4.
8 The 'care of the self' can be conceived of as a specific governmental apparatus used as part of 'governmental rationality' or 'governmentality' to manage populations and the state's impertinent intervention into detailed aspects of our everyday lives (Foucault, 1991c, pp. 102–103).
9 Chapter 4 develops a multi-level, philosophical-analytical framework that incorporates the philosophical study of valuation and political economy with CDA approaches.
10 This principle is explicated in the section 'Micro-meso-macro' of Chapter 4.
11 Fairclough 1992; 1995; 2001; 2000; 2003; 2005; 2006a; 2006b; 2009, 2010.
12 Two concepts of 'value' are at work in Graham's analysis. They condition, and are being conditioned by the other. The first concept of value is perceived as important, necessary, and desirable (Graham, 2002, p. 245). The second concept of value pertains

to the Marxist critique of production, the creation of value via the labour process (Marx, 1973, as cited in Graham & Luke, 2011, p. 106).

The concept of value within the context of this research, while not drawing on Marx, also explores how forms of valuations relate to processes of labour appropriation. The concept of labour appropriation draws on Foucault's (1982a, pp. 777–778) work on the 'modes of objectification which transform human beings into subjects', and how the 'human subject is placed in relations of production and signification'. The concept of value is here is linked to the production of truth (Foucault, 1982a, p. 783).

4 Micro-meso-macro movements

A multi-level critical discourse analysis framework to examine the value of truth

Overview

This chapter presents detailed methods for constructing a flexible philosophical-analytical model through which to apply the analytic principles of critical discourse analysis (CDA) with the methodological approach of genealogy for the interpretation of metaphors of flexibility, diversity, choice, and opportunity across policy texts. Drawing on a theoretical framing from Foucault augmented by Nietzsche's views on valuation, the discussion here sketches a framework for examining ways in which evaluative semantic categories can be linked to sociological theories in order to bring out their relevance for the purpose of critical discourse analysis. This multi-level research framework draws upon a relationship between language analysis, the philosophical study of valuation, and political economy as a composite formulation of values through which neo-liberalism is discursively entwined and progressed through a system of principles of e/valuation. This framework aims to make analytically observable how changes associated with new modes of value determination serve to legitimise inequality.

Principles of truth and valuation in Foucault, Nietzsche, and CDA: policy texts as games of truth

Critical discourse analysis research examining the relation between identities and institutional practices within educational research has tended not to develop the historicity and the epistemological and theoretical depth of Foucault's philosophical principles and methodological insights (see Thomas, 2005, p. 25; Walshaw, 2007, pp. 46–56). However, within the focus of this research, there is the opportunity to offer historically rich readings of the traverse of discourses between and across chronological policy texts and to fully place such analyses within historical and political matrices that influence the emergence of certain epistemological practices. The following section argues that such a genealogical analysis can be achieved through employing a CDA approach to data.

Foucault's (1984b) work on analysing the 'processes of subjectivation and objectivation that made it possible for a subject qua subject to become an object of knowledge [connaissance]' (n.p.), provides an understanding of how (fictionalised) policy narratives are constituted and reconstituted as truths in the multiple layers of the '*games* of truth' (n.p.). Thus, within policy discourse, to borrow Heidegger's (2003a, p. 64) words, truth is a 'multiply-founded' phenomenon. Binding themselves together into *one single* organic world of truth, these narratives influence and direct institutional practices to make the overarching and ultimate conventional Truth of economic growth as the *only* way forward possible. In doing so, they reflect parallel realities with a symptomatic unity, specifically, economic growth as 'the Truth' or as having an independent normative salience. To understand how these truth games are set up in policy discourse and how they are connected with power relations, this section draws together Foucault's with Nietzsche's work around the revaluation and the transvaluation of values[1] where within the discursive work of *games of truth*, valuation *is* the essence of truth (cf. Nietzsche, 1967a, p. 275). This philosophical heterodoxy aims to distil a sort of unity from both.

This *essence* is not constitutional but stands in a conditioning–conditioned relationship to a form of structured Truth based upon the principle of contradiction, where each element of separated 'truth' is necessarily together because they are one (cf. Schopenhauer, 1907, p. 106). The relation of the games of truth to the Truth is that of the condition to the conditioned. Valuations condition and are being conditioned by Truth, and Truth conditions and is being conditioned by valuations. The principle of contradiction is the conflict of conditioning–conditional opposites: economic imperatives that necessitate a differentiated system and meritocracy (as in the discourse of 'equal opportunity') are two conflicting-supporting discourses and can also be considered as an extension of each other. The confluence of their philosophical perspectives is a strong contributing factor in understanding how morality and ethics (as discussed in Chapter 3) are central to legitimising the increasing prominence of inequality in education policies. The question of inequality is related to this research's inquiry into *how* relationships of power and ethics are linked to the games of truth. These contingent relationships necessarily develop and find their form as the research proceeds with analysis.

Here, the problem is in understanding how these truth games are set up in policy discourse and how they are connected with power relations (Foucault, 1997, p. 296). To understand how this Truth is substantiated, this study draws on Nietzsche's work on the revaluation and the transvaluation of values. By enveloping this Nietzschean character, the nature and *value* of truth(s) that alludes to the conventional Truth of the ideology of economic growth continues to be called into question and treated as fiction through interpreted forms of valuations (cf. McKerrow, n.d., p. 6; Nietzsche, 1967a, p. 232). Further, by treating truth as a hyphenated phenomenon (i.e., *conventional* truth), it is then argued that the heterogeneous phenomena of morality that arise from the games of truth cannot be simplified, and that there exist no objective truths that can exist independently. The return is not a monolithic, moral phenomenon.

What is 'truth'?

The sense of truth that is open to critique within the Foucauldian-Nietzschean corpus needs more precise delineation. Policy narratives are 'truths' only in the sense that they are conditions of life for us (Nietzsche, 1967a, p. 278): asserting, in this instance, that economic growth is the (only) way forward as a conditional Truth. This is the foundational principle of all moral rationality. Thus, the preliminary concept of 'truth' is to be exhibited by characterising what is meant by the two components, truth and conditions, and by establishing the interpretation of these *combined* terms in all its necessary variations. Here, then, because the term 'truth' is used in a broad sense, and put to use in various discourses, it is not possible to conceive of 'truth' as a fixed concept with defined properties. Rather, to perceive what truth is, it is necessary to be free of all conceptual conditioning of the past, free of any belief, ideals, imitation and conformity, for they dictate what should be sought or impose on how things ought to be (Krishnamurti, 2005, pp. 53, 64, 211). Hence, in using the term 'truth', it is not to specify any particular philosophical interpretations but that such an analytic interpretation can only be developed from the objective necessity of particular discursive rules and procedures that brings the *being* of ideology into existence. In this sense, truth is a living movement. Valuation, as a form of power, and truth, condition each other reciprocally, and thus always exist at the same time (cf. Schopenhauer, 1907, p. 111).

While Foucault and Nietzsche provide some philosophical perspectives, this discussion builds their insights within a critical discourse *analysis* as a means through which the games of truth and valuations are then laid bare for examination. The strength of CDA is that it not only makes transparent the relations between discourses of truth, but also makes possible the synthesis of the *games of truth* and *valuations* that create and support inequality within the system. Truth and valuation are not independent of each other. Foucault (1984a, p. 127) argues that truth is produced through an ensemble of procedures. Nietzsche (1967a, p. 275) argues that the *essence* of 'truth' refers to: 'The valuation "I believe that this and that is so". In valuations are expressed conditions of preservation and growth'. Combining these ideas draws attention to the interdependence of truth; truth is produced through an ensemble of micro-macro valuations that express the conditions for sustaining economic growth.

From the mutual development of truth and valuation, and their interconnection, what could be called the '*games* of truth' come into being – that is, not the discovery of true things, but the rules (Foucault, 1997, p. 297) according to which truths are given their values discursively. Thus, for example, to examine discourses and metaphors of truth through a critical analysis requires first treating 'truths' in themselves as having no value and recognising that in order to have value they must first be seen as embedded in the (economic) idealism or ideology from which these truths derive their value or non-value (cf. Nietzsche, 1967a, p. 141). This ideology would remain of primary importance in creating value. That is to say, policy claims only have truth values relative to the broader ideology in which they exist, draw upon, and are contributing to. Hence, drawing on these concepts, the discussion here maps out an approach to examine how truths derive their value discursively and in so doing make explicit how, in the realm of discursive strategies, policy discourse is reduced by means of value judgments of the first order to *desirability*. The process through which desirable outcomes are constituted as knowledge and as an assimilation of morals that are both truths and prescriptions (Foucault, 1997, pp. 263, 285) can only be analysed through a precise inquiry. Through the analysis of metaphors, this research seeks to determine what the ethical substance was/is.

Employing an amalgamation of CDA approaches that seek to examine e/valuations discussed in Chapter 3 will make transparent the relations between discourses of truth and valuation. To make 'transparent' is to expose the assumptions underpinning claims for truth through its principles and its rules of procedures (Foucault, 1984a, p. 127) that are rationalised by propositional content. The power of CDA lies precisely in its capacity to expose contradictions and reveal hidden tensions. The combined theoretical and corresponding methodological tools outlined below provide a critical, linguistic, *propositional* method of analysis. As such, in passing from the abstract to the concrete, the approach to CDA is both method-driven and theoretically framed: both theory and method work to inform each other, and are inseparable as the process of methodological shaping finds their form through the analysis. In essence, the approach is designed to make explicit the problem of practices of *institutions of power*, much more than the problem of ideology (cf. Foucault, 1997, p. 290).

In what follows, the study argues that the recurring appearance of metaphors and the values they confer represent an '*approximation of a world of becoming to a world of being*'; this is the supreme will to power (Nietzsche, 1967a, p. 330, italics included). This exercise of power is most succinctly demonstrated in policies where perceived forms of necessary skills should be desirably acquired in view of a constant anticipatory state of potential *becoming* of surrealistic economies (cf. Graham & Luke, 2011, p. 112). In relation to Foucault's concept of power-knowledge-truth, and as a critique of morality, these 'valuations are only consequences and narrow perspectives of this one will: valuation itself is only this *will*[2] to power' (Nietzsche, 1967a, p. 356). This will to power as 'being' is expounded in the form of values and valuation, revaluation and transvaluation (Nietzsche, 1967a). As a form of power, valuation thus plays at once a conditioning and conditioned role for inequality. Social changes associated with new modes of value determination are closely associated with legitimising inequality. An effort is being made then to determine fundamental valuations in policy discourse, and more importantly, their conditions for existence.

Instead of viewing morality as a primary development of this ideology, it is argued that morality invents new *values*, and consequently these values produce new *truths* that give form to this *ideology*. Therefore, ideology and morality are not related causally but are imbricated within a tripartite system. Ideology-morality, values, and truths are *necessarily* allies, and are to be called in question together. In doing so, the analysis is better able to challenge the taken-for-grantedness or dominant logic that economic growth is the (only) way forward, and examine how this ideology dominates morality. One truth that supports and is being supported by the Truth that economic growth is the (only) way forward can never displace another; but all must ultimately be in agreement. Regarding economic growth, then, the problem is to find out how the question of growth could have been made to operate in terms of discourses of truth or *games of truth*, that is to say, in terms of discourses having the status and function of *true* discourses (cf. Foucault, 1980, p. 210, italics included). This is the angle from which to approach the question of inequality. This study is hence directed to an investigation of this philosophical truth through value-creation.

Values and neo-liberalism

Examining what and how desirable outcomes are presented and configured in policy texts involves examining how specific macro (neo-liberal) values are made desirable through supporting, and being supported by, micro valuations. In the analysis of policy texts, this was reflected through a high level of interdependence of different evaluations used to provide coherence for neo-liberal imperatives. The determination of micro values is the fundamental basis for constructing 'truths' that legitimise structural inequality.

The following will first frame political economy as a complex system of values that underpin the politico-economic rationality of neo-liberalism. Second, it will explicate how neo-liberalism as a form of political economy works as a system of principles of valuation and evaluation, in order to begin to formulate an analytical framework designed to highlight how policy texts and discourse cohere by drawing on a particular value system through three interconnected micro-meso-macro levels. This value system is the invisible force that holds everything together. It is through a three-level analytic frame that an understanding of *how* inequality is inbuilt into the education system through the arbitrariness of the argumentative process in policy discourses which press forward to this unity can be made explicit. This unified field theory, developed through the analysis, underlies and gives rise to all the forces in valuations. The unified field is the fundamental ground where all discursive processes merge, and reconciles seemingly contradictory aspects of various fields of metaphorical relations through e/valuations in policy discourses to create a single value system. In doing so, this field reveals the indivisibility of space and time. Here, then, within the value system, everything is connected; and, in theory, any individual form of e/valuation could reveal information about every other e/valuation in policy discourse. This is an allusion to the genealogical method, which looks at the regulatory forces and events that shape discursive practices into a recursive network of power relations.

Here, 'valuation and evaluation'[3] are economic strategies and tactics, or the 'techniques and procedures accorded value in the acquisition of truth' (Foucault, 1980, p. 131) within the political economy framework. Neo-liberal values are related to distinctive organising principles of political economy such that they are normalised through the functional requirements of political economies.

Political economy as a complex system of values

Policy texts reflect highly condensed, abstract, contingent, and arbitrary processes through which policy discourse mounts appeals to truth as 'an end in itself', and through which policy based 'truths' can be asserted without being true. Here, 'arbitrary', in the sense of 'no rational explanation' refers to: first, a discontinuous series of relations between and within policy proposals and propositions which are not in any order of succession. Second, random division and dismemberment, that is, the confusing temporal and paradoxical co-existence and orientation of realis (present) and irrealis (future-oriented, non-existential) states set in juxtaposition to each other. And third, the binary logic underlying categorical designations of learners that form the primary basis for structural changes. Within the context of neo-liberalism, these assertions argue for change to be driven exclusively by changing political economies as a simple and certain way forward, executed through a high level of interdependence of different evaluations to provide coherence (Lemke, 1998, p. 43).

The analysis draws on Graham and Luke's (2011, p. 105) definition of political economy, as the process through which 'values of all kinds are produced, distributed, exchanged, and exercised politically'. Here, though, it is argued that the perceived desirability of a process or a proposed outcome is (albeit not perfectly) synonymous to its 'value' (Graham, 2001a, p. 764; Graham, 2002, p. 228). By this, desirability is key in evaluative meaning but it is *mutually* mediated by the evaluative core dimension(s) of necessity/importance in the process of propagation (Graham, 2002, p. 245; Graham, 2007, p. 121; italics added).

Further, evaluations of desirability and undesirability are dependent on the overall macro value system underlying the text (Thompson & Hunston, 2000, p. 22). Whilst propagating the monolithic ideology of economic growth, the aim of these value-production micro 'systems' (Graham, 2002, p. 245; Graham, 2001a, p. 765) is not economic reductionism. Rather, they build inequality into the system by imposing a moral order of rank among values (cf. Nietzsche, 1967a, p. 314; Nietzsche, 1967b, p. 56). Viewed from a politico-moral perspective, the analysis demonstrates how historically, through the determination of value, policies are used to promote, privilege, and operationalise very specific values (Graham, 2005, p. 126). This operationalisation of values occurs simultaneously through a complex dialectical interdependence with changing economic material conditions. They reflexively rely upon each other. By adopting a historical approach, it is argued that the political-economic macro value-system is entangled in complex configurations of micro values that have evolved over time. Towards this end, an examination of how intersecting constructions of e/valuations are derived in policy extracts is necessary. Here, the political economy approach assumes that the ways in which values are produced and distributed in policy discourse have social effects (Graham, 2001a, p. 765). Further, CDA assumes that language has social effects (Graham, 2001a, p. 765). A synthesis of both will provide a lens through which to view institutional change as driven by the production of values through language (Graham, 2001a, p. 765).

As such, the cohesiveness of policy texts is attributed to a high density of evaluations. In setting out to explore how these e/valuations are foregrounded in policy texts by elucidating the 'complexity of evaluative dimensional interplay' (Graham, 2002, p. 237), this chapter maps a three-layered analysis in order to bridge the complexity of contradictions and the inherently obfuscating nature of language that are constantly on the borders of the arbitrary in policy discourse. And further, to examine how the policy texts cohere by drawing on the same value system that is connected at these three levels. In other words, this chapter sets out a way to examine how the interrelated ethical e/valuations for desirability, necessity, and importance are 'propagated for and from' within the main value system and drawn upon intertextually when proposing action and its outcomes. And relatedly, where contradictions and fragmentations within policy discourse provide a degree of tension that requires a unified value system to maintain the semblance of coherence (Graham, 2002, p. 231). This formulation has a certain practical value because it calls attention to fundamental forces and processes at work in policy discourse.

The discursive formations and transformations traced through this analytic framework then highlight how specific values and outcomes *are made* desirable and where *desirability* is valued in creating historical conditions for economic growth, and where economic growth is the (only) way forward (cf. Nietzsche, 1967a, pp. 194–195). This approach calls into question the *value of this truth* (Nietzsche, 1967b, p. 153). By questioning the value of this truth, this research is undermining its claims to authority over how the world should be organised and how we should live according to policies, and its claims to be absolute (Nietzsche, 1967b, p. 153). The subsequent analysis traces the complex and shifting interplay of the micro evaluative dimensions of metaphors of desirability that are foregrounded throughout policy texts, underpinned by an overarching, macro, large-scale definitive of 'what value is' (Graham, 2002, p. 237–239; Lemke, 1998, p. 38). In this vein, the analysis demonstrates that desirability is seen as the supreme value, yet conditional upon the existence of the complementary concepts of what is important and necessary. As Graham (2002, p. 245) argues, the evaluative chain within and across policy texts propagates, overall, an evaluation of degrees of 'Desirability and Importance for certain propositions upon which imperatives for Necessary action are developed'. The deconstruction of this chain essentially belongs to the formulation of the question of truth and is possible solely within such a formulation. To understand how metaphorical transfers are mobilised through e/valuations, the following section expands upon how these values operate and their guiding key principles to assist in the design of a flexible framework for analysis.

Neo-liberalism as a system of principles of valuation and evaluation

Informed by an understanding of political economy as a complex system of values, this section argues in favour of understanding neo-liberalism as a system of principles of valuation and evaluation. Policy metaphors as existing mechanisms of neo-liberalism flow from this system of principles. Conceptualising neo-liberalism as a system of principles of e/valuation, made operative through discourse, enables a potential merger of political economy and Foucauldian-Nietzschean philosophical concepts by recognising the alignment of both critical perspectives without privileging either (cf. Springer, 2012, p. 134).

The three underpinning values of macro-neo-liberal economics, competitiveness, de/regulation, and market economies are made desirable through micro valuations of what is important; that is, they are seen as necessary to generate desirable educational outcomes in relation to economic imperatives. Here the determination of micro values was highlighted as the fundamental basis for constructing 'truths' that legitimise structural inequality. Through examining what and how desirable outcomes are presented and configured in the policy texts, it was then possible to highlight how specific macro (neo-liberal) values are made desirable through supporting, and being supported by, micro valuations.

Within this transmission, the role of 'necessity' is seen to hold the sole function of pointing out the ontological 'place' for moral phenomenon in the constitution of the *becoming* and *being* of the ideology of economic growth as the only way forward (cf. Heidegger 2003b, p. 260). 'Necessity' here was conceptualised as an abstract category indicating an inner essential relation of two aspects; if the one is important, and *because* the one is, then (*and therefore*) it is desirable (cf. Hegel, 1970, pp. 91–92). Here, then, 'necessity' can be seen as an enduring principle (or truth) that provides the logical basis for structural reforms such that the system of principles creates a common basis from which to hold both policy propositions and proposals to truth logical and reasonable. As such, these conditional values give rise to a *moral* phenomenon built on interpretations rather than facts (cf. Nietzsche, 1967a, pp. 149, 297–305). Further, within the context of meritocracy and the ideology of economic growth as the only way forward, the system of principles of valuation and evaluation illustrates *how* a highly differentiated system can coexist with assertions of equal opportunity. It is with this in mind that the next section now maps out the framework designed to explicate structural inequality through such forms of valuation.

Examining valuation as power: micro-meso-macro movements

This section maps out a methodological framework in which Foucault's and Nietzsche's philosophical perspectives and CDA are deeply integrated within a flexible analytic model. To examine valuation conceptually in all its necessary variations as a form of power, a micro-meso-macro reflexive grid of analysis is conceived of as a guide and structuring principle that makes explicit the reflexive interaction between philosophical theory and data. Here, then, reflexive does not mean to connect and conjoin philosophical ideas with data in a potentially reified way but rather, to explicitly avoid working within a predictable framework that projects rather than seeks to conceptualise a particular (albeit loose, changing) phenomenon. As such, this reflexive framework does not claim to have totalising effects. Rather, it is by and through such analysis that it is recognised analytically that data always contains inconsistent material that is arbitrary, ambiguous, uncertain, fragmented, and disconnected. Herein lies the inescapable paradox – how does language do the work of valuation while being arbitrary (i.e., without supporting evidence) at the same time? The unifying principle between these two dual functions of policy language, valuation and arbitrariness, is their *interdependence*; and this functions as the seat of their coherence. They are both mutually necessary to each other. The hortatory nature of policies is to incentivise[4] and de-incentivise structural changes through perceived market demands at a very broad level. To fulfil this purpose, valuation is necessary to provide a logical basis for a discontinuous series of propositions and proposals and hold them to truth.

Assembling a skeletal framework: on the primacy of movement and undivided wholeness

To design the framework, the following section first draws on Foucault's micro-capillaries of power to formulate the basic multi-level organisation that is necessary to examine valuation as a form of power. This is followed by a subsection which discusses the principle of thematic condensation employed in the meso-macro movement. The next subsection suggests that forms of 'valuation' should be examined through the notion of 'movement' as the guiding principle of this analytical framework in order to offer a more fluid, explicit approach to the circumspect interpretation of and the interplay between micro techniques and macro strategies that supports Foucault's argument that 'power is everywhere' (Foucault, 1981a, p. 93).

Micro-meso-macro

The micro-meso-macro grid formulated here makes explicit the interaction between philosophical theory and data through CDA. Employing CDA supports the examination of historical conditions which motivate the *ongoing* conceptualisation of the philosophical-theoretical framework explicated through the analytical work (cf. Foucault, 1982a, p. 778). That is to say, the architectural grid outlined here emerged through the process of data analysis. The task of the micro-meso-macro movement is then to start from the analytical parts and to derive the value system through abstraction, explaining this system as the result of interactions of micro-macro valuations (cf. Bohm, 1980, p. 179).

Analysing the data thus requires consideration of various interpretive, fluid possibilities, and shifting positions. Moreover, this openness to variation may in turn lead to unexpected unities within fragmentation. For example, it became clear that as the analysis of policy texts progressed, the policy discourse was primarily axiological; that is, there was a particular Value that policy discourse was propagated from and drawn upon that appeared to provide the primary coherence for texts that are constantly on the borders of the arbitrary (Graham, 2001b, p. 25). This value system draws on forms of relation to oneself and others from within which policy discourses emerge, are framed, and articulated.

This value system remains hidden until a layered analysis of successive themes is brought to bear on it. On the basis of an integrated structure, levels of analysis together can present a semblance of coherence which can serve as a point of departure for a process of deduction.

The analytic framework embeds the principles of Foucault's micro capillaries of power and valuation as a form of power. By variously using micro (i.e., the overall theme that emerged from analysis of texts), meso (i.e., specific policy texts being the primary empirical material), and macro (i.e., large-scale orders of several texts across several years) as interim stages, the analysis in Chapters 5 to 7 was able to trace the *evolution* of underpinning values through metaphors of flexibility, diversity, choice, and opportunity, and in the process, highlighted and examined the dimensions of these metaphors. Further, this method systematically exposed how such values are transported and propagated through metaphors and their metaphorical relations through three interconnected levels. Specific macro (neo-liberal) values are made desirable through supporting, and being supported by, micro valuations within and through these metaphorical relations. Significantly, metaphors are used to bridge, connect, and smooth over contradictions, and provide the appearance of logical cohesion. Within their relations, interpretations of what is necessary, important, and desirable are conceived as propositional truths, and shown to be moving within an evolving structure made possible on the basis of, or corresponding to, the material (economic) Truth (cf. Heidegger, 1961, n.p.). The grid then highlighted ways in which values are transcendental, that they are interconnected through micro movements within an overall yet necessary truth. The relations between what is necessary, important, and desirable are interlocked among themselves as a primordial totality. From these interpretations arises the disclosure of *necessity* and, as a result, the possibility of valuations being transposed into structural changes (cf. Heidegger, 1961, n.p.).

Assembling this framework begins with Foucault's argument that power 'does not emanate from some central source but circulates throughout the entire social body down even to the tiniest and apparently most trivial extremities' (Fraser, 1981, p. 278; cf. Foucault, 1980, pp. 96, 131–132). Thus, (institutional) power is understood as functioning at the capillary level via a plurality of micro-practices in policy discourse (Fraser, 1981, p. 279). For Foucault, these micro techniques are integrated into what he calls 'global or macro-strategies of domination' or 'large-scale orders' (1980, p. 142) that concern the (re)production of life in modern society (Fraser, 1981, pp. 276–278). It is important to note that both 'micro techniques' and 'macro strategies' are not constituted as a dichotomy, nor is one the mere inversion of the other. They are interchangeable and permeable. What Foucault provides is the basis for the discourse-analytic investigation of relations between the micro and the macro. However, he did not make explicit the transition or *movement* between the micro and the macro or provide a grid of analysis by which the apparatuses of power which underpin and drive these relations can be empirically examined.

Here, then, the study develops and employs a micro-meso-macro architecture or trajectory in order to not only elucidate the extremities of power using a historical framework (Foucault, 1980, p. 117), but also untangle and determine the global or macro strategies of domination through micro discursive practices. Without reducing them to finite relations, the meso level serves to make explicit the transitional link between the micro and the macro, and to comprehend organic change through the seamless and unbroken lineage of translation and transmission of movements. The analytical structure is built around the meso level, where the micro and macro are two perspectives that reveal the structural aspects of the changes in inequality that draw on the utilisation of the metaphor. Metaphors and movements are thus seen to move in unison as the combined essence of what constitutes the lineage transmission. This framework of translations and transmissions traces the conditions for inequality to exist. The preservation and promulgation of metaphors are of central importance for the (full) transmission of inequality to occur.

The meso level, then, lies between the micro and macro regions where even though its role is mainly an intermediary one, it is nonetheless fundamental as it makes explicit the transitional link between the micro and macro. Micro-meso denotes a middle space, between the micro powers, on one hand, and half-philosophical and half-empirical interpretations of the transvaluation of values on the other. This middle space is where the power of transvaluation resides, where the modulation of values changes according to a culture that institutes an initial separation from the micro powers, freeing itself 'sufficiently to discover that these orders are perhaps not the only possible or the best ones' (Foucault, 1973, p. xx). As such, micro-meso is a guiding mechanism that opens and closes particular conditions of possibility for the relational pair of metaphorical transfers and transvaluation of values to exist. It provides an elastic relationship to valuation as a form of power. Meso as architecture, then, works to structure and mediate the boundaries, as well as regulate the flows, of transvaluation. The entirety of the value system flows from the transvaluation of values. It is in the realm of this value system that the functional transformation between statements of fact (propositions) and demands for action (proposals) is operationalised (cf. Graham, 2005, p. 120).

It is then through these micro movements that the analytic themes for subsequent meso and macro movements become analytically visible. The thematic movements open up subsequent analytic possibilities. This value system bridges and integrates these three levels of analysis. While the micro-level constitutes the overall themes that emerge from the analysis of a group of texts, the meso-level is sensitive to the discourse under this theme and calls for the detailed study of language use in a specific micro-context, and the macro-level is interested in finding broader patterns and going beyond the details of the text examined at meso-level to examine similar texts which are grouped under the same micro theme (Alvesson & Karreman, 2000, pp. 1133–1134).

Here, first, it is not supposed that the same pattern of things is necessarily repeated at all levels; and second, it is not supposed that the general pattern of levels that has been identified thus far must necessarily continue without limit. The method that is presented here is oriented towards understanding how the two 'interact'. Through this process, a model of power that draws on a dispersed network of metaphorical apparatuses within these three layers emerges (Foucault, 1980, p. 71). The most immediate benefit of this framework is its capacity to synthesise disparate parts of evolutionary discourse into a unified framework, enabling, for example, the possibility to connect valuations with institutional coordination and change.

While the micro-meso movement constitutes the analysis of a single text, the meso-macro movement provides the analysis of several texts linked together through theme and time. The micro-meso and meso-macro and the transition between these two movements can trace the evolution of a policy as it develops while at the same time it is projecting ideological consistency. This movement within and through (discussed in more detail in the following two sub sections: 'Mining the esoteric depths: a CDA of thematic metaphorical flow in the meso-macro movement' and 'Power as "movements"') the levels provides a way of examining a policy in formation as it discursively attempts to maintain a fundamental consistency through time while the context continues to develop and shift. Meso-macro is thus focused on the intersection of underpinning principles explained or justified while being reconceptualised in relation to a policy. Hence, to bridge the micro-macro gap, that is, in order to understand an evolution, there is a need to look at both micro-meso and meso-macro linkages.

The meso theme that emerges from the analysis of the micro analysis provides the theme for the subsequent macro analysis. In so doing, the analysis shows how the micro discursive practices can provide a subsequent analysis in understanding, and exploring, how inequality is re(produced) at the macro level. As illustrated throughout the analysis in Chapters 5 to 7, the connections and extensions of micro and macro valuations through metaphorical apparatuses of power within the meso-macro movements are seen to delineate general conditions of domination, reflected in relatively stable configurations that give form to a unitary strategic form of value regularity (cf. Foucault, 1980, p. 142). Thus, a kind of telescopic analysis, building up from types of valuations, is possible where these are embedded within and build upon each other in the multi-layered framework. As forms of valuation enter into the mechanism, these become amenable to the evolving discourse and amenable to critical analysis. Analysing pervasive metaphorical apparatuses of power through their micro techniques is then the starting point for understanding its movements, functioning, and developments (Foucault, 1980, p. 138).

Of particular significance within the meso-macro movements is an explication of thematic condensation that arises out of evaluative condensation (Graham, 2002, p. 237; Lemke, 1995, pp. 60–61) by functionally collapsing connected texts of similar themes and metaphors across texts. This process is neither restricted, nor subjected, to a linear time frame. This method of examining the wielding of thematic and metaphoric chains draws on Lemke's (1998, p. 43) idea that:

> what is a proposition at one point in a text readily becomes 'condensed' … as a participant at another, and participants (especially abstract nominals) are often meant to be correspondingly 'expanded' by the reader into implied propositions through reference to some known intertext, as well as through reference to the immediate co-text.

Here, then, e/valuations mobilised through metaphorical transfers can propagate from one element of policy text or separated elements of policy text(s) to another to become part of, or create, connected, cohesive chains (cf. Lemke, 1998, p. 50). Being able to analytically trace this shows how systemic valuations can reinforce each other through the chaining of metaphorical formations. Moreover, a key part of the regulation of flows within movements is in the actual work that metaphors do: of creating, ordering, and ultimately giving valuation to policy narratives or 'games of truth'. In this way, an analysis centring on metaphors allows the possibility of looking at their relations with surrounding discourses and sees how these complex relationships construct certain representations of the world to produce new values. And how these representations of the world and values determine the new, necessary conditions of possibilities where such possibilities tend to be mediated by *desire*.

Within this framework both (thematic, multi-level) movements and metaphors stand in a conditioning–conditioned relationship, where transformations are seen as a sign of modification in the conditions of formation and play of statements that are accepted as truth. The utilisation of *metaphors, movements, valuations* is necessary as conditions to attain comprehensive forms of dominion that support inequality. Inequality is thus analytically based in the specificity of these existing conditions. The notion of 'conditions' here should be taken in the broad sense: how a value comes to be defined, then, is not the result of objective fact but is rather a discourse-mediated consequence of unified heterogeneous elements.

Mining the esoteric depths: a CDA of thematic metaphorical flow in the meso-macro movement

The thematic condensation in the meso-macro movement enables an examination of the esoteric dimensions of policy metaphors within the same theme, and their transformative possibilities through evaluative propagation, within and between texts in various themes. 'Esoteric' here indicates inner, successive, multiple, layered meanings. The meaning of these policy metaphors is thus capable of indefinite extension (cf. Bohm, 1987, p. 102). Through an esoteric interpretation, these metaphors can be seen as enduring principles that provide the logical foundation from which to hold unequal structural reforms as a justifiable form of ethical practice. The meso-macro theme is seen as a dynamic, indivisible, wholeness-in-motion, a 'metaphorical superfluidity', in which metaphorical relations move together in an interconnected, non-linear process. This movement illustrates the concept of transcendent unity that gives rise to the main value system. Further, the esoteric approach, when used within the two broad consecutive levels of the micro-meso and the meso-macro, indicates the nature of truth that is constructed through the metaphor within texts of the same theme; that is, one truth *conceals* other truths through the process of continual flux during the transitional movements.

Truths constructed in policies are in a state of unending flux of *enfoldment* and *unfoldment* as they intermingle and interpenetrate each other (cf. Bohm, 1980, pp. 184–185) throughout discourse, giving form to manufactured realities that support policy proposals and propositions. In order to explicate the principles of thematic condensation as a living organism with conditioning-conditioned (discursive) elements, this discussion draws on the work of Bohm (1980, pp. 173, 183)[5]: that 'at any given one moment, one of these (truths) may be unfolded but in the next moment, this one (truth) enfolds to be replaced by the one that follows'. Enfolded elements of (two) truths may merge and flow together to unfold a new truth (cf. Bohm, 1980, p. 174). The process of thematic condensation is thus *sensed immediately* as the presence together of many different but interdependent multidimensional discursive transformations of truths (cf. Bohm, 1980, p. 199, italics included). The texts under analysis contain implicit and explicit uses of the metaphors. In some texts, these metaphors are explicitly adapted and their meanings become redefined, while in others they are implicitly drawn upon through the chaining of metaphorical relations, yet, performing the same work in steering structural inequality. The unceasing movement of these truths or policy narratives – propelled through forms of valuation, either consecutively or simultaneously – brings the continuous *being* of ideology into existence. One may thus expect the unending revelation, or development, of new forms of truths as the analysis progresses. Being able to analytically trace the movement of these metaphors shows how the different levels of esoteric dimensions of the metaphors of flexibility, diversity, choice, and opportunity provide a sustained moral basis for inequality. These meso-macro movements make explicit the relationship between the meritocratic education system and the reproduction of inequality.

These metaphors do not hold inherent static meanings in themselves; their various meanings are continuously shaped and reshaped through surrounding discourses under the same broad theme throughout texts from the same year or from different years. They are mutually interdependent on surrounding discourses for their in situ meaning and for their existence. Through the chaining of metaphorical relations by 'condensing' or putting together layers of texts side-by-side, referred to here as 'co-texts', it is argued that these metaphors do not have any meaning when used separately. Their meaning only arises when they function together with the immediate (the text which they occur), and broader (co-texts) surrounding discourses. Grasping an infinitely complex, indivisible, whole of a particular phenomenon can then be made possible. By drawing on the analogy of water in a current, the turbulent play of forces in policy discourse that condition our existence takes the form of swirling vortices of valuations within metaphorical relations that live in a spherical space caused by eternal, recurrent, spiral movements (cf. Nietzsche, 1967a, p. 547). Here, then, within these metaphorical relations, are 'truths' that transcend time and (historical) contexts, making time spherical (rather than linear). This 'spherical' quality of time is based on a perceptual shift that implies the properties of continuity and non-locality.

Such a conception goes beyond a mechanistic analytical approach, which emphasises a step-by-step consecutive temporal sequence; rather, it entails an implicate order, in which everything is folded into everything within an indefinite range of conditions, thereby allowing the simultaneous investigation of historical discursive formations and transformations, in which policy texts are no longer understood or analysed as separate and historically distinct. Each discursive part is thus, in a fundamental sense, internally related in its basic function to constantly enfold and unfold the whole through simultaneous engagement with all the other discrete parts. The micro, meso, and macro regions emerge as external, secondary approximations formed through the transmissions occurring in this deeper implicate order (Bohm, 1987, pp. 13–15). Thus, the full and consistent application of the micro-meso-macro movement makes sense only in a context in which one refrains from assuming the absolute, distinct, and final character of any discrete discursive part.

Metaphorical relations flow as one interdependent, ever-changing whole instantaneously. Thematic condensation extends the analytic work of CDA by making explicit how metaphors 'inter-be'. This approach to analysis involves, first, an examination of a single text under a particular theme at the micro-meso level. Second, it involves the examination of several texts under the same theme at the meso-macro level. The movement between the two illustrates the transitional elements of change and the reconceptualisation of metaphoric interpretation. A metaphor is thus a building block of a theme, and the (repeated) use of metaphor (s) makes up a theme. Flexibility, diversity, choice, and opportunity can thus be conceived as thematic metaphors. The metaphor as a device at a micro-meso level then takes on a meso-macro structure when it is repeated in ways (which can include a combination of metaphors) that thread the theme throughout texts. Thus, the notion of 'movement' within the meso-macro level is about tracing the esoteric dimensions of metaphors within and between the same theme. These micro-meso and meso-macro levels are thus necessary to understand the dimensional depth of these metaphors. By implication, then, a metaphor itself has a micro-meso-macro structure. Metaphors and metaphorical relations are parts of a whole with no independent existence. Because they are perceptive abstractions from the whole, the micro-meso-macro framework provides a way of explicating the multiple dimensions of a metaphor.

Tracing the movements of particular metaphors through the micro-meso-macro levels illustrates their role as a functional device to help transmit and sustain themes. The repetition of metaphors themselves gives a kind of macro resonance; that is, they build meaning. And yet, these meanings are contingent on the surrounding discourses through which they interweave and interpenetrate each other, within texts. In the meso-macro movement, metaphors take on multi-dimensional meanings, through which themes are sustained. Where the micro-meso demonstrates one specific instance of how the metaphor operates, the meso-macro demonstrates the metaphor's capacity to operate in multiple ways.

A defining aspect of the metaphorical apparatuses as an exercise of power is their grouping of heterogeneous elements of games of truths and valuations into a common philosophical network of desirability. The apparatus is the 'system or relations that can be established between these elements' (Foucault, 1980, p. 194). What this analytic framework seeks to identify is 'the nature of the connection that can exist between heterogeneous elements' in this apparatus (Foucault, 1980, p. 194). These elements are also conditions for the insertion of subjects into the games of truth.

Repeated elements of these metaphors and their metaphorical relations appear to be randomly arranged, but through analysis they come together as thematic movements to create a complex and seemingly never-ending pattern that presses forward to a system of value regularity. That is, in tracing the problematisation of truth in policy discourse in analysing how metaphorical relations function in unrelated spheres, the genealogical method recognises 'that unity derives from a dispersion of singular events' (May, 1993, p. 74). Here, then, the analytical framework is able to highlight how policy and historical text-based metaphors operate as apparatuses of power through inciting the development of productive forces characteristic of neo-liberalism and its value system, which advocates support for competition, de/regulation, and market economies. This framework provides a grid of analysis which makes possible an analysis of power of a very complex field (Foucault, 1980, pp. 194–199; 1984a, p. 144).

However, while an abstract value system within any given policy texts is possible, the form it takes in any particular policy or series of texts continues to be an abstract unity until it finds its concrete form in the analysis. A three-layered analysis thus helps to highlight in detail the contradictions in discourse and explore how texts provide coherence by drawing on the same value system embedded and connected throughout the three levels. Contradiction is dissolved through a value system of regularity. An understanding of micro-meso-(meso)[6]-meso-macro relations in policy texts through such a discourse framework enables a mapping of the heteroglossic relations among different valuations to identify the overarching value system. With this multi-level framework in place, the following section illustrates the notion of 'movement' within and through the analytic framework.

Power as 'movements'

In order to construct a framework to examine *thematic metaphorical flow*, what follows elucidates the notion of fluid movements in policy discourse through power as an overarching movement that is conditional upon, and conditioning, the movement of metaphors.

(I) POWER AND SUBJECTIFICATION

To further explicate the notion of heterogeneity, Foucault (1980, p. 201) argues that 'in order for there to be a *movement* (of power relations) from above to below there has to be a capillarity from below to above at the same time'. The micro-meso-macro levels within this framework developed through the analysis are conceptualised as (philosophically) free, cyclical, *living* 'movements' to reflect the mobile, circulatory workings of power through metaphorical apparatuses as an open, more-or-less coordinated cluster of relations (Foucault, 1980, pp. 131, 199; 1986, p. 77; cf. Nietzsche, 1974, p. 82). Hence, through the notion of 'movement', the analytical framework embeds a fluid approach to the circumspect interpretation of, and the interplay between, micro techniques and macro strategies, giving analytic substance to Foucault's argument that 'power is everywhere' (Foucault, 1981a, p. 93). In other words, a movement is a heterogeneous moral phenomenon not wedded to limited categories. In this way and in order to make genealogy and CDA work together, the data assembled will have to be seen as and treated as 'living' in the sense that more data can be, and should be, added in the examination of evolving discursive change (Anais, 2013, p. 131). In relation to this, the analysis explores different aspects of the value system through tracing particular themes. This value system works by a set of conditions which are then potentially unlimited. More data can be added to explore how conditions are modified; that is, elementary conditions may take the form of several modifications. On the one hand, for discourses to have such 'constructive or performative effects' (Fairclough, Jessop & Sayer, 2004, as cited in Fairclough, 2010, p. 292) means they are *in continual flux* – they are fluid boundaries that are variable, indeterminate forms, and constitutive within each other. They are connected as an interdependent, inseparable web, subject to alteration, and not firmly set and congealed.

Through the analytical grid of analysis, the objective here is to create a history of the different modes through which a policy makes and addresses policy-formulated subjects (Foucault, 1982a, p. 777). The grid formulated here supports the examination of historical conditions which motivate the conceptualisation of the theory explicated through the analytical work (Foucault, 1982a, p. 778).

(II) CIRCULAR MOVEMENTS WITHIN ANALYTICAL FRAMEWORK

The architectural grid of three sets of three[7] micro–meso–macro movements cannot be balanced if it has to reflect dynamic, continuous and intertwining circular movements or the flow of circulatory system. This framework does not refer to an algorithm of permanent and complete grid of classifications that draws clear and definitive lines of division between movements. Instead, it presents an infinitely open organic fractal. The spatial dimensions of the structure have an irregular, interrupted, or fragmented shape. It is reflective of meandering rivers, subjected to unexpected unities as it traces the flow of the movements of fragments of metaphorical relations, from moment to moment, as though each moment is simultaneously its own infinity, *in infinitum*, connected to the past, present, and future states. Considering that truth is a major theme to be analysed in this work, the irregular structure reflects the increased problematisations of truth. This irregularity suggests that the examination of truth cannot and must not be reduced to some kind of mechanical procedure or pattern of conditioning as the analysis progresses. Even though the architecture is a means of structuring initial identifiable patterns, it becomes more fragmented. Recognisable structural inconsistencies are made explicit in several thematic movements. Perfect consistency in the analytical process would imply mechanical repetition, the establishment of and the attachment to a habit which risks relegating the exploration of truth. Further, to view the architectural grid as a fixed set of patterns would suggest that it is incapable of adaptability or pliability.

It is precisely these non-mechanical, fluid features that give e/valuative formations their analytical and practical force. To that extent there is no necessarily adequate or perfect fit between the forms of problematisation of truth, and the assemblage of forms of valuations which construct the shape eventually taken by the grid. Hence this grid allows for a constant and detailed problematisation of truth, a differential valuation of this truth with regard to the (ethical) subject, and a continuous repositioning of the subject in relation to social, civic, and political activities (cf. Foucault, 1981c, p. 101).

(III) METAPHORS AS FLUID MOVEMENTS

By employing the multi-layered architectural grid, Chapters 5 to 7 examine what is termed as 'Metaphorical realism', 'De/regulation', and 'Political economies of surrealism' respectively as micro movements within which policy metaphors act as a form of translatable micro-power. By examining the dissemination of these three themes as micro-powers, an implicit model of power that draws on a dispersed network of metaphorical apparatuses emerges (Foucault, 1980, p. 71). In this way, metaphors are also movements and also facilitate further movement such that the analysis examines how the metaphors of *flexibility, diversity, choice,* and *opportunity* transmit and put in motion relations of domination through their successive discursive transformations (cf. Foucault, 1980, pp. 95–96).

Policy extracts that drew on the utilisation of metaphors and reflected the three-stage micro-meso-macro themes were selected for analysis subsequently after each theme emerged at each stage. These themes can only be admitted after rigorous analytical examination. Once recurring proposals and propositions drawing on metaphorical relations are distilled into thematic patterns, organisational and evaluative coherence between systematically produced proposals and propositions can be assessed. The policy texts can then be analysed at the semantic level to determine the lexico-grammatical features that precipitate schemas of valuation (Graham, 1999, pp. 493–495). In doing so, this historical inquiry serves to grasp the points where *change* is constructed as possible and *desirable* in policy discourse (Foucault, 1995, p. 316). As Anais (2013, p. 129) argues,

> a genealogical approach never involves the generation of data according to a logic of beginning, middle, and end, it involves the collection of a wide range of source materials in order to discern socially and historically contingent patterns and events where existing practices are invested with new significations, or where they are co-opted and redeployed towards new ends.

Further, to elucidate historically determinable phases of the various forms of structural changes, the study explores how these changes are linked to modes of educational-political rationality and ethos, or what Foucault (1997, p. 256) refers to as 'ethico-political choice' made within the parameters of the existing system. By being sensitive to the recurrence of events, the purpose of the genealogical approach is not to trace the gradual curve of the evolution of neo-liberal-ethics, but to isolate the policy discourses where they engaged in different roles to give rise to forms of moralities (cf. Foucault, 1986, p. 76; Foucault, 1977, p. 140). The isolation of different points of emergent moralities in these policy extracts does not conform to successive configurations of an identical meaning (Foucault, 1986, p. 86); rather, they result in a main value system – a system of relations between valuations that is intricately and broadly related to Foucault's perspective on 'ethics'.

Chapter 5 proposes that metaphors, conceptualised apparatuses of power, turn (idealised/politically induced) images of the system into multiple organisations of truths that create and support inequality. Metaphors serve as a critical principle of institutional differentiation. Chapter 6 further explores how metaphors have been highly influential in giving a particular shape to an imagined, albeit self-evident economic system. Specifically, it examines how these metaphors are doing *ideologising* work to obscure the agent or agency involved in generating desirable outcomes. Finally, Chapter 7 examines how metaphors are doing *ideologising* work to bring together realities that appear to have limited logical relationship or rational link, to produce conditions of emerging political economies that permit new knowledge and new truths (cf. Adonis, 2005, p. 41).

When considered philosophically, each level of these metaphorical micro-meso-macro movements contains the forms of its earlier states of existence. By this, it is argued that this trans-substantial motion in the form of temporal *metaphorical transfers* (Graham, 2001a, p. 770; 2005, p. 123; Lemke, 1998, p. 45) among evaluative dimensions continues throughout all stages, altogether, and all at once integrated. The philosophical *movement* of metaphors involves the positioning of contextualised elements in new sets of relations within the recontextualised context, which entails a transformation of both these elements and the valuation of these metaphors. Working together, they contribute to the constant *becoming*, internal transformation, *streaming towards* the continuous intensification, and *being* of the ideology of economic growth (Nasr, 1996, p. 649; cf. Nietzsche, 1909, p. 109). As such, while a 'movement' is self-contained as a distinct part in each of the micro-meso-macro analytical sections, these three movements are interrelated thematically, such that even the individual movements exert a cumulative effect. What is also important to note is that although these metaphorical elements exist in one realm, and though they may interact, they are not related causally. Rather, both cause and effect occur simultaneously whereby the effect of metaphorical transfer is inherent in the cause. The cause cannot be detached from the effect and so a relation of causality can be established in either or all directions and where the reproduction of metaphorical relations accompanies many other structural transformations, of which it is at once the effect, the relay, and the instrument. However, it is not the aim of this research to reduce the structural transformations suggested in the texts essentially to the phenomenon of metaphorical transfers.

(IV) METAPHORICAL SUPERFLUIDITY

This idea of causal sequence and linear determinism is, here, replaced by the notion of *metaphorical superfluidity* that illuminates the concept of conditionality where each lives in an intrinsic movement of its own that gives way and converges and presses forward to a system of value regularity. Here, water-fluid dynamics and the movement of water as rapidly flowing streams are the primary analogical methods of analysis. An imperative to analyse evaluative meaning flows directly from the fluid position briefly outlined above. In order to overcome the false notion of a fragmentary analytical movement, this analogy of a flowing stream enables the conception of a total, whole movement (cf. Krishnamurti, 1978a, pp. 161–162). The *metaphorical* superfluidity is the simultaneous movement of the individual metaphors, the collective stream of metaphors and their surrounding discourses, the metaphorical relations that pull them forward, and the path of least resistance (laying stress on greatest adaptability) that they find. Hence, superfluidity indicates that everything moves together in an interconnected process. Since values, e/valuations, and the transvaluation of values are formulated through such metaphorical relations, this process highlights the relativistic elements of truth as being adaptive in the long run; that is, there is no coherent theory of truth (Medina & Wood, 2005, p. 12). This fluid movement is not, however free; every movement is necessary, compulsory, and is systematically calculated (Nietzsche, 1909, p. 106). Hence, *movement* can also indicate the transfer of a particular metaphor with a certain power from one particular extract to another, and for that reason, (neo-liberal) metaphors, as micro-mechanisms of power, can also act as the vehicle for transmitting a wider power that serves to enlarge and maximise the effects of power (cf. Foucault, 1980, pp. 72–73, 101).

Superfluidity thus indicates the constant, seamless transitioning of connected movements, the ongoingness and recognising that the boundaries between movements are so inextricably interrelated that it is not possible to make absolute distinctions or assume a rigorous classification between the micro, meso, and macro. That is, the micro-meso-macro is not a causal or sequential argument, but a structure with interchangeable components. They are conceived as *attacca*, that is, without any break between the current movement and the next movement. So although distinctions between micro-meso and meso-macro movements are possible, the metaphorical resources and relations that facilitate thematic condensation across texts often make such distinctions difficult and the search for such distinctions illusory. And indeed, such distinctions appear to be more obfuscatory than explanatory. Rather, by always treating trajectories as interdependent, it is still possible to examine these trajectories, realising that as the analysis progresses, their parameters become blurred as the analysis synthesises the structural implications of their relatedness that appears to be contingent upon a broader, more invisible, more important value convergence. Indeed, through not attempting to separate these trajectories, the boundaries – conceptual and temporal – between them are dissolved through the ubiquity of a main value engendered by the ideology of economic growth, and more importantly, the immediacy of micro-macro e/valuations. Considered in detail, these analytical themes do have a certain intelligibility. Within this organic phenomena, metaphorical relations move between the porous divide of the simultaneous separateness and interdependence of the analytical themes. In these themes that develop, become accentuated, and gather strength, one can discern a different type of modification: it concerns the way in which institutional practices define the relation of the subject to their 'ability', and to economic imperatives.

Furthermore, in examining the inter-connectedness of policy metaphors, their trajectories, and their surrounding (philosophical) discourses, it is important to recognise the immortality of their movements. Each metaphorical-evaluative transference conditions a sequence of metaphorical-evaluative transfers in the same series, a circular movement of transmissions within various combinations of series is thus demonstrated: metaphorical relations as circular movements that repeat themselves infinitely and play their game of truth *in infinitum* (Nietzsche, 1967a, p. 549, italics included). These processes again reflect Foucault's (1986, p. 74, italics added) argument that '"Truth" is linked in a *circular* relation with systems of power (through valuations) which produce and sustain it, and to effects of power which it induces and which extend it'.

As a corollary to all this, it is hence important not to consider these thematic movements as three separate domains but three 'transcendentals'. In order to develop their potential in constructing complex relationships, these thematic movements call and build upon the play of relations of the other through discursive (deep inner) contradictions or alignments, discontinuities or/and fragmented disjunctures for 'new' concepts to emerge. These new concepts can be collectively conceptualised as 'fragments'. In order to explicate the notion of 'fragments' as conceptualised in this research, the discussion here draws parallels with Graham's (2001b) analysis. There appears, for instance, to be: first, a complete and distinct disjunction between the values in policy discourse that suggest the possibility of opportunity for all and the institutional practice of equity. Second, there appears to be an arbitrary division and dismemberment in terms of the confusing temporal orientation of realis (present) and irrealis (future-oriented, non-existential) states that are set in juxtaposition to each other, appearing as complementary rationales in creating and presenting political imageries. Third, necessity for institutional and regulatory action is premised upon the *desirability* in meeting the *perceived* needs of certain political economies which apparently does not exist or has not yet existed by identifying the kinds of commodifiable labour in these economies. Within these fragments, what holds for evaluative condensation also holds for thematic condensation that gives rise to each movement (Graham, 2002, p. 237; Lemke, 1995, pp. 60–61). Nevertheless, even though movements can appear as distinct, they intersect in a web so dense that they cannot be dissociated (cf. Foucault, 1980, pp. 86–87, 111–112). As such, these movements are not necessarily purely successive. In this sense there exists a stronghold of competing genres held in contradictory tension within the games of truth or policy narratives, within the context of surrealistic economic landscapes that converge to create and sustain the ideology of economic growth. Despite the transformative moments that punctuate policy discourse, currents of continuity can be observed: the repeated exhortation of metaphors elucidated through the architectural grid, the form and formlessness of realities, and images of political economies that unfold endlessly.

Arguably then, discursive strategies build in/tangible structures and determine the possibilities of the *present* that are seen to continually flow through the metaphorical relations being modified as the discourse unfolds and continues to flesh out the main value system. The term 'flow' highlights the continually changing structural possibilities within policy discourses that are realised. That is, there is a (living) movement of change only when there is a constant flow (cf. Krishnamurti, 1978a, pp. 106–107). The thematic movements in the analytical chapters flow into each other; they are inter-related and ultimately transcend their own distinctions. Hence, even though the thematic movements are operating in a field of fragmentation, within each fragment there is the whole mechanism of all fragments (cf. Krishnamurti, 1978a, pp. 129–130). By weight of references to history, past and present, these (porous) movements are infinite by virtue of interconnectedness.

While sustaining this ideology, these movements can be conceived as component parts of a general evolutionary analysis of *desirable* change (Dopfer et al., 2004, p. 269). In these *systems of dispersion* (cf. Foucault, 2002, p. 41), the moment of negotiation and transition is constant. The analysis argues that as a rule of action in political struggle, the opaque (in the sense of how it appears as self-evident) ideology of economic growth as the (only) way forward is and can only be sustained through this fragmentation. Fragmentation or discontinuity is an integral component of unified discursive formations that allude to this ideology. These formations are co-dependent; they inter-be, and are unified by a richness of diversity. By demonstrating the ellipses of fragmented discourse, the analysis illustrates that this phenomena of rupture, of discontinuity (cf. Foucault, 2002, p. 4) means that discursive formations are not stable; they create the conditions for their own change, are their own simulation, and in the process, reflect ideological hybridity in legitimation strategies (cf. Mulderrig, 2009, p. 108). Because of this nature of fragmentation in policy discourse, and in order to grasp the specificity of mechanisms of power in their detail and complexity so as not to fall into the trap of a unitary discourse (Foucault, 1980, pp. 83–86, 145) prematurely, the analytical structure adopts an aphoristic style. Although this structure may not appear systematic, the phenomenon of conceptual recurrence makes elements of a system detectable. Arguably, then, the work of the analysis is not fragmentary even though it may appear to be in fragments.

However, any *new* discursive regime in policy discourse can be found to be aligned with the underpinning value at the systematic core. New discursive regimes of truth then are not merely superstructural – of legitimating and reinforcing social and structural inequality; they are conditions of the formation and development of the evolving (policy) discourse. Thereby the framework places the initial focus of analysis and critique on the *discursive practices* rather than the analysis and critique of the ideology. For as Foucault (1986, p. 76) points out, it is not through 'reducing an entire history and genesis to an exclusive concern for (economic) utility' that we could understand the phenomenon of power, and how it is imbricated within the history of morality. Rather, a rigorous analytical examination of the discursive practices in texts that set the conditions for the historical constitution of subjects in the games of truth become foregrounded and through this *how* games of truth are linked to relationships of power (Foucault, 1984a, p. 127; 1997, p. 285).

This idea of the multi-layered analysis provides for a very loose yet complex conception of the workings of policy discourse. This conception, which interacts with and is embedded within the philosophical study of valuation, necessarily remains vague until any analysis is carried out, yet the aim is to be able to demonstrate that an on-going *becoming* and *being* of the ideology of economic growth can be shown to be reliant upon the connections between metaphorical relations and structural inequality operative simultaneously. As such, this research orientation can be considered as a 'bricolage' that is concerned with a non-systematic use of a range of tools by integrating multiple methodological approaches with diverse theoretical and philosophical concepts of the various elements encountered as the data unfolds (Kincheloe, 2001, p. 682). Using these approaches when and as required in the analysis will enable a better conceptual grasp of the complexity of discursive strategies that are employed in policy discourse (cf. Kincheloe, 2001, p. 679). This synthesis would enhance the level of multiple, nuanced interpretations of discursive strategies in policy discourse, and where appropriate, developing from these approaches. Analysis that relies on a prescribed set of analytical and theoretical tools risks imposing ideologies onto texts (Rogers, 2004a, p. 14). Further, it may also neglect other possible interpretations of discursive strategies that are operative as the data unfolds. Employing a pre-existing system will make the analysis more and more mechanical, and produce increasing conflict between *what is* and the system being applied (cf. Krishnamurti, 1978b, p. 57).

Summary

In order to explore the subtle complexity of metaphors and how their work is threaded through policy, this chapter has constructed a multi-movement architecture for a critical discourse analysis of political economy through micro, meso, and macro shifts within a complex network system of values. This conceptual three-level fluid interactional grid combines individual text discourse analysis and philosophical-theoretical discourses within a methodological approach designed for the critical analysis of connected (policy) texts as part of a critique of the value of truth (Nietzsche, 1967b, p. 153) through forms of neo-liberal e/valuation. The framework, rather than providing an algorithm of a permanent and complete grid of classifications that draws clear and definitive lines of division between movements, presents an infinitely open organic fractal with spatial dimensions of the structure as having an irregular, interrupted, or fragmented shape subjected to unexpected unities as it traces the movements of fragments. Further, the notion of 'movements' reflects the circulatory workings of internal power mechanisms of policy discourse.

The general aim here is to present historical policies as a theory of unified whole, making clear the reasons which led to its adoption. By thus showing that the micro-meso-macro movements are interrelated to form a unified totality, through using a plurality of discourse-analytic approaches that are dynamically related (cf. Bohm & Peat, 2010, p. 44), this chapter hopes in some measure to foreground a functional aspect of each discursive part as internally related in its basic function to constantly enfold and unfold the whole through simultaneous engagement with all the other discrete parts. This framework is thus a form of dynamic unity within plurality (cf. Bohm & Peat, 2010, p. 243). Herein lies a potential for a continuously creative approach to analysing data so that any abrupt discontinuity of thematic patterns is not inevitable.

Highlighting and maintaining the essential notion of a fluid movement of and between text, texts and discourse, the three-layered analysis that is suggested provides a methodological frame by which to examine how texts cohere by drawing on a central or core *value system* that is connected as truth throughout these three levels. In mapping this out it is argued that this conceptual three-level fluid interactional grid provides a subtle and dynamic framework for drawing out and examining the interconnections within and through discourses, providing the possibility of tracing intersecting constructions of macro-micro valuations. By framing the analysis through, between, and within the micro-meso-macro levels, this framework retains the essential point that temporal *metaphorical transfers* continue throughout all stages where they contribute to the constant *becoming* and *being* of an underpinning ideology in which a taken for granted 'truth' is established and drives the action as the (only) way forward.

Adopting a genealogical approach of problematisation and informed by both the principles of political economy and neo-liberalism, three thematic movements emerged from the analysis of 'ethics: or *philosophy of desirability*' as elucidated in Chapter 2. Drawing on the micro-meso-macro framework, these three themes are: 'Metaphorical realism' (Chapter 5), 'De/regulation' (Chapter 6), and 'Political economies of surrealism' (Chapter 7). The analyses in these three chapters provide a critical reflection on the ab/uses of neo-liberal economic discourse within ethics; in particular, they provide an understanding of the micro mechanisms (capillaries of power) and ethical dimensions of neo-liberal control. This control works through the systematic recurrence (Foucault, 1972, p. 60) of policy metaphors of 'flexibility', 'diversity', 'choice', and 'opportunity' within the context of multiple, changing political economies to engender public legitimacy. To illustrate this, the next chapter will firstly employ the notion of 'Metaphorical realism' in order to focus attention on how these policy metaphors do *ideologising* work to varying degrees, in the service of contributing to and sustaining systemic educational *inequality* through forms of valuation.

Notes

1 'Transvaluation of values' here is not to be understood as Nietzsche's concept of bringing about 'a triumph of opposite values' (Nietzsche, 1924, p. 178) but the trans-substantial motion in the form of temporal *metaphorical transfers* (Graham, 2001a, p. 770; 2005, p. 123; Lemke, 1998, p. 45). In relation to the ongoing conceptualisation of the

methodological framework within this study, it is proposed that the entirety of the value system flows from the transfers of micro-macro valuations through the propagation of metaphors.

2 'The will is not a single entity but more like a constantly shifting federation or alliance of drives' (Nietzsche, 1967a, p. 381).

3 There is considerable sociological literature conceptualising and theorising valuation and evaluation within the workings of the market that is beyond the scope of this study (see, for example, Carruthers & Stinchcombe 1999; Zelizer 1979; 2011) – the focus here is on how modes of value determination are situated and mobilised within the discursive processes in the documents, rather than a treatise on these theories. However, it is relevant to note that Lamont (2012, p. 205) considers valuation practices as 'giving worth or value' and evaluative practices as 'assessing how an entity attains a certain type of worth'. Evaluation is therefore conceived as an act of valuing – though it is more than this as it includes a possible action of arguing for a valuation. Thus, in policy discourse, it is possible for both valuation and evaluation to be interchangeable and interdependent as each conditions and is conditioned by the other.

4 How budgets are made and how resources are allocated (in Singapore) are decided on the basis of policies (Quah, 1984, p. 119).

5 To elaborate, this research draws on Bohm's account of how the general structure of matter may be understood in terms of enfoldment and unfoldment to the *implicate order* (from a Latin root meaning 'to enfold' or 'to fold inward'), the central underlying theme of which is the notion of 'unbroken wholeness of the totality of existence as an undivided flowing movement without borders' (1980, pp. 172, 177–180).

6 '(meso)' here emphasises its intermediary role as explicated in the 'Micro-meso-macro' section above.

7 There are three themes and each is analysed at three levels.

5 Theme 1

Metaphorical realism

Overview

Chapter 5, the first of the three micro movements, proposes and employs the notion of 'Metaphorical realism', in order to focus attention on how the metaphors of flexibility, choice, diversity, and opportunity do *ideologising* work to varying degrees, in the service of contributing to and sustaining systemic educational *inequality* through both micro and macro valuations. In its philosophical dimension, 'Metaphoric realism' proposes that these metaphors are apparatuses of power, where power includes forms of valuations that serve to turn idealised and politically induced images of the system into multiple organisations of truths that support inequality. These truths shape and retain competing economic imaginaries and massive abstractions; that is, they construct the illusion of desirable realities. Further, a three-layered analysis of these policy extracts reveals correlations between these metaphors and an organic arrangement of micro-macro valuations that hierarchise these metaphors relative to capitalism-corporatism (Graham & Luke, 2011, p. 106; cf. Foucault, 1997, pp. 90–91). In doing so, the analysis provides a critical reflection on the ab/uses of neo-liberal discourse and an understanding of the mechanisms and ethical dimensions of neo-liberal control through the *eternal-systematic* recurrence (Foucault, 1972, p. 60) of policy metaphors in texts.

The first micro movement discusses the overarching examination of three micro-meso and meso-macro movements: 'Flexible curriculum for different categories of pupils', 'Flexible system for VITB trainees', and 'Diverse pathways for talents'. These movements examine how policymakers persistently use metaphors as the 'ideological' foundation for inequitable opportunities. Paradoxically, while the education policies claim to implement flexibility, diversity, choice, and opportunity as necessary responses to different 'categories' of pupils – 'VITB trainees' (Extract 14, line 6) and 'talents' (Extract 23, line 2) – the analysis suggests that these metaphors allow for the possibility of legitimising increasing inequalities. As such, these metaphors can be seen as 'ideological' in the sense that they are *ideologising* economic-material rationalities to provide legitimacy and cover for the consolidation and extension of asymmetries of knowledge access.

Flexible curriculum for different categories of pupils

This key theme investigates under what conditions systemic inequality first existed and makes clear the linkages between the use of metaphors and the reproduction of inequality. Specifically, it examines the need for a transition between two dichotomous systems – from rigid to flexible – in order to cater to students' needs (in the micro-meso movement) and economic needs (in the meso-macro movement).

Micro-meso movement: genesis of a 'flexible' curriculum

This section begins with the 1979a MOE report before tracing the rhetoric and genesis of a '*flexible* curriculum'. This report was the first to propose an explicit form of ability-based streaming. In the extract, the 'present rigid education system' (line 2) is strategically presented as *undesirable,* to be replaced by a 'flexible' (line 4) system. The following analysis examines the way the metaphor of flexibility builds rationalities for a flexible curriculum.

The analysis of this single section illustrates how this metaphor can be seen moving through and between the micro and meso discourses in the sense that a 'flexible' curriculum (line 4) is positioned as not only a necessary response but more importantly, constructed as an ethical, sustainable, sorting mechanism to cater for 'different categories of pupils' (lines 4–5).

In Extract 5, the evaluations within this text depend on a single variable which must be assigned textually (Lemke, 1998, pp. 48–49): the desirability of a *flexible* curriculum. The rest of the elements of the text receive evaluations on the dimension of desirability indirectly once a value is assigned to this keystone.

In order to make a coherent link between the second sentence and the sentences that precede it, there is an assumption that the solution to a 'rigid' (line 2) system with 'the use of absolute standards' (line 3) lies in a 'flexible' curriculum (Fairclough, 2001, p. 69). Drawing on Martin and Rose's (2007, pp. 116–131) discourse on conjunctions, *if* is a condition, indicating probability, which serves to

Extract 5 1979a MOE report

Lines	*Extract*
1	To set absolute standards at PSLE, it would be necessary to work backwards
2	from the GCE 'O' Level Examination. In the present **rigid** education system,
3	the use of absolute standards would mean fewer pupils entering secondary
4	schools. If the curriculum is to be **flexible** enough to cater for different
5	categories of pupils, it would mean longer years of study for some pupils.
6	These extra years would either be spent in primary schools or secondary
7	schools, depending on the standards stipulated for the PSLE.

Source: MOE, 1979a, p. 4-3.

link the thought 'it would mean longer years of study for some pupils' (line 5) with the condition under which it would have done so, 'If the curriculum is to be *flexible* enough to cater for different categories of pupils' (lines 4–5). This statement constructs the idea that there are different categories of pupils and drawing from the previous utterance, 'the use of absolute standards would mean fewer pupils entering secondary schools' (lines 3–4) raises the *desirable* need of attending to this difference in order to increase the number of pupils entering secondary schools. This proposition of reform to ensure an increase in the number of pupils entering secondary schools alludes to the notion of ethics through inclusive (albeit differentiated) practices. The understanding that this is possible is brought forth by the proposal for a '*flexible* curriculum' which constitutes a revision in both the amount of time spent in school, differentiated standards for 'some pupils' (line 5) and more importantly, provides a preliminary understanding of the historical systematic exclusion of these pupils.

Meso-macro movement: moving towards social-economic discourse

Having examined the work of the metaphor of flexible as it moves within and through the micro-meso level of a single text, this section now turns to this theme within and through the meso-macro level of policy as it appears and reappears in the 1979b–2008 policy extracts. While the previous micro-meso analysis showed the undesirability of a rigid education system, the following meso-macro traces the desirability of a flexible system across Extracts 6–13, further reinforcing the key role of this metaphor in providing a rationale for an inequitable system. To bridge the macro-micro gap, the meso-macro movement highlights the way the theme of flexibility moves from the non-economic to economic and enters into a field of social-economic discourse.

In Extract 5, the causal relation between structural problem and policy solution is represented in terms of necessity. While the metaphor of *flexibility* is used within *non-economic* discourse of the micro-meso movement, the analysis of the meso-macro movement here outlines the impetus for a reworking of the system as it transfers metaphorical meaning from an evaluative government to abstract economic forces (Mulderrig, 2009, p. 110). Here, then, the colonising spread of economic discourse in policy is in a potentially problematic relationship with what might reasonably be called the ethics of policy discourse through the production of 'values'. That is, this economic discourse implies a relational-hierarchical organisation of values associated and imbricated within the discourse of a flexible/rigid system. On closer inspection, this interfaced hierarchy is still more intimately woven. Through an explication of thematic condensation, this hierarchical arrangement of e/valuation includes related semantic labels of desirability and importance/necessity, *all of which* might appear as predicates of elements in the extract (Graham, 2002, p. 245).

From the initial use of flexibility, the following analysis can then trace this through a series of policy texts (Extracts 6–13), where flexibility as a positive value serves to underpin the necessity for institutional change tied to desirability for change. The effects of the change result in a new *flexible* system.

Extracts 6–13 Flexibility through MOE policy texts, 1979b–2008

Does the present system, successful as it is, give general satisfaction? Undoubtedly no – neither in quality nor in quantity. This discontent, divine though it may be, emerges clearly from the 'Report on the Ministry of Education', the recommendations of which were subsequently endorsed by Parliament and are currently being implemented. In future, therefore, the system of schooling will be more **flexible** ... The implications for the curriculum of these reforms alone are considerable, though their prime intention is to augment, as they undoubtedly will, the quantity of those who will succeed in passing the PSLE and of those who subsequently will obtain three passes at the 'O' level.

(Extract 6, MOE, 1979b, p. 6)

In addition to the above factors, educational policy makers in Singapore must also grapple with general educational issues which are present in all societies and in all educational systems. The most difficult of these issues is how to design a **flexible** education system which will stretch the abilities of the brightest children and at the same time provide encouragement and opportunities for advancements for those who are less academically inclined.

(Extract 7, MOE, 1991a, n.p.)

For pupils in the lowest ability range (20%) who, at present, are most likely to be streamed to the Monolingual and Extended courses, the system has not been as effective in helping them to progress up the educational ladder. Greater attention to these least academically able pupils is hence necessary. Improvements to the primary school system can be made by customising education to suit the ability of each pupil rather than to subject all pupils to the diet provided in broad educational streams. This will require **flexibility** and responsibility to be given to principals and teachers whose judgment will be crucial in tailoring the most appropriate educational package for their pupils.

(Extract 8, MOE, 1991a, p. 11)

JC curriculum should be structured more **flexibly** to better cater to the students' strengths and interests and equip them with skills, knowledge and outlook to participate and contribute fully in society and economy.

(Extract 9, MOE, 2002, p. 9)

JC students will benefit from a new broader and more **flexible** GCE 'A' level curriculum from this year, which will allow those with talent and interest in particular areas to pursue them in greater depth.

(Extract 10, MOE, 2006, p. 1)

... MOE has in recent years introduced various initiatives to bring about greater diversity and **flexibility** in the education system As students have different strengths and interests, these efforts are aimed at allowing our students to develop their potential to the fullest and *ensure* that they are well-prepared for future challenges.

(Extract 11, MOE, 2006, p. 5)

One advantage of a polytechnic 'high school' is that it allows greater **flexibility** for the polytechnics to focus on curricular and pedagogical innovations from as early as secondary one to cater to students with clear intent on an applied education.

(Extract 12, MOE, 2006, p. 21)

The new university could exercise **flexibility** in structuring courses so that students with relevant prior learning could progress at a faster pace.

(Extract 13, MOE, 2008a, p. 21)

In Extracts 6–13, the benefits of a *flexible* system as opposed to the present system are introduced here arbitrarily as a string of desirable 'facts' – appearing as unquestionable effects of a flexible system (Graham, 2002, pp. 248–249). The prospect of the present system in giving 'general satisfaction' (Extract 6) is denied based on the 'Report on the Ministry of Education' (Extract 6). The syntactic progression of necessity (Graham, 2002, p. 247) (the importance) of structural reform and educational institutions thereof depends on a single metaphorical variable that has been assigned textually. This operates, as Graham (2002, p. 246) points, through 'syntactic propagation', which 'occurs when an evaluative stance towards an element in the clause transfers its evaluation to another element'. In this case, it is the high degree of evaluations for desirability of *customisation* that automatically flows from a *flexible* system. These will allegedly offset the negative effects (i.e., 'the system *has not been as effective* in helping them to *progress up the educational ladder*' – Extract 8) of a *rigid* system (Extract 5, line 2).

The decrepit state of the present system is acknowledged in the implied need for Singapore to 'grapple with general educational issues which are present in *all* societies and in *all* educational systems' (Extract 7), and 'design a flexible education system which *will* stretch the abilities of the brightest children and at the same time provide encouragement and *opportunities* for advancements for those who are *less academically inclined*' (Extract 7). Both of these statements reinforce the futility of maintaining the present system. Next, 'the system' (Extract 8) which has 'not been as effective' (Extract 8) calls for the solution through 'customising education to suit the ability of each pupil rather than to subject all pupils to the diet provided in broad educational streams' (Extract 8). Furthermore, this system allows the ability to 'cater to students with clear intent on applied education' (Extract 12).

Cogently, similar to the argument mounted in Extract 7, which emphasises the importance of investing in those who are deemed more capable, while a flexible system '*will* allow those with talent and interest in particular areas to pursue them in greater depth' (Extract 10), it would 'help them (pupils in the lowest ability range) to progress up the educational ladder' (Extract 8). A policy framework that is designed to facilitate the positive effects of a flexible system hence becomes necessary. The outcome of all these evaluations, positive and negative in polarity, is necessity – as the metaphor of flexibility further enters into a field of irrealis social-economic discourse, that is, 'JC[1] curriculum should be structured more flexibly ... to participate and contribute fully in society and economy' (Extract 9).

Specifically, Extract 9 proposes a flexible curriculum that not only is able to 'better cater to the students' strengths ...' but allows students 'to *participate and contribute fully* in society and *economy*'. Further, in Extract 11 'these efforts are aimed at allowing our students to develop their potential to the fullest and *ensure* that they are well-prepared for *future challenges*'. Full participation propagates necessity for flexible-institutional 'reform'. These instances demonstrate the pervasive work of *metaphorical transfers* among the evaluative semantic dimensions and, here, the closely related semantics of (catering to) ability (cf. Lemke, 1998, p. 45).

Graham (2002, p. 232) observes that, in cases where a prediction (representing desirable) outcomes follows a verb like 'ensure' (Extract 11), it elides the future orientation of the predicate, thereby construing it as the unquestionable result of the government's (MOE) action, rather than a possible future effect. As a result, 'diversity and flexibility in the education system' takes on the appearance of inevitability; that is, 'the managed action is represented as if it were already accomplished, rather than being a possible future outcome, thereby reducing room for negotiation over the matter' (Mulderrig, 2011a, p. 55).

The analysis above illustrates how the notion of flexibility can be traced through the permeation of a series of policy texts and analysed through a multi-layered, superfluid, critical approach highlighting the infusion of 'ideological truths', in the sense that it is *ideologising perceived* learner capabilities and economic-material rationalities to provide legitimacy and cover for the consolidation and extension of asymmetries of knowledge access. The metaphor of flexibility, thus, provides a legitimising truth through metaphorical transfers that propagate the necessity for flexible-institutional 'reform'.

Flexible system for VITB trainees

As an expansion of the previous section's micro-meso movement, the following analysis of the 1991 MOE report traces the way the metaphor of *flexible* is used to justify differed access for VITB trainees. The argument for differed access as a moral imperative and as a form of social and labour inclusion is projected and developed in 1991 with a proposed upgrade to vocational training. The analysis identifies a commitment to vocational education and training as a means to 'better meet the needs of school leavers and the economy in the 1990s' (Extract 14, lines 4–5).

Within the context of a system of educational meritocracy that espouses equal opportunities and equity perspectives, an important aspect of the role of policy documents is to justify and sustain the distinction and differentiated treatment made between students who will undertake the university pathway and those who will have to undergo vocational training. Given the potential for

Extract 14: 1991b MOE report, upgrading vocational training, Vocational and Industrial Training Board

Lines	*Extract*
1	The proposed changes will help to upgrade the status and quality of
2	vocational and technical training in Singapore. The wider options of
3	vocational **choices** through a more **flexible** system of full-time institutional
4	training and apprenticeship schemes will better meet the needs of school
5	leavers and the economy in the 1990s. There will be better **opportunities**
6	for VITB[2] trainees to achieve higher-level **skills** and progress to further
7	education and training.

Source: MOE, 1991b, p. x.

a negative response to this from within the frame of meritocracy, one might expect considerable effort to be invested into mitigating or justifying this proposal. Within the meritocratic principle frame of 'equal opportunities', this second key micro-meso theme examines the discursive strategies through which proposals and propositions for vocational training are justified through more opportunities for progression.

The role of vocational and technical education in fostering and securing social inclusion through a broadly workfarist strategy is articulated in the discourse of opportunity, choice, and skills through a more *flexible* system. This system is seen to benefit individuals through 'longer years of study' (Extract 5, line 5), employers, and the nation as a whole (Mulderrig, 2009, p. 57). The discussion in the next section offers an initial conceptualisation of how vocational education provides *necessary* educational and economic access for students who are 'less academically inclined' (Extract 7). Importantly, it provides an understanding of how a sustainable educational trajectory for 'VITB' (Extract 14, line 6) can be thought about and rationalised through a '*flexible* system' (Extract 14, line 3). Here, the context is inclusive educational and ethical practices, through the rhetoric of labour participation. The relations between opportunity, choice, and skill in Extract 14 propagate evaluations of a more abstract and broad order. They do so within, across, and *beyond* the propositional content of the text. This section explores how the notion of social inclusion in relation to labour participation is contextualised through meeting the broader objectives of government and industry, emanating from irrealis time and spatial dimensions of meeting 'the needs of school leavers and the economy in the 1990s' (Extract 14, lines 4–5).

Justification for differentiated treatment within the social inclusion and equity orientation is made through what can be conceptualised as two key moments or subdivisions – what is referred to in the following analysis of Extract 14 as 'sub micro-meso-macro movements'. The problem of securing equality of opportunity for VITB trainees in a highly differentiated system is resolved through both moments simultaneously. Specifically, this section illustrates how this metaphor moves between two sub micro-meso movements that draw on the primary metaphoric principle of 'opportunities'. These sub-movements function as discrete building blocks of explicit structural discrimination.

Overall, this theme engages in an investigation of the concept of 'equal opportunities' and its intersection with educational policy and practice in relation to VITB trainees. Within the frame of meritocracy, it is unfair if some learners get more opportunities for educational achievement and progress (Satz, 2007, p. 629). The analysis of the two simultaneous sub micro-meso-macro movements demonstrates how the playing field is levelled, and the competition for society's occupations and academic progression is fair even for VITB trainees.

Discourses of opportunity and choice

The first sub micro-meso movement (see below) illustrates how VITB students will *receive* opportunity in the new economy, an irrealis state, through the provision of choice in a more flexible system. Further, this provision of choice will also transit paradoxically into *creating* opportunities for Junior College/Upper Secondary/University students through the metaphor of diversity in the sub meso-macro movement.

In considering flexibility as an organising principle in terms of the metaphorical work that it does, the sub meso-macro movement identifies its relationships with the metaphors of diversity and choice. As such, different metaphorical complexes are in play at different levels of thematic abstractions; flexibility, choice, and diversity are elaborated in a range of metaphorical systems. Here, the metaphors of diversity and choice subordinate themselves to flexibility, which itself determines the structure within which flexibility, diversity, choice, and opportunity belong together.

Sub micro-meso movement: opportunity and choice for VITB students in relation to manpower demands

Extract 14 assumes that the expansion of the vocational education sector and the provision of 'better' *opportunities* (line 5) will lead to the acquisition of higher-level skills and progression to further education and training (lines 6–7). Graham (2001a, p. 772) argues that '*opportunities* are always *desirable* potential realities for someone and thus imply the *necessity* for a certain amount of action for the opportunities to be moved from potentiality (*irrealis*) to actuality (*realis*)' (italics included). By deploying *process metaphors* (Graham, 2001a, p. 767) of 'choices' and 'flexible' (line 3) and by exercising *potentiality* embedded in nominals such as 'opportunities' (line 5), policy authors actively exercise the tense system to represent future and imagined or *irrealis* (potential) states (e.g., 'will better meet the needs of school leavers and the economy in the 1990s', lines 4–5) as if they actually existed in the here and now. These broadest of evaluative orientations are expressed implicitly and explicitly in the data where there is an explicit recognition that 'choices' (line 3) are *desirable*. In order to make a coherent link between the second and third statements, the underlying assumption, or 'truth' is that 'the wider options of vocational *choices* through a more *flexible* system' (lines 2–3) will lead to 'better opportunities' (line 5), 'higher-level skills' (line 6) and 'progress to further education and training' (lines 6–7). It is also assumed that a 'flexible system' is an existing reality (i.e., 'through a more flexible system', line 3).

In order to underpin these logical truths, the extract as a whole lists 'texture relations of equivalence' (Fairclough, 2010, p. 288) among elements. Drawing on Fairclough's (2010, p. 285) approach, by 'texturing' elements as equivalent, the analysis of the policy report focuses on 'the *work* that is done textually, that is, the textual *working up* of that relationship'. In this case, 'equivalent elements are co-hyponyms' (Fairclough, 2010, p. 288); for instance: 'wider options' (line 2), 'more flexible system' (line 3), 'better opportunities' (line 5) are co-hyponyms of 'change' (line 1) (the superordinate term). As such, in the case of texture, these elements are 'linked through a text to form a (cohesive) 'chain' by virtue of their semantic relations to one another' (Lemke, 1998, p. 50). These elements are key to the configuration of vocabularies of 'flexible' (line 3) and its implicit relation with 'status and quality' (line 1). The second sentence of this particular extract explicitly foregrounds the pairing of 'flexible' and 'economy', and its last sentence effects a further merger between the vocabularies. This time, 'flexible' (line 3) is glossed with a conjunction of an expression that belongs to the vocabulary of 'better opportunities' (line 5) (i.e., 'higher-level skills and progress to further education and training' lines 6–7). The total configuration that results is the linguistic facet of a major strategic conjunction in policy: between the promotion of a 'flexible' system of full-time institutional training and apprenticeship schemes and, beyond, a vocationally-geared education system.

Further, the metaphorical construction of the 'flexible system' (line 3) as attending both to the needs of the 'school leavers' (lines 4–5) and 'the economy in the 1990s' (line 5), is illustrated through the phrase: 'The wider options of vocational *choices* through a more flexible system' (lines 2–3). The phrase also alludes to the intended processes and ideological attachments of '*choices*' (lines 2–3) (Fairclough, 1992, pp. 195; 2001, pp. 99–100). This recommendation, based on common-sense assumptions, gives coherence and social meaning to the metaphorical representation of 'flexible system' and suggests the systematic redistribution of opportunity through 'wider options of vocational choices' (lines 2–3), which 'will help to upgrade the status and quality of vocational and technical training in Singapore' (lines 1–2).

Indeed, as Graham (2001a, p. 772) argues, 'opportunities' (line 5) are pre-evaluated *desirable* potentialities to varying degrees, even if those potentialities are not available. This extract demonstrates the interrelatedness between evaluations of *desirability* and *importance* for realising opportunities. The hortatory function of policy is expressed in *necessity*: 'a more flexible system' (line 3) is required to 'provide better *opportunities*' (line 5). There is also subtle reference to *degrees of desirability* where *opportunities* are concerned; for some, namely this 'excluded' group that receives an education of a perceivable 'lower' status, *opportunities* can be *improved* (lines 1–2). That is, by providing '*choices* through a more *flexible* system' (line 3), students who undergo vocational and technical education will have improved opportunities and 'progress to further education and training' (lines 6–7). 'Choice' here is construed as intrinsically desirable for this 'excluded' group, rather than envisaging a more egalitarian system of 'equal' status (Mulderrig, 2012, p. 715). The evaluative orientation is explicitly expressed as the *necessity* of making sure everybody can at least *receive* opportunity spaces in the new economy, at individual, national, and international levels: to 'better meet the needs of school leavers and the economy in the 1990s' (lines 4–5).

As Mulderrig (2003, pp. 108–109) states, this kind of argument is based on a nested set of premises: (1) that this economic context should and does determine the nature of educational practice and content; and (2) that an education system tailored to the economy is the *right* of each child. Prospects for greater *flexibility* through wider vocational options is construed as an expansion of opportunities closely linked to greater labour participation. In such emphases, a 'more flexible *system*' (line 3) is not justified in terms of increased choice ('wider options of vocational *choices*', lines 2–3) for the student, but in terms of the need of the educational institution to recreate, restructure, and maintain itself at the competitive edge of an economic market. Contradictorily, 'rather than offering more choice through the increasing commodification and performativity of knowledge', a constriction of choice to the student is made to cater to market demands and reap financial gain (Nicoll, 1998, pp. 301–302). The weaving together of apparently contradictory rhetoric redefines ethics as the widening of *opportunity* to enter into competition (Mulderrig, 2007, p. 143).

Driven by an economic imperative, the trend of reducing the process of teaching into systems (lines 2–5) was projected as an unavoidable phenomenon when viewed in the nation's best interest. By the same token, this proposition assures the recipients of the message that the status and quality of vocational and technical education in Singapore will not only be upgraded, but that the '*wider options*' (line 2) through a 'more *flexible* system' (line 3) 'will better meet the needs of school leavers and the economy in 1990s' (lines 4–5). The definite article, *the* in '*The* wider options of vocational choices through a more *flexible* system' (lines 2–5), triggers the presupposition that there exist wider options of vocational choices (Fairclough, 2006a, p. 2). This presupposition, however, also has the characteristic that it holds under negation, that is, '*proposed* changes will help to upgrade the status and quality of vocational and technical training' (lines 1–2), suggesting a slippage between the *potential* and *actual.*

However, given that this recommendation for 'full-time' (line 3) *vocational* training has profound implications in the climate of a competitive knowledge-driven economy, policymakers seek to rationalise why these changes are necessary. Even though the use of 'help to upgrade' (line 1) at the beginning of the paragraph acknowledges that the 'status and quality of vocational and technical training' (lines 1–2) are low, the 'needs of school leavers and the economy' (lines 4–5) leave policymakers with no other choice, and a 'more flexible system' (line 3) is proposed as it 'will better meet' (line 4) those needs. The use of the modal verb 'will', and a repeated emphasis on the word 'better' in 'will *better* meet the needs' (lines 4–5) and the modal verb in 'There *will be* better opportunities for VITB trainees' (lines 5–6) suggests a validity that is synonymous with almost a status of fact.

Sub meso-macro movement: transitioning towards creating opportunities for junior college/upper secondary/university students

Like the sub micro-meso movement, the metaphors of opportunity and choice are also operationalised in policy texts 1991a–2012. The analysis highlights that there was a movement in the evaluative chain in how the metaphor of opportunity is linked and the focus is on its use with the metaphor of diversity. The previous sub micro-meso movement illustrated how VITB students would *receive* opportunity in the new economy, an irrealis state, through the provision of choice in a more flexible system. Through a new metaphorical chain of opportunity and diversity, what was construed as inevitable manpower demand in relation to the *choices* available for VITB students in the above subsection, now translates into *opportunities to be created* for Junior College/Upper Secondary/University students, further reinforcing the key role of metaphors in providing a rationale for unequal forms of opportunity for different learners.

The movement within the sub meso-macro theme in creating opportunities for Junior College/Upper Secondary/University students is first illustrated through the choices that are made available for students of VITB. The first section of the analysis below highlights the way the theme evolves around the desirability of opportunity through choice for students of VITB. In Extract 15, there is the interrelatedness between evaluations of *desirability* for realising *opportunities.* The evaluative dimension of factuality is expressed in positive, high-degree evaluations for *Probability* (Graham, 2001a, pp. 770–772): 'Opportunities for advancement from NTC-2[3] to higher level VITB courses, to further education in the polytechnics and the universities, will also be made available to students who meet the requisite standards.' Here, opportunities are pre-evaluated potentialities and are positively evaluated for *desirability.* There is a subtle reference to degrees of *desirability* where opportunities are concerned; for some, 'particularly those from the Normal (Technical) course', *opportunities* can be *advanced.* That is, they must be made to appear more *obviously desirable* than they currently are. Thus, there is an express need to advance opportunities by means of *making available* higher-level educational pathways. Further, an evaluative dimension of desirability is further propagated for the *necessity* of making sure this particular group can at least receive *opportunity* in the new economy through the provision of *choice.*

Following Graham's (2002, p. 249) analysis of propagated value as syllogistic, a kind of evaluative 'syllogising' is going on through Extracts 15, 16, and 17. The evaluations of particular elements in the extract do not merely obviously 'add up' to an overall evaluation of desirability for the benefits of vocational education,

Extracts 15, 16, and 17: Choice and opportunities through MOE policy texts 1991a–2006

Depending on their abilities and aptitudes, secondary school leavers, particularly those from the Normal (Technical) course, will be offered 2–3 year full-time courses leading to a NTC-2 qualification. In addition, pupils with GCE O-levels will be able to choose from a wide range of higher level vocational courses. **Opportunities** for advancement from NTC-2 to higher level VITB courses, to further education in the polytechnics and the universities, will also be made available to students who meet the requisite standards.

Besides these full-time courses, a more comprehensive apprenticeship scheme will be structured. This will complement the institutional training programme and provide a wider **choice** of occupational options to better meet the needs of the industry.

(Extract 15, MOE, 1991a, p. 24)

To achieve a better match between occupational **choices** of school leavers and manpower needs of the industry, wider options in the vocational training system will be made available.

(Extract 16, MOE, 1991b, p. 16)

We are providing for greater **choice** in the curriculum in mainstream schools. Elective Modules (EMs) for Normal course students have been introduced to allow for more practical, hands-on learning and to expose students to possible courses of study at the ITE.

(Extract 17, MOE, 2006, p. 1)

even though the 'choice' and 'opportunities' of introducing VITB courses are laid out according to a certain (neo-liberal-industrial) axiology, inter alia, 'employment opportunities'. The evaluations across three policy documents are not merely heaped one upon the other; they are set in (conditional) opposition to one another, and at times, to themselves, in a kind of *sic et non*. In the following analysis, positive degrees of desirability are foregrounded, drawing on the discourse of opportunity and choice.

Extracts 15, 16, and 17 are functionally collapsed onto each other to see how they draw on the propositional and evaluative meaning of opportunity and choice in relation to vocational training over the years. While 'Opportunities for advancement' are made according to 'requisite standards' (Extract 15) and 'occupational choices of school leavers' (Extract 16) and 'greater choice in the curriculum in the mainstream schools' (Extract 17) are 'made available' (Extract 16), the *choices* are in themselves subordinated to the 'manpower needs of the industry' (Extract 16) and the 'possible courses of study at the ITE' (Extract 17).

Here, a string of desirable 'facts' – apparently the unquestionable effects of choice(s) – are counterposed to the possibility that they are subjected to the external demands of industry and course availability. These positive facts are constitutive of 'choice' of a different kind. Choices may increase, but the choices available to VITB students and school leavers will come from the manpower needs that industry inevitably creates.

Further, in Extracts 18, 19, and 20 below, desirable opportunities are problematised to bring forth an evaluated proposal: there needs to be 'shift' (Extract 18) in 'the focus of education' (Extract 18) if opportunities are to be realised for Junior College/Upper Secondary students. Here, the metaphor of diversity is transferred from the exogenous effects of 'fitting people to specific jobs' (Extract 18) for VITB students to the endogenous necessity for a system that enables the creation of '*opportunities*' (Extract 18), 'to respond effectively to the challenges of the twenty-first century' (Extract 20), and 'the sophisticated economy' (Extract 20) for Junior College/Upper Secondary students. Thus, a policy framework that is designed to facilitate the positive effects of diversity becomes necessary. So, what was construed as inevitable manpower demand in relation to the *choices* available for VITB students now becomes *opportunities to be created* for Junior College/Upper Secondary/University students.

Here is the central *sic et non* proposal on which the evaluative chain rests (Graham, 2002, pp. 230, 250). Note that the nominal *diversity* (Extract 18) is evaluated both as a substance and as an actor in a material process; it has intrinsic properties as a source of 'opportunities' that can '*better position* Singapore for the future' (Extract 20). Thus, the necessity of change in the 'next phase of development in our education system' is established based on the desirable effects of diversification is transferred and translated to (re)positioning Singapore. Therefore, adjustments to the system and its benefits are necessary to better position Singapore's economy.

In Extract 18, the orientation towards *development* foregrounds the future orientation of policy (Graham, 2005, p. 123). Development is presented as a substance rather than a process, because it compresses an enormous amount of

Extracts 18, 19, and 20. Diversity and opportunities through MOE policy texts 2002–2012a

We should build on the strengths of the current system, and transit to the next phase of development in our education system. The focus of education must shift from efficiency to **diversity**, from knowing to thinking, and from fitting people to specific jobs to equipping them for lifelong learning and creating their own **opportunities**.

(Extract 18, MOE, 2002, p. i.)

The recommendations present bold moves that will enable Singapore's university sector to continue to meet the needs of our fast-changing economy, while also providing more **opportunities** for young Singaporeans who can benefit from tertiary education.

(Extract 19, MOE, 2008a, n.p.)

For Singapore to respond effectively to the challenges of the twenty-first century, our university sector must be one that is high-quality, student-centric, and able to accommodate the growing **diversity** of choices and pathways sought after by our young people and our increasingly sophisticated economy.

We believe that our recommendations will enable Singapore's university landscape to become more **diversified** and vibrant, provide more **opportunities** for Singaporeans to develop to their full potential, and better position Singapore for the future.

(Extract 20, MOE, 2012a, p. 13)

social and technological processes into a noun. In this context, development is defined by particular attributes: it is about the transformation of the system ('the focus of education must shift from efficiency to diversity') and involves people changing how they think (*'fitting people to specific jobs* to equipping them for lifelong learning and creating their own *opportunities*', Extract 18). Further, it is an irrealis substance, a potentiality that can only emerge at some time in the future, and only then if people adopt certain behaviours and think in new ways. Here, then, we see the interrelatedness between the metaphor of *diversity* for realising *opportunities*. With this, the function of policy is again expressed in necessity: the focus of education ***must shift*** from efficiency to diversity.

There is also a reference to a higher degree of *desirability* where *opportunities* are concerned for Junior College/University students, as opposed to Normal (Technical)/vocational students: 'from *fitting* people to specific jobs to equipping them for lifelong learning and *creating* their own *opportunities*' (Extract 18). Further, Extract 19 suggests that 'The recommendations ... will enable Singapore's university sector to continue to meet the needs of our *fast-changing economy*, while also providing more *opportunities* for young Singaporeans who can benefit from tertiary education'.

In Extract 20, the interrelatedness between the metaphor of diversity and the realisation of opportunities is again demonstrated. Drawing on Lemke's (1998, p. 44) approach to analysing attitudinal meaning, here, the mental process 'believe' projects a proposition and at the same time evaluates it for warrantability. The same evaluation is then carried forward within the proposition by the epistemic modal auxiliary '*will* enable'. Coupled with this are evaluations of desirability that a diversified landscape will 'provide more opportunities', allow 'Singaporeans to develop to their full potential' and thus 'better position Singapore'.

Raising *opportunities* is presented throughout the extracts as the main objective for all participants in education. Evaluation is propagated for the necessity of making sure everybody can at least recognise opportunity (albeit irrealis) spaces in the new economy, at both national and international level (Graham, 2001a, p. 772). They are unquestionably desirable potentialities, even if those potentials are not available or equal for all.

Discourses of opportunity and skills

The second sub micro-meso movement concerns the discourse of opportunity and skill. This theme helps to construct the idea of inequality of opportunity and how it further translates into a sub meso-macro movement that traces evaluations for the acquisition of differentiated skills to meet the demands of ir/realis states.

Sub micro-meso movement: skills for better opportunities

This section further explores how policy discourse constructs inequality of opportunities for differed learners through the logic of ethics. More importantly, the analysis illustrates further the slippage between the irrealis (potential) and realis (actual) states in the argument for how the acquisition of skills through 'vocational and technical training' (Extract 14, line 2) leads to the expansion of opportunities. The main theme of this section draws attention to the argument that providing 'better opportunities' (Extract 14, line 5) in the economy in the 1990s and 'higher-level skills' (Extract 14, line 6) is presupposed through a 'more flexible system' (Extract 14, line 3). In relation to the first sub micro-meso movement, it seeks to further explore how these arguments have been utilised to justify special and segregated educational provisions for VITB trainees, paradoxically, within the discourse of economic inclusion through labour participation.

Central to the argument of flexibility, in the discourse of opportunity and choice in Extract 14, is that an increased focus on the learner and choice in vocational education supports individual and economic goals (lines 2–5). Further, within the discourse of equity of access, a 'more *flexible* system' (line 3) is tied to the universal humanistic views of education (Nicoll, 2006, p. 21) and of social desirability as it enables 'VITB trainees to achieve higher-level skills and progress to further education and training' (lines 6–7). In line with Mulderrig's (2008, p. 162) analysis of the discourse of *skills*, when students from the Normal Technical (NT) stream are enjoined to participate and be included, they are primarily represented as engaged in the acquisition of skills. Within the extract, the discourse of *skills* (line 6) collocates with 'better opportunities' (line 5) and 'progress' (line 6), suggesting skills are functionally specific for 'further education and training' (lines 6–7). This then expresses an operational relation, constructed as a commodity to be used for improvement. This discourse of *skills* also helps to operationalise a 'workfarist regime' (Mulderrig, 2008, p. 167) by representing the acquisition of higher-level skills through VITB as essential to both economic growth and social inclusion within the context of higher education. By working ethics into a discourse of social inclusion, ethics is redefined as the *provision of opportunities* to participate in the labour market (Mulderrig, 2009, p. 52).

Sub meso-macro movement: expansion of skills for opportunities and developing the ability of the brightest children

Similar to the sub micro-meso movement, the metaphors of opportunity and skills are also operationalised through the 1991a and 2002 texts in relation to meeting the demands of changing political economies. The previous analysis of the sub micro-meso movement identified the construction of an argument for the acquisition of technical skills to expand opportunities for the VITB students. The following sub meso-macro movement traces these metaphors and how their interaction transitions into a different form of useful skill that Junior College/ Upper Secondary students have access to in order to meet the demands of a changing economy, further reinforcing the key role of the metaphor of 'flexible' in providing justification for a differentiated system.

To illustrate this, the theme first highlights the way the analysis revolves around the desirability of expanding opportunity through the acquisition of skills. In line with Graham's (2001a, p. 770) analysis of evaluative meaning and annotation, the following policy extracts involve a great deal of *metaphorical transfers* among the evaluative semantic dimensions of a *flexible* system and lexical metaphors of 'opportunity' and 'skills'. The general result of *metaphorical evaluative transfers* in these policy genres is to create evaluations for high degrees of necessity in re-skilling, which are almost invariably transferred – quite directly – from high degrees of importance in relation to changing types of (global) political economies, and intertextually from expressions of high degrees of desirability for given outcomes, contextualised as 'opportunities'.

These metaphorical transfers, which contribute to the emergence of arbitrary relations, bring distinct operations into play by making certain skills synonymous with opportunities. In doing so, Extracts 21and 22 below introduce a space of differentiation; that is, they introduce the principle of rules to be followed. This principle is being understood as specific powers attached to the true, through a system of values (cf. Foucault, 1980, p. 132). And, for this operation, the politico-economic apparatus has recourse to two great schemas: the politico-moral schema of skill hierarchy and the economic model of force applied for full employability. The effect of evaluative transfers from claims of *warrantability*, typical of technocratic propositions, to the implied *necessity* for certain actions can be seen in the following examples:

In Extract 21, a high modality truth claim is being made for an imperative: '*To be* prepared for life in a modern industrialised society like Singapore, children *must acquire* the basic technical skills'. In this way, evaluations for *importance* become translated directly into *necessity* in the policy genre. Through the relationship between an irrealis object – that is, the advent of a technological environment – evaluative meaning is transferred metaphorically from *importance* to *necessity*. An explicitly evaluative (axiological) justification for the proposition is then given, which is also cast as a statement of fact: it will enable them to function effectively in a technological environment. The evaluation of desirability rests on the semantics of both necessity and warrantability: it is desirable for children to acquire basic

Extracts 21and 22: Skills and opportunities through MOE policy texts 1991a and 2002

To be prepared for life in a modern industrialised society [warrantability: desirability: necessity: importance] like Singapore, children must acquire the basic ***technical skills*** [importance] which will enable them to function effectively [necessity] in a technological environment [warrantability: desirability] (lines 1–3) ... The most difficult of these issues is how to design a **flexible** education system which will stretch the abilities of the brightest children and at the same time provide encouragement and **opportunities** for advancements for those who are less academically inclined [warantability: necessity: importance: desirability] (lines 12–15).

(Extract 21, MOE, 1991a, n.p.)

Greater emphasis should also be placed on ***communication skills*** [necessity: importance], which remain a weakness for many of our students, and will become [warrantability] increasingly important [importance] in a globalised economy and as **opportunities** grow [warrantability] in the *service* industry.

(Extract 22, MOE, 2002, p. ii)

technical skills. And this implied proposition becomes more desirable insofar as the skills will enable them to function effectively in a technological environment is highly warranted as true or likely. One could say here that necessity and warrantability are functioning as metaphors for the desirability of the implied action; but even here the full situation is more complicated (Lemke, 1998, p. 49).

In the same Extract 21, describing the *necessity* for agentless, nominalised action, 'a *flexible* education system which *will*' allows the exhortation to pose as a fact. The extract provides an explicitly evaluative (axiological) justification for the proposition, which emphasises an evaluative dimension of factuality through the modal verb 'will': a *flexible* education system which '*will* stretch the abilities of the brightest children and at the same time provide encouragement and *opportunities* for advancements for those who are less academically inclined'. The *desirability* of the system is presupposed; it is presented as given, a 'truth'. Cogently, the abilities of the 'brightest children' 'will' be the focus for development while those who are 'less academically inclined' are provided with the provision, but not certainty of 'advancements', through the metaphor of 'opportunities'.

In Extract 22, a high modality truth claim is being made for an imperative for effort on someone's part to see that 'Greater emphasis *should also be placed* on communication skills', the *desirability* of which is presupposed (Graham, 2001a, pp. 770–771). An expansion of the proposition into Lemke's (1998, p. 37) rank-shifted probe would demonstrate more clearly how these evaluative dimensions become condensed in these processes: the statement might be expanded because it is very important/necessary that 'greater emphasis should be placed ...'. An evaluation for *Truth* can be construed because, as typical of the policy genre, the whole extract is agentless: 'will become *increasingly important* in a globalised economy and as *opportunities grow* in the service sector'. The evaluative dimension of factuality is expressed through high degrees of *probability* by drawing on the demands of an irrealis object – the globalised economy and its relations with the service industry (Graham, 2001a, pp. 770–771). Even where it was proposed that something should be done in relation to increasing importance in a globalised economy, by whom or how opportunities would grow in the service sector is not made explicit (cf. Lemke, 1995; McKenna & Graham, 2000, as cited in Graham, 2001a, p. 771). What is made explicit though, is first the relationship between an irrealis object (the advent of a globalised economy) and the service industry. Second, how evaluative meaning is transferred metaphorically from importance to necessity. And last, a further inclusion of a relational proposition: *Greater emphasis should also be placed on communication skills.* Thus, communication skills will necessarily play a central role in the globalised economy. This claim provides an even stronger evaluation of *necessity* for future action upon the education system. This metaphorical transfer serves to define and regulate what counts as 'useful' knowledge as that which can be translated into an economic gain within an irrealis economy. Students under the Junior College/Upper Secondary education pathway are given access to this knowledge.

Two sub-movements

Changes in the parameters of the two sub micro-macro movements account for how 'equal opportunities' is defined in *particular spaces* (cf. Sen, 1992, p. 14). These two sub-movements are distinct but thoroughly interdependent. Both these sub-grids are related to the central argument of 'equalising' structural 'opportunities' (as a focus on fairness) for VITB trainees through the provision of skills and choice to proceed as far as the individual is able. There is an effort on the part of policymakers to 'equalise' opportunities, within the context of differed educational pathways. The egalitarian aspect of meritocracy could then be seen to be sufficiently addressed under the conditions of these existing provisions. These measures would not only make it possible to push through a differentiated system, but also undermine any resistance against the credibility of meritocracy.

Corresponding to the construction of economic globalisation and its associated labour demands as having two areas, Extract 14 weaves together two different discourses of and through the metaphor of *flexibility*. In relation to meritocracy, the principle of equality of opportunities is extended through making the success of those who undergo vocational training conditional on the implementation of these essential reforms. Here, the justification of inequality of relative disparity in dis/advantages of pupils is made to rest on the equality of opportunity and choice, taken to be more basic in this meritocratic system. This equality, in what is seen as the 'base', is invoked for a reasoned defence of the resulting inequalities within the education system. It is not the intention here to comment on how convincing this defence is but rather to highlight the discursive role of the metaphor in *ameliorating the tension* of providing equal opportunities within a differentiated system. The important issue in this theme – flexible system for VITB trainees – is the nature of the discursive strategies of justifying inequality through equality. That is, borrowing Sen's (1992, p. 20) words, 'inequality in one space tends to go, in fact, with inequality in another'. This paradox does, in fact, introduce some internal tension in the meritocratic discourse, since the derivative importance of progression depends on the respective opportunities to convert skills and choice into the fulfilment of the respective economic-industrial demands (cf. Sen, 1992, p. 19). The problematisation of skills and choice through the two sub-movements is crucial to analysing inequality.

The analyses illustrated how the two sub micro-meso-macro movements are textured together through the discourse of *opportunity*. This is of central importance in relation to examining inequality within *a meritocratic system* that proclaims '*equal* opportunities for each student to learn and to achieve his or her potential' (Wong, 2000, n.p.). The discursive strategies employed within these narratives provide cogent arguments for exclusion from the mainstream educational pathway. Further, a relationship of subordination of opportunity-choice-skill to flexibility is textured as the relation between policy action and implicit global reasons for this action. The analysis shows that *opportunity, choice*, and *skills* from the two sub micro-meso movements and their macro translations belong more broadly to the metaphor of *flexible*. Having a *flexible* system is intrinsically linked to not only the provision but the expansion of opportunity, choice, and the acquisition of skills for VITB students. This conflates an intimate relationship between the desire and possibility of self and national progress. The analysis above makes explicit how policymakers put forth a substantial justification for how and why VITB should exist and how it is delivering opportunities even for those who are not undergoing the mainstream education.

The analysis illustrates that in both these two sub micro-meso movements outlined above, the discourse of *opportunity* is presented metaphorically as the spatial aspect of irrealis states, as the result of hypothetical ways of 'being, seeing, and *enacting* new spaces' (cf. Fairclough, 2000 cited in Graham, 2001a, p. 771, italics included). Within the extract, the formulation of opportunities through the discourse of choices and skills alludes to the moral and equity principles of labour inclusiveness. However, the phenomena to which *opportunity* refers in enabling students to progress need not even exist – now, or in the future. Nevertheless, while there is a relationship between *desire* and the expansion of opportunity, they are not the same, and they do not necessarily operate in tandem. Towards this end, the analysis highlights the high evaluative polarity and importance of *opportunities*. The ethical-political discourse of 'opportunity' and how ethical practices are implicated in the nexus of contractual discourse of 'common social responsibility' through the metaphor of 'diversity' will be explored in the next section.

Diverse pathways for talents

The two previous key themes – 'flexible curriculum for different categories of pupils' and 'flexible system for VITB trainees' – examined the use of the metaphor of 'flexible' to build arguments for differentiated access for the lower stratum of academic achievers. The third key theme – 'diverse pathways for talents' – is concerned with the metaphor of 'diversity' and examines the way it legitimises privileged access for those with exceptional achievement.

Micro-meso movement: contractual-ethical discourse for talent investment

The following analysis of the 2003 policy speech, 'The Next Phase in Education: Innovation and Enterprise' by former Acting Minister for Education T. Shanmugaratnam, examines the way the metaphor of 'diversity' is operationalised to build the logic for privileged talent access through the ethical-political discourse of 'opportunity'. The purpose of this section is to identify the rhetorical and linguistic devices of a speech that provide functional force for the legitimation of privileged access. The analysis of this single section illustrates how this metaphor can be seen moving through and between the micro and meso discourses of 'ideological' in the sense that it is *ideologising* economic-material rationalities to provide legitimacy and cover for the consolidation and extension of asymmetries of knowledge access through not only curriculum changes, as discussed in the previous themes, but also a shift in cultures. As such, this speech provides empirical insights into the *revaluation* and *trans-valuation* of values through shifting cultures. How Singaporeans are positioned in the midst of global, cultural shifts that demand social transformation is of central importance in the analysis of this text. The insights are categorised according to the actions they represent, based on the 'mode of subjectivation, that is, the way in which people are invited or incited to recognise their moral obligations' (Foucault, 1997, p. 264).

Unlike the analytical procedure employed previously, this movement involves the analysis of a speech as opposed to an extract from a policy document and does not have parallel micro-meso-macro movements. Here it is argued instead that the speech accords special attention to the contractual-ethical discourse of common social responsibility through three discursive strategies. The analysis of this text is divided into three lateral sections, indicating the progression of the argument. First, by claiming shared values; second, by employing the hegemonic role of 'we' in a neo-liberal context that purports inclusion and shared responsibilities for the benefit of 'all'; and third, the need for enterprise culture and the transvaluation of the macro value of competitiveness. In relation to moral obligations, the care of the self occurs through the concern for the truth (Foucault, 1997, p. 295); that is, investment in talent would serve self and national interests.

In Extract 23, Shuanmugaratnam mounts an argument that it is in 'our' interests that talents should get privileged access to knowledge because that is how 'they' create more jobs for the rest of 'us'.

Claiming shared values

In order to distil this construction of the narrative, this first section of the analysis focuses on the way in which Shanmugaratnam actualises some pedagogical access and privileged access to knowledge for 'diverse talents' (lines 1–2) and 'Singaporeans who are exceptional in their own way' (line 5) by drawing on the metaphor of 'diverse'. Further, this section examines more broadly how this ethical practice is implicated in the nexus of contractual discourse of 'common social responsibility' and the ethical-political discourse of 'opportunity' through the hegemonic use of 'we'.

Extract 23: 2003 Speech by former Acting Minister for Education, T. Shanmugaratnam

Extract
In our next phase of development, we [?] will need more **diverse** talents, and Singaporeans of different moulds. We [?] need a **culture** that respects exceptional achievement, whether in science research, in business, the professions, the arts and other areas of life. Only if we[E] nurture Singaporeans who are exceptional in their own way, can we [?] be the natural hub for talent and enterprise from all over the world, and become ***one of the leading cities in Asia***. This is the way in which we [?] can hold our own against other major cities and grow **opportunities** for all Singaporeans.
We are therefore creating more **diverse pathways**, starting with the secondary school and junior college system, where we are opening up to integrated programme schools, various specialist schools and a few private schools, and to mainstream schools who wish to adopt an alternative curriculum.

Source: Shanmugaratnam, 2003, n.p.

In the extract, 'diverse talents' (lines 1–2) and 'diverse pathways' (line 10) are terms that are ideologically contested and thus become the focus of ideological struggle (Fairclough, 2001, p. 95) in the belief that 'the next phase of development' (line 1) should be exercised in the interest of talent investment. Here, then, the extract centres on the growth and development of 'talents' (line 2) through the educational institution, at the expense of academic equality, evident in the vocabulary for these meanings: 'culture that respects exceptional achievement' (lines 2–3), 'nurture Singaporeans who are exceptional' (line 5), 'hold our own against other major cities' (line 8), 'grow opportunities for all Singaporeans' (lines 8–9). More specifically, this ideological struggle draws upon pre-existing classification schemes that are in part systems of evaluation (Fairclough, 2001, pp. 96–98). One is a scheme for the development of talent – 'We need a culture that respects exceptional achievement' (lines 2–3) – which is constructed on the belief that talents should be nurtured even if such a policy creates a society of differential access to resources, that is, a non-meritocratic one. The second scheme is for ways of evaluating the culture of respecting exceptional achievement within the Singapore context; it is implicit in the collocations 'hold our own against other major cities' (line 8), and 'grow opportunities for all Singaporeans' (lines 8–9). The complete verbal phrase here is an idiom: grow opportunities for all Singaporeans, where 'opportunities' marks the desirability and *all* amplifies its degree (Lemke, 1998, p. 49). Here, then, the text proposes that there is a general acceptance that a *standard* discourse of meritocratic based system of equal opportunity is in need of challenge through it having a reactionary effect of failing to engage with national and economic needs.

As Fairclough (2001) indicates, in both cases, this classification scheme constitutes a particular way of projecting some aspect of educational-ethical realities that are built upon a particular representation of 'exceptional achievement' in that reality (p. 28). If a diagnosis of meritocratic-based education is incurably problematic in meeting the national and economic needs of all Singaporeans (lines 8–9), then the entire strategy of providing equal opportunities in education is deeply impaired, even if every conceivable alternative in the world were available. What follows from this argument is that a system which nurtures *diverse* talents (lines 1–2), and therefore the creation of *diverse* pathways (line 10) is necessary for the pursuit of economic growth and for becoming one of Asia's 'leading' cities (line 7). Further, greater attention to economic policy concerns is found in terms such as 'development' (line 1), 'diverse' (line 1), 'exceptional' (lines 3, 5), 'hub' (line 6), 'talent' (lines 2, 6), 'enterprise' (line 6), 'leading' (line 7), and 'opportunities' (line 9). This entails rendering *diverse* educational practices amenable to competition as a condition of progress (Mulderrig, 2008, p. 156). This form of economic model stresses competition and is motivated by profit through inequality. Within this instance, ethics is paradoxically redefined as the *right* to succeed in an open competition by enabling talent investment (Mulderrig, 2007, p. 143).

In order to strengthen the argument for greater *inequality*, the extract makes categorical predictions and expert assertions about economic possibilities in the use of *can* (Fairclough, 1992, p. 173). That is, 'Only if we nurture Singaporeans who are exceptional in their own way, *can* we be the natural hub for talent and enterprise from all over the world, and become one of the leading cities in Asia' (lines 4–7). Here, even though the use of *can* expresses tentative possibility, something that is possible, this lexical choice implies doubt that Singapore will be a hub for talent and enterprise *unless* particular conditions are met. This is hence brought forth by the proposal of mass instruction through even more differentiated systems: 'We are *therefore* creating *diverse* pathways' (line 10). The conjunction 'therefore' links the two paragraphs in terms of purpose or reason – the message that comes across is one of reassurance: more *diverse* pathways are there for a good reason (Fairclough, 1992, pp. 171–172).

Moreover, inequality is not only tied to competitiveness but also ethical practices. In order to 'become one of the leading cities in Asia' (line 7) acknowledges that countries and regions in Asia are in competition for growth in measures of well-being – that is, 'science research, in business, the professions, the arts and other areas of life' (lines 3–4) – and that inequality between countries is part of the economic order. Success in this order is realised by winning economic competition. This establishes an implicit system of obligation between the 'non-talent' and the 'talent': the 'non-talent' has the right to have employment opportunities, but they must accept the moral constraint of 'confinement' (Foucault, 1967, p. 48) in being denied privileged access to knowledge. It is in this context that economic and moral demands for confinement are formulated (cf. Foucault, 1967, p. 57), and developed within an institutional character through the legitimisation of unequal access. In this form of globalisation then, there is nothing morally wrong in creating more diverse pathways that support and increase inequality. The grounds for the claim that Singapore will need more diverse talents of different moulds (lines 1–2) to 'become one of the leading cities in Asia' (line 7) contain a set of assumed goods in the economic system: through 'integrated programme schools' (line 12), 'various specialist schools' (line 12), 'few private schools' (lines 12–13), and 'mainstream schools with alternative curriculum' (lines 13–14). These schools are implicated as a means to achieving economic growth and promote conformity to the logic of the need for more *diverse* pathways (line 10) in the 'next phase of development' (line 1). Hence, 'opening up' (line 11) the system 'to nurture Singaporeans who are exceptional' (line 5) is desirable, important, and therefore morally *necessary*. Subsequent reforms continue this trend, permitting the continued expansion and diversification of an educational market.

Moreover, as all countries need to become more 'competitive', as a *virtue*, then its *necessary* outcome, inequality, cannot be a moral wrong; nor is there a principled way within this economic system of identifying a point at which inequality becomes so extreme as to be morally wrong. And since inequality may mean that certain countries, regions, and people will benefit and some will lose from this economic system, it cannot be morally wrong for the system to benefit some while impairing others. Taking away educational opportunities from some will allow improved 'opportunities for *all*' (lines 8–9). Also, the means envisaged to achieve this are formulated in a familiar neo-liberal way (Fairclough, 2006a, p. 9) as talent investment by nurturing 'Singaporeans who are exceptional' (line 5).

The hegemonic role of 'we' in a neo-liberal context: inclusion and shared responsibilities for the benefit of 'all'

To enable improved opportunities for all at the expense of some, the Minister draws on the hegemonic role of 'we' to constitute inclusion and shared responsibility in ensuring the economic and social success of Singaporeans. Mulderrig's (2011b, pp. 568–569) approach to the hegemonic role of 'we' in manufacturing consent suggests that the success of the discursive strategy in legitimating policy rests on semantic slippage across the different types of *we* (inclusive, exclusive, ambivalent 'we'). Extract 23 illustrates how the strategy of using the different forms of 'we' or exploiting the semantic pronoun 'we' can be used to legitimate a neo-liberal model of citizenship through the assumption of a shared consensus from which prescriptions for success can be validated. This particular extract provides significant insight into socially significant aspects of change in the relational identity of self in legitimising unequal practices.

In the extract, the ambivalent *we* textures a hortatory evaluation about the role of education in socialising Singaporeans for the 'next phase of development' (line 1). 'Only if *we* nurture Singaporeans who are exceptional … can *we* be the natural hub … and become one of the leading cities in Asia' (lines 4–7) paints a picture of the global economic context for education policy in which shared responsibility in nurturing exceptional Singaporeans (line 5) is paramount. The next sentence juxtaposes this citizenship argument with an economic responsiveness discourse of education, where the emphasis is on nurturing talent to enhance (economic) opportunities for all Singaporeans.

While not explicitly conflating them, this textual arrangement construes a close relationship between citizenship and shared responsibility for the common and greater good. The semantic slipperiness of 'we' helps construct an apparent consensus on the nature of the world we live in: 'Only if we [exclusive] nurture Singaporeans who are exceptional in their own way, can we [ambivalent] be the natural hub for talent and enterprise from all over the world' (lines 4–7) and the inescapable responsibilities this creates. In turn, this supposedly inexorable context of global economic competitiveness – so that 'we can hold our own against other major cities and grow opportunities for all Singaporeans' (lines 8–9) – is used to preface and legitimise policy proposals for greater diversity, 'whether in science research, in business, the professions, the arts and other areas of life' (lines 3–4). These ambivalent and exclusive uses of *we* form a rhetorical structure and discursive strategy whereby government policy decisions on education effectively become harder to criticise since their legitimacy rests on global economic forces apparently for the common good of all Singaporeans.

The second strategy this speech deploys to justify greater diversity involves the use of a further embedded nominal group that functions as the qualifier: *one of the leading cities in Asia*. The subject of the clause *we* in the sentence, 'Only if we nurture Singaporeans who are exceptional ... can *we* be the natural hub for talent and enterprise ... and become one of the *leading cities in Asia*' (lines 4–7), is thereby constructed as the equivalent to the entity *leading cities*. This equivalence draws on the logic of a neo-liberal value system, which is also triggered by the attributes *enterprise, hub*, and *leading*. These approaches help construe a positively evaluated state of affairs which Singaporeans would 'naturally' wish to sustain. As Mulderrig (2011b, p. 568) argues, 'through this type of evaluative statement, a nation state is represented as equivalent to its economic system, and ascribed characteristics whose value is intertextually derived'.

Notably, the attributes *enterprise, hub*, and *leading* do not semantically encode a positive or a negative value in the same way as a lexis whose chief semiotic function is evaluation (for instance *excellent* or *poor*) (Mulderrig, 2011a, p. 56). In the extract, a leading city in Asia is one which is valued on the basis of the scale on which it is able to operate. The value triggered is one of power relative to other economies, achieved through geographical 'Asia'. Similarly, the predication *leading* again values the entity in terms of power, this time through its ability to direct and affect others, triggered by the attribute 'hub'. These two dimensions of evaluation are coherent only within the structural framework of competitive activity, the basic form of social relation around which capitalist economic activity is organised. Taken together, the evaluative components of this clause are therefore derived intertextually from a neo-liberal discourse of competitiveness (Muntigl et al., 2000 as cited in Mulderrig, 2011b, p. 568) – wherein 'economies are represented as less confined to national territory, but rather operating across an increasingly transnational or "global" competitive terrain, and where national economic success is measured in terms of relative market position' (Mulderrig, 2011b, p. 568).

Enterprise culture and the transvaluation of the macro value of competitiveness

The equivalence between country, nation, and full employability is tied with a positive construction of competition. The discourse of this policy extract is unquestionably oriented towards changing the nation's attitudes and behaviours (Graham, 2001a, p. 766). In his speech, Shanmugaratnam indicated the need for a culture that respects exceptional achievement (lines 2–3). In this there is an attempt to *revalue* such a culture that respects exceptional achievement positively by the government aiming to identify and equip some people to succeed in the next phase of development. Transforming the culture is a part of that – through establishing positive attitudes towards *nurturing those with identified talent*, for instance, so that people accept unequal educational access.

Similar to the above analysis on transitioning towards creating opportunities for Junior College/Upper Secondary/University students for 'the next phase of *development* in the education system' (Extract 18), the orientation towards *development* (Extract 23, line 1) here foregrounds the future orientation of policy (Graham, 2005, p. 123). Development is presented as a substance rather than a process, because it compresses a massive amount of social and technological processes into a noun ('whether in science research, in business, the professions, the arts and other areas of life' lines 3–4). In this context, development is defined by particular attributes: it is about the transformation of society and involves people changing how they think (lines 2–3). Further, it is an *irrealis* substance, a potentiality that can only emerge at some time in the future, and only then if people adopt certain behaviours, and think in new ways. There is an overt idealist philosophy of desirability (cf. Nietzsche, 1967a, p. 181) underpinning the ideology of economic growth here: people must first change *how they think and what they believe* for development to happen. According to this logic, underdevelopment is merely a function of people thinking incorrectly (i.e., a culture that respects *equal*, rather than *diverse*, opportunities for achievement).

The representation of the global economy as competition between nation states (lines 6–7) leads to a priority and explicit commitment for the government. The focus is upon Singapore as a whole, as a national community. The representation of the global economy as a field for intensifying competition for survival and comparative advantage between nation states not only entails a focus on national unity through a 'culture that respects exceptional achievement' (line 2–3); it also leads to elements of nationalist discourse (Fairclough, 2000a, p. 35) as the 'the natural hub for talent and enterprise from all over the world' (line 6) and 'one of the leading cities in Asia' (line 7). The point is that this 'culture' has come to be understood in moral terms which emphasise that inequality is the other side of nationalistic 'achievement'. Talent investment hence is projected as not only desirable but necessary: because it is probably an indispensable part of how Singapore develops economically (line 7).

A moral discourse is also combined with the contractual-conditional discourse of 'only if' (line 4), 'can we be' (lines 5–6), and 'This is the way in which' (lines 7–8). Such expressions draw attention to assumed incompatibilities while at the same time denying them – they go against the expectations of a conventional egalitarian discourse while at the same time conflating it through such phrases as growing *opportunities for all* (lines 8–9). The principle of *opportunities for all* is extended through policy discourse to making all success (individual and nation) conditional on the implementation of essential reforms. Through this, the meaning of *ethics* shifts through the omission of *equality*, in the sense of equality of educational access and outcomes and its substitution by *opportunities.* Here, then, the ideology which underlies policies for 'inclusion through opportunities' relies upon the ideology of an irretrievable slide into division, and thus sustaining a regime of equal opportunity is constructed as a way that will not meet the diverse national and economic needs of the nation (lines 5–7). This is an important step – perhaps the crucial step – in the logic of this culture. This logic provides a basis for inclusive/exclusive politics (Fairclough, 2000a, p. 34).

Within this argument, nurturing *diverse* talents (lines 1–2) through *diverse pathways* (line 10) is rated in terms of economic efficiency and social impact within the local context, and is positively evaluated in binary-driven classification schemes (i.e. talents vs non-talents). Hence, sustaining a regime of equal opportunity is constructed as not totally satisfying in the way it addresses diverse national and economic needs and the difficulty in nurturing talents (lines 5–7). The notion of talent investment as a form of ethical practice in which the broader society is implicated will be further explored in the following subsection.

Meso-macro movement: moving towards nurturing talent through diversity, opportunity, and choice for the future economy

The previous section examined the work of the metaphor of diversity as it moves within and through the micro-meso level of a single text. The following analysis traces this theme within and through the meso-macro level of policy as it appears and reappears in the 2002 and 2012 policy reports.

The previous analysis of the micro movements demonstrated how the metaphor of diversity builds rationalities for privileged talent access through the ethical-political discourse of 'opportunity'. The following meso-macro movement traces its expansion across Extracts 24, 25, and 26, further reinforcing its key role in providing an ethical rationale for talent investment. Specifically, the analysis highlights the way the theme of diverse pathways for exceptional achievement evolves in a policy discourse around the necessity of diversity for nurturing talent in curriculum design needed for the future economy.

Unlike previous meso-macro movements, the process of thematic condensation is set up differently here. Instead of functionally collapsing parts of connected texts like the previous meso-macro movements, the analysis here is focused on the transference of multiple aspects of talent investment through an explication of several full texts. This enables an examination of how confluent and diverging issues in relation to privileged opportunities within a frame of meritocracy are negotiated.

Extract 24: Diversity to widen students' intellectual horizons in the 2002 MOE policy text

Extract
The Committee's proposal for the JC curriculum to place greater emphasis on thinking and process skills addresses the need for a more innovative outlook and greater adaptability among our young. By providing a stronger multi-disciplinary grounding, the new JC curriculum will also widen the intellectual horizons of our students.
The introduction of greater **diversity** into the education landscape recommended by the Committee is also timely. The move towards a less uniform system will **open up** new options and **opportunities** to cater to the different talents and strengths of our students. Greater **diversity** will also be a source of strength and innovative ideas for the education system.

Source: MOE, 2002, n.p.

Extract 24 is from a 2002 policy report and constructs an argument for greater diversity in the Junior College curriculum to widen the intellectual horizons of the students (lines 4–5). In order to distil this construction of the narrative, the analysis focuses on the necessity for systemic change that would enable the expansion of opportunities for talents. Further, the analysis draws on the work of Graham (2001a) and Lemke (1998), to examine how diversity is implicated in the contractual discourse of 'common social responsibility' in how it contributes by adding value to the education system.

The effects of evaluative transfers from claims of *warrantability* to the implied necessity for certain actions can be seen in the following:

> The Committee's proposal for the JC curriculum to place greater emphasis on thinking and process skills **addresses the need** [warrantability: necessity: importance: obvious] for a **more innovative outlook and greater adaptability among our young** [desirability]. By providing a stronger multi-disciplinary grounding, the new JC curriculum **will also widen** [warrantability] the **intellectual horizons of our students** [desirability].
>
> (Extract 24, MOE, 2002, n.p.)

In line with Graham's (2007, p. 121) discussion of significance as an evaluative resource for proposals and propositions, Extract 24 is concerned with propagating the *significance* of 'a less uniform system' (lines 7–8) by proposing that an institutional structure that embraces differences not only strengthens the system but also supports innovation. The evaluative semantic of significance suggests that there are two forms being evaluated in this extract: a less uniform system is both a proposition – statements that can be tested for truth, and a proposal – a request for action. A high-modality truth claim is being made for a curriculum imperative that '*addresses the need* for a more innovative outlook and greater adaptability among our young' (lines 2–3), the desirability of which is presupposed. According to Lemke's (1998, p. 37) rank-shifted probe, various evaluative dimensions of the proposition become condensed in these processes: the statement might sensibly be expanded as it is necessary, important, and obvious for the Junior College (JC) curriculum to 'place greater emphasis on thinking and process skills' (lines 1–2). An evaluation for *warrantability* and *truth* can be construed because not only is the whole text agentless, but an explicitly evaluative (axiological) justification and desirability for the proposition is also given, which is also cast as a statement of fact: '*will also* widen the intellectual horizons of our students' (lines 4–5). While the predicate of *truth* would seem to belong to the broader semantic domain of *warrantability*, in this context it is an evaluation for *desirable* outcomes which the text deploys to propagate the significance of a 'less uniform system' (lines 7–8). This is further evidenced when the text deploys the resource of *significance* that semantically embraces *necessity* by claiming that this system is responsible for *opening up* new options and opportunities (line 8). The evaluative chain deployed here is underpinned by the assumption that students from the JC have different talents and strengths, and that it is therefore *important* to institutionally regulate their intellectual development. This importance feeds into the necessity of systemic change.

The phrasal verb *open up* (Extract 24, line 8) appears to function as a material process, a 'singular doing' (Halliday, 1994, as cited in Graham, 2001a, p. 768). This process metaphor relates to two highly condensed, extremely abstract nominal groups that compress myriad, complex, and massive processes into static things: 'new *options* and *opportunities* to cater to the different talents and strengths of our students' (lines 8–9). Following Graham's (2001a, pp. 768–769) approach, the metaphorical scope of 'open up' can be replaced by other processes that retain the semantic sense of the proposition: 'The move towards a less uniform system will open up, (i.e. promises, offers, brings, or creates) new options and opportunities' (lines 7–8). These choices that retain the original semantic sense of the proposition would occupy positions on the verbal [promises]; abstract-material [offers]; and material [brings, creates] planes of Halliday's process typology (Graham, 2001a, p. 768). In other words, the process metaphor lets an abstract and highly compressed nominal group actor-like thing ['The move towards a less uniform system'] grammatically loose by having for its object an irrealis, highly compressed nominal group, 'open up' (line 8). The evaluative dimension of factuality is further expressed in positive, high-degree evaluations for *probability* or *warrantability*; that is, 'Greater diversity will also be a source of strength and innovative ideas for the education system' (lines 9–10) (Graham, 2001a, p. 770). There is clearly a colonising imperative in all of this as opening up the system 'to cater to the different talents and strengths of our students' (lines 8–9) is desirable, important, and therefore necessary *as a source of strength for the education system* (line 10). That is to say, new options and opportunities are desirable traits that will enable new kinds of education.

Following on from the 2002 extract, in the following two extracts taken from the 2012 policy document there emerges a struggle to restructure hegemony within the discourse of higher education through the transvaluation of the macro values of market economies and de/regulation. First, in Extract 25, an emphasis on '*diverse* workforce profile' (line 5) is central to the argument in providing privileged access for a certain segment of the student population, legitimising increasing inequality of access to higher education.

Here, the main theme of the paragraph draws attention to the needs of market economies. Focusing on this part of this extract, even though the use of the adverbial 'but' (line 2) (Asher, Benamara, & Mathieu, 2009, pp. 284–287) acknowledges that a degree education will benefit a growing number of students, practical considerations involving the 'industry's requirements for a diverse workforce profile' (line 5) within the context of market economies left policymakers with no other choice *but* to provide certain segments of the student population 'from a broader range of educational backgrounds, with different aspirations, abilities and learning preferences' (lines 3–4) with 'more opportunities ... to contribute to the country's development' (lines 6–8). The use of the modal verb 'will' in 'This *will* also better meet industry's requirements' (lines 4–5) and 'we *will* enable them to contribute to the country's development' (lines 6–7), gives the suggestion a validity and a high-degree evaluation for *warrantability* that are synonymous with almost a status of fact. Providing a certain segment of Singaporeans with 'more opportunities' (line 6) is desirable, important, and therefore necessary 'to contribute to the country's development' (line 7).

The argument signals an ideological struggle and the true situation brought about by the 'industry's requirements for a *diverse* workforce profile' (line 5). The objective is to argue that the public cannot expect an increase in publicly-funded degree places to cater to a growing number of students, for industry's requirements would only negate that pursuit. As such, the society that practises this system of allowing an indiscriminate increase in publicly-funded degree places that does not cater to 'students

Extract 25: More opportunities to meet a diverse workforce profile in the 2012a policy text

Lines	*Text*
1	An increase in publicly-funded degree places will cater not only to a growing
2	number of students who are able to benefit from a degree education, *but* also
3	to students from a broader range of educational backgrounds, with different
4	aspirations, abilities and learning preferences. This will also better meet
5	industry's requirements for a **diverse** workforce profile. In providing
6	Singaporeans with more **opportunities** to fully actualise their potential, we
7	will enable them to contribute to the country's development and provide them
8	with a greater stake in the nation's success.

Source: MOE, 2012a, p. 4.

from a broader range of educational backgrounds … preferences' (lines 3–4) is misguided about reality. This argument hence establishes a common ideological ground in which streaming students' education opportunities and outcomes through diverse pathways is conceptualised as being highly desirable within the context of industry's requirements and where the absence of such a regulation may result in severe consequences for the national interest, in ensuring the 'country's development' (line 7) and the 'nation's success' (line 8). This ideology of access has a strong flavour of favouritism that privileges the stance of inegalitarianism.

Here, then, we see the interrelatedness between the metaphor of *diversity* for realising opportunities and the function of policy expressed as necessity: to better position Singapore for economic success. This argument is further reinforced in the following extract where policymakers put forth ways for a certain segment of the population to receive more opportunities to realise their and Singapore's potential.

Configured around a discourse of *diversity* and *choice*, Extract 26 draws on notions of ability, curriculum, and opportunity to examine further the discursive positioning of 'talent' in relation to educational privileges.

Extract 26 is preoccupied with growth and development of the 'spread of talent' (line 4) through the educational system, evident in the vocabulary of these meanings: 'more *choices*' (line 8), 'more can be done to increase the *diversity*' (line 9), 'to develop their full potential' (line 10), and 'provide a better fit with their learning preferences and interests' (lines 11–12). Specifically, similar to the analysis (in the section 'Claiming shared values') of the schemas that evaluate the culture of developing talent and respecting exceptional achievement, this ideological struggle also draws on what Fairclough (2001) argues as pre-existing classification schemes which are in part

Extract 26: Diversity and choice to cater to talent in the 2012a policy text

Lines	*Text*
1	To better cater to students from a broader range of educational
2	backgrounds, with different aspirations and learning preferences. The pre-
3	tertiary education system has **diversified** its options to better cater to the
4	spread of talent and preferences over the years, with the introduction of the
5	Integrated Programme (IP), specialised schools such as the Singapore
6	Sports School (SSS) and School of the Arts (SOTA), NUS High School for
7	Mathematics and Science, and the School of Science and Technology
8	(SST). While more **choices** have also been introduced in the tertiary
9	landscape, more can be done to increase the **diversity** of articulation
10	pathways for young Singaporeans to develop their full potential, through
11	introducing different degree pathways that would provide a better fit with
12	their learning preferences and interests.

Source: MOE, 2012a, p. 17.

systems of evaluation (pp. 96–98). One is a scheme by which 'talent' may be harnessed, 'While more *choices* have also been introduced in the tertiary landscape, more can be done' (lines 8–9), which is constructed on the belief that talents have an immense capacity to acquire knowledge. Another scheme is for ways of evaluating 'diversification of options' (line 3); it is implicit in the collocations, '*diversity* of articulation pathways for young Singaporeans to develop their potential' (lines 9–10), 'introducing different degree pathways that would provide a better fit with their learning preferences and interests' (lines 11–12), the *desirability* of which is presupposed. Further, there are also evaluations of desirability in relation to *choice* and *diversity* through amplification (Lemke, 1998, pp. 44, 51): 'more' (lines 8 and 9), 'increase' (line 9). Embedded within the texts is the assumption that whatever develops '*their* full potential' (line 10) and 'provide[s] a better fit with *their* learning preferences and interests' (lines 11–12) is perceived as a desirable and important (perhaps necessary) outcome for any future action on the part of the government. 'Their' refers here specifically to 'talent' (line 4).

The thrust of these policy extracts as movements draws on the metaphor of diversity to create e/valuations for high degrees of *necessity* in relation to institutionalising not only diverse, but also privileged pathways for talents. The general result of these metaphorical evaluative transfers as they move within and through the meso-macro and above the micro-meso in the policy texts, is to create evaluations for high degrees of *necessity* in relation to institutionalising diverse pathways for talents, which is almost invariably transferred – quite directly – from high degrees of *warrantability, importance*, and intertextually from expressions of high-degree evaluations for *desirability* for given educational outcomes in relation to economic growth and development (Graham, 2001a, p. 770).

Summary

This chapter employed the notion of 'Metaphorical realism', indicating the work of metaphors in establishing a current state of affairs and projecting a desirable future. This notion was placed within a conceptual three-level, fluid and interactional grid in order to examine the interconnections within movements and to give a dynamic account of the intersecting constructions of micro-macro valuations to generate desirable outcomes.

Through this framework, the analysis demonstrates *that* and *how* value determination through the use of the metaphors are used in creating the inter-osculation of realities and legitimising inequality. Specifically, the analysis highlighted that metaphors, as apparatuses of power, promote the development of productive forces characteristic of capitalism which advocate support for macro-neo-liberal values that propagate inequality (cf. Foucault, 1980, p. 158). Economically considered, the transliteration of meritocratic discourse into the metaphor of diversity pinpoints how the appeal of *development for all* necessarily also demands the advance of inequity for the sake of the whole (cf. Nietzsche, 1967a, pp. 155–157).

As an expansion of the discursive arguments made in Chapter 2 for inequality, the analysis drew upon the discursive analytic to understand how policy texts associate particular systems and access for different categories of pupil. In relation to how the human subject fits into certain games of truth (Foucault, 1997, p. 281), the analysis has provided a continued understanding of how discursive processes function to produce and locate 'VITB trainees' as requiring institutional segregation and 'talents' as requiring privileged access. These learner categorisations run parallel to the earlier conceptions of 'slow' and 'fast' learners respectively. The phenomenon of identity as a categorical imperative permits forms of institutional practices to be legitimated as truths and regulations. The analysis above continued to explore how the objectification of these subjects has made possible increasing divergences in curriculum and opportunities that arise from policy discourse, and how these changes are linked to modes of value determination that serve to legitimise inequality. The formations and definitions of subjects implicated institutional structures and a moral practice (Foucault, 1997, p. 116): that is, institutional changes are 'responsive' to learner categories.

This (re)establishment of subjects as a domain of knowledge [savoir] is associated with changes in institutional practices and the ethical attitudes that concerned it (Foucault, 1997, p. 116). The analysis has established the role of politics and ethics in the establishment of subjects as a particular domain of scientific knowledge [connaissance], and how this is associated with institutional and ethical practices (Foucault, 1997, p. 116). Significantly, both the utilisation of metaphors, and their metaphoric relations that allude to the irrealis states of political economies, provide the conditions for differed learner access. The discursive strategies employed subsequently build a sustained case for streaming.

Enormous amounts of evaluative detail have been unpacked from the policy extracts. The analysis has highlighted a special emphasis on the simultaneous processes of truth production and reproduction, supporting and being supported by means and modes of value distribution, in the form of meritocratic inequality. The analytic framework helps expose how values are propagated at multidimensional levels of perceptive abstraction. Further comparative work will be necessary, however, to see what kinds of different and/or specific forms of axiological configurations emerge through the use of metaphors within the broader micro-discursive practices of de/regulation and political economies of surrealism. In order to examine further *how* inequality has been built in to the system through local-global economic imperatives, the constant allusion of policy discourse to the macro values of de/regulation and market economies as desirable within the broader context of economic competitiveness and micro valuations will be explored in the following two analytic chapters. Chapter 6 will specifically examine how de/regulation can serve to obfuscate state responsibility with respect to policy trajectories that propagate meritocratic inequality.

Notes

1 Junior College.
2 Vocational and Industrial Training Board.
3 National Technical Certificate Grade 2.

6 Theme 2

De/regulation

Overview

In order to further explore how metaphors have been highly influential in giving a particular shape to an imagined, albeit self-evident, economic system, this chapter – the second micro movement, 'De/regulation' – builds on the analysis in Chapter 5 to examine how the metaphor of flexibility performs *ideologising* work that obscures the agent or agency involved in generating desirable outcomes. More importantly, this regulatory 'crisis' involves a lack of (state) agency in discourse, effectively underplaying the potential of active agents. This amounts to a shift from traditional concepts of 'state responsibility' to new 'school accountability' in which the relationships between state, school educators, and individual interests have become redefined and obscured through new discourse strategies. *The separation of accountability from responsibility* is a corollary outcome of separating state from control and school from state (cf. Graham & Luke, 2011, p. 110). *Accountability* here is referred to as a literal duty of care in the academic career projection of students. *Responsibility* is referred to as moral liability for decisions taken about how the school curriculum is formulated and what educational outcomes are specifically meant to be achieved.

This second micro movement involves three micro-meso and meso-macro movements or themes: 'Transformation of a "single-curriculum" to a "flexible" education system', 'Flexibility as a condition for creativity', and 'Flexibility to group pupils and decentralising state responsibilities'. These movements are concerned with how state responsibility has been seemingly diffused by the exhortation of metaphors. In addition, this chapter explores how the lack of agency can serve to obfuscate state responsibility with respect to policy trajectories. By devolving power to schools, the lack of (state) agency in discourse underplays the potential of active agents. As Fairclough (2000a, pp. 120–121) argues, decentralisation 'does not imply an abandonment or weakening of control from the centre, but a transformation in the nature of central control'. Devolution to school leaders and teachers hence in no way entails relinquishing state control. This strategy reinforces an order of information and discourse on decentralisation while at the same time obscuring its central agent(s) and implication on structures.

Within this focus, the significance of policy discourse on school leadership, and state ambiguity as a central dimension of structural organisation (particularly in the changing economies) are highlighted. In particular, the analysis illustrates the *necessity* for agentless, nominalised action of state decentralisation (Graham, 2001a, p. 771). It is through this that state interests have become redefined and obscured through discursive strategies (Graham & Luke, 2011, p. 104).

Transformation of a 'single-curriculum' to a 'flexible' education system

The analysis of the first key theme makes explicit how a 'flexible system' is represented as an abstract agentless nominalisation and is re-concretised through a conceptual metaphor that casts it as a malleable object. The analysis examines how policymakers support their position of a *flexible* education system. Further, the work of this metaphor facilitates an orientation to a general depoliticisation of responsibilities in relation to decentralisation and within a frame of ethical practices.

Micro-meso movement: flexibility to tailor to pupils' needs

This section develops an analysis of how the metaphor of *flexibility* works in the 1979a MOE report to build rationalities for an education system tailored to pupils' needs. The analysis illustrates how this metaphor can be seen as moving through and between the micro and meso discourses of how a flexible system as a mechanisation of education that lacks agency has been constructed as an ethical, sustainable, differentiating machinery to cater to 'differences in absorption capacities and rates of learning of the pupils' (Extract 27, lines 2–3). Further, it illustrates how such discourse, through the use of the metaphor of *flexible*, has shaped educational reform.

The central tension between the centralising and decentralising tendencies of two dichotomous systems is also a tension between two different modes of ethical modes of practices. Framed by a dichotomy of learners – 'above-average' (Extract 27, line 6) and 'below-average' (Extract 27, line 7) – pupils, the analysis here elucidates the arguments made based on a binary logic of which education system best delivers enhanced ethical practice for Singaporean students who are the paradigmatic subjects of this dilemma. Further, it illustrates how the metaphor of flexibility is implicated in the construction of suitable, albeit necessary access to educational opportunity premised on certain rationalities that promote devolution of state responsibilities.

The binary logic of Extract 27 below constructs a polarising 'single versus flexible curriculum dilemma'. The 'single-curriculum' (line 1) education system is thus strategically implicated in the discourse as undesirable. More importantly, policymakers provide an understanding of how a sustainable educational trajectory for different categories of children can be conceptualised and rationalised through a *flexible* education system. This view of rationality exclusively in terms of *flexibility* will be scrutinised using data that explicitly manifests the weaknesses of a 'single-curriculum' education system. It is important to note that by holding the 'single-curriculum' education system responsible for 'high failure rates' (line 9), agency is obscured.

The crisis is explained in Extract 27 as the effect of weaknesses of the 'single-curriculum' system (Fairclough, 2006b, p. 44). The attribution of responsibility can be made clear by looking at how agency and responsibility are represented here. In the narrative, the 'system' that streams 'pupils according to merit into different classes and schools' (lines 3–4) is represented as processes without agents. The agents or agencies that resulted in high failure rates are not identified.

Grammatically, there is an *intransitive* verb – 'streamed' (line 3) – representing a *transitive* action (some agent acting upon the entity at issue here, i.e. pupils), which moreover has as its subject 'this rigidity in the system' (line 6), the reifying *nominalisation* of another transitive action. To put the point simply: the agent or agencies who did the streaming and who were responsible for the 'high failure rates' (line 8) are not salient. If we look back at the first sentence of the paragraph, we again find the nominalisation of actions: 'does not take into consideration differences in absorption capacities and rates of learning of the pupils' (lines 1–3). All these reified actions are negatively *evaluated* (Fairclough, 2003, pp. 215, 171–190) either with *evaluative adjectives* – 'same' (line 5), 'failure' (line 8) – or through the *negative connotation of* the *noun* – 'rigidity' (line 6). To the degree that problems associated with a 'single-curriculum' exist, the solution lies in introducing *flexibility*. Interestingly, agency and the processes involved around the discourse of a 'flexible' (line 10) education system that determined stipulated desirable outcomes are obscured. In other words: 'high failure rates could be reduced if the education system is *flexible* enough to cater for the different categories of pupils' (lines 9–11). How this has been made possible will be further explored in the next section.

Extract 27: 1979a MOE report

Lines	*Text*
1	The '**single-curriculum**' education system does not take into
2	consideration differences in absorption capacities and rates of learning
3	of the pupils. Although pupils may be streamed according to merit
4	into different classes and schools, all are required to cover the same
5	syllabus within the same period and to sit for the same examinations.
6	This **rigidity** in the system tends to favour the *above-average pupils*,
7	penalising the *below-average pupils* and the *slow learners*. This
8	resulted in high failure rates. In 1976, 41% of the PSLE candidates
9	and 40% of the GCE 'O' candidates failed. These high failure rates
10	could be reduced if the education system is **flexible** enough to cater
11	for the different categories of pupils.

Source: MOE, 1979a, p. 4-1.

Meso-macro movement: moving through value and devaluation of flexible and centralised systems

Like the micro-meso movement, the metaphor of flexibility is also operationalised in the 1979b, 1987, and 1991a policy reports. The following analysis illustrates how the metaphor is implicated in the construction of a suitable, albeit necessary, curriculum that is tailored to the learner as a form of ethical practice, and to promote the devolution of responsibility to school educators. This provides further evidence for the key role of this metaphor in providing rationalities for an unequal system. By collapsing several texts together, the analysis of this theme traces the movement through co-texts to examine further the discursive positioning of a 'flexible' system in relation to a centralised system.

The analysis tries to grasp the essential connection between *value* and *devaluation* of *flexible* and *centralised* systems respectively. Describing the necessity for agentless, nominalised action allows the exhortation of *flexibility* to be posed as a fact.

Following Graham's (2001a, pp. 770–771) analysis of the generic tendency in policy towards necessity, which is transferred intertextually from expressions of high degrees of desirability for given outcomes, in Extract 28, we see a high

Extracts 28, 29, and 30: Comparison of flexible and centralised systems through MOE policy texts 1979b–1991a

The areas in which the Ministry requires expert assistance include:-
Definition of the system of curriculum development
The present system is **centralised** in the Ministry which develops and defines in detail all curricula for schools. There is, however, significant variation in the ability and performance among pupils within a school and among schools. The Ministry needs expert advice on the degree of **flexibility** to be given to schools and teachers so that they can adapt the prescribed curricula to suit the ability of their pupils and the aims of the school.

(Extract 28, MOE, 1979b, p. 17)

The Minister acknowledged that our system was a highly **centralised** one. It had come about as a result of history, the only intention being was to ensure that all our schools maintained proper standards and contributed to the general well-being of the country. The end result was that schools tended to develop into stereotyped units, activating themselves on instructions from the central authority, with limited **flexibility** and freedom to strike out on their own, capable though they were of this. It was hard to tell one school from another. This state of affairs was likely to prevail as long as schools were rigidly bound to a **centralised** system, and even schools, which had come to establish a certain standing for themselves would be penalised and denied the prospect of greater achievements.

(Extract 29, MOE, 1987, p. 2)

For pupils in the lowest ability range (20%) who, at present, are most likely to be streamed to the Monolingual and Extended courses, the system has not been as effective in helping them to progress up the educational ladder. Greater attention to these least academically able pupils is hence necessary. Improvements to the primary school system can be made by customising education to suit the ability of each pupil rather than to subject all pupils to the diet provided in broad educational streams. This will require **flexibility** and responsibility to be given to principals and teachers whose judgment will be crucial in tailoring the most appropriate educational package for their pupils.

(Extract 30, MOE, 1991a, p. 11)

modality of truth being made for an effort on someone's part to decide 'on the *degree of flexibility* to be given to schools and teachers so that they can adapt the prescribed curricula to suit the ability of their pupils and the aims of the school', the *desirability* of which is presupposed. Even where we are told that the Ministry *needs* expert advice, we are not told by whom (cf. Lemke, 1995; McKenna & Graham, 2000 as cited in Graham, 2001a, p. 771). After the proposal for action by unnamed agents, we are also given an explicitly evaluative (axiological) justification for the proposition that favours a *flexible* system through decentralisation, which is also cast as a statement of fact: 'The present system is *centralised* in the Ministry which develops and defines in detail all curricula for schools. There is, *however*, significant variation in the ability and performance among pupils within a school and among schools' (Extract 28).

This claim is further reiterated in Extract 29: 'This state of affairs was likely to prevail as long as schools were rigidly bound to a *centralised* system, and even schools, which had come to establish a certain standing for themselves *would be* penalised and denied the prospect of greater achievements.' Here we see how evaluations for importance become translated *directly* into *necessity* in the policy genre. What we see is the relationship/tension between an *irrealis* object (the advent of a flexible system), evaluative meaning tending to transfer metaphorically from *importance* to *necessity*, and the smuggling in of a second exhortation by what seems like a relational proposition: with a flexible system, prescribed formula can be adapted by schools and teachers to suit the ability of pupils and aims of the school (Extract 28). The *desirability* of this is reiterated in Extract 30: 'Improvements to the primary school system can be made by customising education to suit the ability of each pupil rather than to subject all pupils to the diet provided in broad educational streams. This will require *flexibility* and responsibility to be given to principals and teachers whose judgment will be crucial in tailoring the most appropriate educational package for their pupils'. Within this argument, there is also a contractual discourse of 'responsibilities and rights' which will be explored in more detail in the section 'Meso-macro movement: moving towards flexibility to raise performance'.

Flexibility as a condition for creativity

The construction of flexibility as the necessary solution for a 'rigid' system (Extract 27, line 6) is also evident in this second theme, which involves an emphasis on the importance and necessity of flexibility for creating the conditions that make creativity possible. While the micro-meso movement explores how flexibility, as an ethical practice is necessary for creativity, the meso-macro movement continues to trace the argument for decentralisation as an integral condition for realising creativity and how this transits into providing a rationale for enhancing the creativity of junior college students.

Micro–meso movement: decentralisation for creativity

The following analysis of the 1987 MOE report examines the role of the metaphor of *flexibility* in developing a justification for decentralisation through the ethical-political discourse of 'creativity'. This metaphor can be seen moving through and between the micro and meso discourses. In doing so, education is redefined on the basis of *decentralisation* through greater autonomy.

In Extract 31 below, the crisis of *centralisation*, and the recommended solution of *decentralisation* (reduction in the power of main gatekeeper) through 'flexibility' by the Ministry are explained as the effect of its weaknesses and strengths. Building on the 1979 report's focus on reducing high failure rates, here in the 1987 report, other desirable movements/outcomes become prominent within the discourse of 'flexibility' – 'environment for creativity' (line 3), 'independent thought to emerge' (line 3), 'more effective educational agencies' (lines 5–6), 'greater autonomy to schools' (lines 7–8), 'creativity and innovation progress' (line 8). Of particular interest are evaluative statements about desirability and undesirability, about what is good and what is bad. As such, the analyses of modality and evaluation involve analyses of how the world is represented, of the un/desirability of these representations in relation to the metaphor of *flexibility*, and of how an authoritative voice on such realities is constructed. Towards this end, the 'evaluation' of *flexibility* refers to the ways in which policymakers commit themselves to positive values of this metaphor and concerns the policymakers' commitment to flexibility as desirable (Fairclough, 2003 as cited in Thomas, 2009, p. 212). Interestingly, the agency and the processes involved around the discourse of *flexibility* are again obscured. As such, state commitments appear as disintegrated and contradictory.

Drawing on Fairclough's (2006b, pp. 44–45) analysis suggests that the attribution of responsibility can be made clear by looking at how agency and responsibility are represented here. The recommendations, 'the need to generate conditions in schools' (lines 1–2) and 'create an environment for creativity and independent thought to emerge' (lines 2–3) are represented as processes without agents. The agents or agencies that generate conditions or create an environment are not identified. There was simply 'the need to generate conditions in schools' (lines 1–2); the action on the part of some agents/agencies (who are

Extract 31: 1987 MOE report, *Towards Excellence in Schools*

Lines	*Text*
1	In July 1986, he (the Minister for Education) argued the need to generate
2	conditions in schools which would allow for greater **flexibility** and so create an
3	environment for creativity and independent thought to emerge. Rather than
4	have schools function only on the basis of instructions from the **centre**, he
5	encouraged to advance proposals of their own, to convert themselves into more
6	effective educational agencies. Again, in August of the same year, he developed
7	further on this concept by expressing his belief that the granting of greater
8	autonomy to schools would pave the way to creativity and innovation progress.

Source: MOE, 1987, pp. 2–3.

responsible for generating conditions in schools) is *nominalised* (Fairclough, 2003, pp. 143–144, 220) as 'conditions', and thereby transformed from an action into a reified event. These 'conditions' would then 'allow for greater flexibility' (line 2). This is a strange and mystifying formulation of what would more transparently be represented as two actions with responsible agents: for example, 'a, b, generate conditions in schools c, d, that e, f, which would allow for greater flexibility'. Grammatically, the *intransitive* verbs, 'generate' (line 1) and 'create' (line 2), represent a transitive action (some agent acting upon the entity at issue here, i.e. flexibility). Moreover, it has as its subject 'the granting of greater autonomy to schools' (lines 7–8), the reifying *nominalisation* of another transitive action. In other words: who has the responsibility for generating the 'conditions in schools' (line 2) which would allow for *flexibility*? These reified actions are positively *evaluated* (Fairclough, 2003, pp. 215, 171–190) either with *evaluative adjectives* ('greater', 'creativity', 'innovation') or through the positive connotations of nouns ('progress') (lines 7–8).

It can, however, be inferred that agents or agencies in this case are internal to the Ministry (Verschueren, 1999, as cited in Fairclough, 2006b, p. 45). First, the agent is identified through the recommendation of 'Rather than have schools function only on the basis of instructions from the centre' (lines 3–4). Second, this can be seen in how schools are imbued with agency to make them more autonomous (in which case they are passive agents) through the 'granting of greater autonomy' (lines 7–8). Hence it is the 'schools' which are responsible for 'generating conditions' (lines 1–2) which would allow for 'greater flexibility' (line 2) and for paving the way for 'creativity and innovation progress' (line 8). This move, which semantically encodes greater freedom and/or less coercion in accordance with the principle of school autonomy, suggests a market-based school reform (Mulderrig, 2011b, p. 571). Based on this argument, within the context of an educational market, responsibility and blame are covertly placed on principals and teachers (Fairclough, 2006b, p. 45) if they fail to 'generate conditions which would allow for greater *flexibility* and so create an environment for creativity and independent thought to emerge' (lines 1–3).

This emphasis on human as opposed to institutional agency suggests that these agents are blameworthy. Specifically, this strategy encourages a narrow perspective that discourages attention to both major and structural influences on actions and outcomes (Edelman, 1995, p. 70). It is also important to note that the absence of agency results in the diffusion of responsibility on the part of the Ministry of Education. In this way, the sense of responsibility can also be diluted by a lack of 'central' control.

Meso-macro movement: moving towards enhancing the creativity of junior college students

The previous micro-meso movement examined the *necessity* of flexibility in creating conditions for creativity and the subsequent decentralisation of education. The meso-macro movement continues to trace this theme in the 1987 and

2002 policy reports. Building on the metaphorical relations of flexibility, this movement traces decentralisation as an integral condition for realising creativity and how this transits into providing a rationale for enhancing the creativity of junior college students. In addition, the analysis identifies the process by which flexibility becomes increasingly implicit and diffused. In other words, the metaphor plays an implicit character as it becomes diffused across the policy texts while still retaining its fundamental role in driving the rationale of the policy. This tendency is more obvious in the analysis of how a political economy of surrealism works (in Chapter 7).

Drawing on Graham's (2001a, pp. 771–772) analysis of opening up future spaces, it is clear that the creation of conditions in schools through decentralisation which would allow for greater creativity is positively evaluated for desirability. Creativity itself is pre-evaluated as desirable potentiality; this implies the necessity for a certain amount of action for the *conditions which would allow for greater creativity* to be moved from potentiality (*irrealis*) to actuality (*realis*). These broadest of evaluative orientations are expressed implicitly and in the data.

The analysis of Extracts 32 and 33 provides an illustration of how creativity and decentralisation are desirable. Here we see the interrelatedness between evaluations of *desirability* and *importance* for realising creativity. The hortatory function of policy is again expressed in necessity in these extracts.

Following Fairclough's (1995, p. 148) analysis, the authority of the Ministry is marked through high-affinity epistemic (or 'probability') modalities that are *desirable*:

In Extract 33, the frequency of clauses with the modal auxiliary *will* marks futurity plus high-affinity epistemic modality. In terms of transitivity, the passive verb 'will have to ground', 'have to evolve' are agentless; the process is not present in the surface of the grammar, and the nominalisation (methods) is also agentless. In other words, these verbs lack an explicit agent. However, in each case the institution is the implicit agent: it is the Ministry, or schools that 'ground students in a range of fundamental subjects'.

In relation to Extracts 32 and 33, we see the confusion of causal circularity in which regulation and deregulation in relation to creativity are concerned (cf. Graham, 2001a, p. 776): 'greater autonomy has been *devolved* to principals' (deregulation) (Extract 32). But this deregulation is juxtaposed with regulation through instances of deontic ('obligation') modality which relates to the discourse-producer's view of something as desirable or undesirable (Thompson & Hunston, 2000, p. 5) as

Extracts 32 and 33: Creativity through MOE policy texts 1987 and 2002

greater autonomy has been *devolved* to principals [is required] on the assumption that centralisation had *stifled* initiative and **creativity**. Within the broad confines of national education policy, principals *have* considerable latitude in the management of schools, usage of funds collected by and allocated to school, structuring the teaching programme from prescribed syllabuses, admission of pupils at levels other than at certain points and the selection and use of teaching materials.

(Extract 32, MOE, 1987, p. 69)

We *should move* to a JC curriculum aimed principally at developing thinking skills, and that engages students in greater breadth of learning ... In the knowledge economy, an ability to draw on different disciplines *will be at* a premium. The JC curriculum *will have* to ground students in a range of fundamental subjects and help them to think in inter-disciplinary terms. We *should also* provide space for students with an exceptional ability for an area, and a passion for the subject, to pursue it beyond the regular curriculum. In addition, teaching and assessment methods *have to evolve*, to groom and enhance a capacity to learn and explore independently and **creatively**.

(Extract 33, MOE, 2002, p. ii)

illustrated in Extract 33: 'We *should move* to a JC curriculum aimed principally at developing thinking skills', 'We should also provide space for students with an exceptional ability for an area', 'teaching and assessment methods *have to evolve*, to groom and enhance a capacity to learn and explore independently and *creatively*'. A dichotomy is established between the space of (state) agency and (human) agency.

Devolution to principals – that is, deregulation – *requires a clear regulatory framework* which can be considered as a set of regulations. But the processes of regulation and deregulation will necessarily get further confused because 'structuring the teaching programme from prescribed syllabuses' (Extract 32) is set against the *desirable* outcomes of the Ministry. To add to the confusion, as shown below, the development of the curriculum, teaching and assessment methods will make it more difficult when it shifts to an economic discourse within the nexus of 'rapidly changing demands of the knowledge-intensive economy' (Extract 34). Paradoxically, even more (agentless) regulation will be required for continuing deregulation; that is, the curricular governance and implementation are indicators of a mixing of centralised and decentralised modes of curricular administration in education systems. In a similar manner to what Astiz et al. (2002, p. 66) have argued, this analysis demonstrates that regulation/deregulation are indeed mixing as a result of what has been attributed as economic globalisation processes:

For example, in a subsequent section of the report, Extract 34, the necessity for regulation is projected through predication that a curriculum that 'tended to over-emphasise content and *did not* sufficiently stress creativity, independent thinking and

Extracts 34 and 35: Regulatory action through MOE policy texts 2002 and 2008

There was a general sentiment that junior college students were at present inadequately prepared for the rapidly changing demands of the knowledge-intensive economy. Although the present curriculum was rigorous and exacting, it tended to over-emphasise content and did not sufficiently stress **creativity**, independent thinking and analytical skills. Other skills and competencies such as communication skills, courage to venture and perseverance essential in today's globalised world were also lacking in many JC students.

(Extract 34, MOE, 2002, p. 35)

The expanded university sector must help power Singapore's next phase of growth by providing high-quality graduate manpower. It must be able to provide our young people with high levels of knowledge and skills, as well as impart a spirit of innovation and **creativity** that they will need as Singapore's economy moves up the value chain and into new growth areas.

(Extract 35, MOE, 2008a, p. 2)

analytical skills' is an *un-desirable constraint*. This constraint will be cast off to enable new kinds of education for students to be 'adequately prepared for the rapidly *changing demands* of the knowledge-intensive economy'. Further, in Extract 35, the expansion of the university sector is explicitly linked to 'Singapore's next phase of growth' and is required to 'impart a spirit of innovation and creativity' (Extract 35). All this *necessity* for regulatory action is predicated upon the desirability, inevitability, and importance as conditions of creativity that are *desirable* for the irrealis spaces of the 'knowledge-intensive economy' (Extract 34) and 'new growth areas' (Extract 35).

Flexibility to group pupils and decentralising state responsibilities

The third key theme builds on the analysis of the previous two to explicitly focus on the role the metaphor of flexibility plays in diffusing state responsibilities. While the micro-meso movement explores how this diffusion relates to raising pupils' performance, the meso-macro movement continues to trace the argument for decentralisation as necessary in the interests of both school educators and pupils.

Micro-meso movement: flexibility for educators

The following analysis of Extract 36 examines the way the metaphor of *flexibility* appears in the 1991a MOE report in such a way to support devolution of state responsibilities to school educators through the ethical-political discourse of 'raising performance' (line 2). The analysis illustrates how this metaphor is drawn upon to develop an argument that state de/centralisation is desirable.

Instructively, the notion of 'flexibility' (line 9) presupposes an underlying conception that sets the condition for not only positive outcomes, but ethical practices. Building on the previous argument that within the context of an educational market, responsibility and blame is covertly placed on the educators who work within the schools, the following examines how 'teachers and principals' (line 8) are imbued with this agency of assuming responsibility in 1991 for 'raising the performance of all pupils' (line 2) through the discourse of *flexibility*. Complicit in this discourse is the invitation of teachers and principals into the authoritative centre, subtly dispersing state responsibility and obligation. Here, the discourse of 'flexibility' explicitly redefines not only education, on the basis of ability-based educational practices; it also redefines the agents responsible for *desirable* outcomes.

In Extract 36, the policy proposes an explicit separation from Primary 1 onwards, leading to increased pedagogical heterogeneity. The proposal recognises the notion of learning differences as a fundamental tenet in the provision of compatible teaching pace. More specifically, the policy of 'formal streaming' (lines 6–7), is constructed as a resolute, authoritative, transformative remedy for addressing differed learning abilities and assumed to provide some degree of pedagogical stability through learner compatibility. The general rationale for policymakers is that early intervention can lead to improved performance, and that the 'lowest 20% of the ability range' (line 3) would most benefit from this move.

Extract 36: 1991a MOE report, *Improving Primary School Education*

Lines	*Text*
1	The proposed improvements to primary education will be a refinement of
2	the present system aimed at raising the performance of all pupils especially
3	those in the lowest 20% of the ability range. These will provide for a 1-year
4	preparatory programme and 6 years of primary education to all pupils. The
5	improved system will be structured in three stages, viz: a 1-year preparatory
6	stage, a 4-year foundation stage and a 2-year orientation stage. Formal
7	streaming of pupils will take place at the end of the foundation stage at P4
8	instead of the present P3. However, teachers and principals will have the
9	**flexibility** to group pupils of similar learning abilities together and provide
10	them with compatible teaching pace from P1 onwards. At P5 and P6, three
11	language learning streams will be available with the provision of fourth
12	stream if there is demand.

Source: MOE, 1991a, p. 14.

In trying to address the problem of difference, reforming school practices from Primary 1 onwards appears to be the one over-arching programmatic orientation capable of 'raising the performance of all pupils' (line 2) (Fraser, 1995, p. 93). This polemical discourse suggests that in conceptualising the nature of the over-arching educational issue – to raise 'the performance of all pupils especially those in the lowest 20% of the ability range' (lines 2–3) – policymakers subscribe to the argument of a 'flexible' (line 9) system. This system is informed by a commitment to early institutional segregation, which institutionalises groups of similar learning abilities, and promotes the fundamental tenet that different children have different capacities to acquire knowledge. Whereas late formal streaming 'at the end of the foundation stage at P4' (line 7) tends to undermine group differentiation, policy-makers promote it judiciously through the metaphor of 'flexibility'. Through this metaphor, they aim to overcome this ideological struggle through devolution of responsibility, that is, by allowing 'teachers and principals to group pupils of similar learning abilities together and provide them with compatible teaching pace from P1 onwards' (lines 8–10). This ideological position of the policymakers and the impetus for early recognition of learning abilities suggests that those truly committed to 'raising the performance of all pupils especially those in the lowest 20% of the ability range' (lines 2–3) should accept the early streaming concept in its entirety. From a national perspective, state decentralisation through *flexibility* to group pupils according to their abilities in schools is efficient: it allows educators to align suitable pedagogy better catered to the individual student.

The use of the metaphor of flexibility thus establishes a common ideological ground in which providing learners with 'compatible teaching pace from P1 onwards' (line 10) is conceptualised as being highly *desirable* within the context of differed abilities. This ideological ground is presented as natural, common sense. To sum up, an analysis of cohesion in this text provides a way into its mode of argumentation and mode of rationality (Fairclough, 1992, p. 174), and so into the educational-ethical voice and ethos that are constructed in it.

Meso-macro movement: moving towards flexibility to raise performance

The previous micro-meso movement investigated the role of the metaphor of *flexibility* in supporting the argument for devolution of state responsibilities to school educators to raise pupils' performance, and also how this has been projected as ethical. In the meso-macro movement, policy texts from 1987 to 2002 are analysed in order to further examine how flexibility is used to decentralise state responsibilities and as a rationale to group pupils and provide them with customised programmes, further legitimising inequality as a form of ethical practice. Yet, this meso-macro movement highlights that an explicit use of the metaphor is not needed to decentralise state's responsibilities.

The policy of decentralisation has become a key aspect of educational restructuring. In the following extracts, decentralisation of educational control and decision-making is clearly evident. This move towards greater devolution through expert management by school leaders increased in momentum after 1987, and is perceived as not only desirable, but absolutely necessary. More importantly and paradoxically, the analysis demonstrates how the state attempts to maintain control over the policy process through moral evaluations while decentralising responsibilities for its implementation.

Moral e/valuations help legitimise state regulation (Mulderrig, 2009, pp. 103–104). This process can be clearly seen in Extract 38. The moralised activity is objectivated; that is, 'greater autonomy and latitude [should] be given to principals *to transfer pupils* from one course to another as and when the principals think that their pupils would benefit by the move. The principal [must] be given ***authority to run his*** [1] ***own school***'. This legitimised activity then becomes the agent of two effect verbs: 'to transfer pupils' and 'to run his own school'. Paradoxically, the moralised activities are realised in a finite clause 'selection and appointment of principal', and the nominalisation 'ensure that they use their authority in the interests of their pupils and teachers'. While these instrumental

Extract 38: Devolution to principals in 1987 MOE policy text

The report recommends that more autonomy be given to principals so that they would have sufficient scope to function effectively and plan good programmes for the development of their pupils. For example, greater autonomy and latitude should be given to principals to transfer pupils from one course to another as and when the principals think that their pupils would benefit by the move. The principal must be given authority to run his own school. Under such circumstances, great care has to be exercised in the selection and appointment of principals, to ensure that they use their authority in the interests of their pupils and teachers.

(Extract 38, MOE, 1987, p. 69)

rationalisations appear to be simply rational justifications for particular courses of action, this appearance of reasonableness, within an ongoing tension between regulation and deregulation derives from the implicit set of normalised moral values they trigger. The pragmatic and positive values triggered here are those of an autonomous devolution to make decisions on pupils' academic pathways that depends upon providing principals with 'greater autonomy', 'latitude', and 'authority'. Moreover, the final relative clause, 'use their authority in their interests of their pupils and teachers', reinforces the basis of the legitimation with a second 'strand' of rationalisation that draws on a discourse of morality. Thus, the legitimation draws on a moral managerial concern in Extract 38. It renders why we should positively value the authority given to principals – because it is not only *necessary for* principals to be 'effective' but is more so in 'the interests of pupils and teachers'.

The necessity of meeting the needs of pupils articulated in the 1987 policy expands in 1991 to the need to tailor 'the most appropriate educational package for their pupils' (Extract 39) and 'group pupils of similar abilities together in order to provide a more customised programme' (Extract 40). In the 2002 document, there is now involved a need 'to customise their programmes and initiatives to suit the needs of their students more flexibly and responsively' (Extract 41).

Extracts 39, 40, and 41: Flexibility as increasing devolution of responsibility through MOE policy texts 1991a and 2002

For pupils in the lowest ability range (20%) who, at present, are most likely to be streamed to the Monolingual and Extended courses, the system has not been as effective in helping them to progress up the educational ladder. Greater attention to these least academically able pupils is hence necessary. Improvements to the primary school system can be made by customising education to suit the ability of each pupil rather than to subject all pupils to the diet provided in broad educational streams. This will require **flexibility** and **responsibility** to be given to principals and teachers whose judgment will be crucial in tailoring the most appropriate educational package for their pupils.

(Extract 39, MOE, 1991a, p. 11)

Formal streaming will take place at the end of P4. However before P4, principals and teachers will have the **flexibility** and discretion to group pupils of similar abilities together in order to provide a more customised programme. At P4, schools will assess pupils' performance in English, mother-tongue and mathematics, making use of the Ministry's item banks to ensure a measure of comparability of standards across schools. All pupils will then advance to the next stage of primary education, the orientation stage, where they will be placed in one of three language learning streams but will remain in the same school. As is the present practice, schools will advise parents on the appropriate stream for their children but parents will have the final say as to which of the streams they wish their children to attend at P5.

(Extract 40, MOE, 1991a, p. 17)

We have moved towards greater customisation within the education system as we seek to maximise the full potential of our students. At the school level, school leaders have been given greater autonomy in key areas such as personnel management and development, finance, use of resources and programme development. Schools are able to customise their programmes and initiatives to suit the needs of their students more **flexibly** and responsively.

(Extract 41, MOE, 2002, p. 3)

Extracts 37 and 38: Contradiction between forms of power in the 1987 MOE policy text

We recommend that once appointed, principals in our schools be given greater autonomy in deciding school matters. Should independent schools be established, the authority to appoint their principals should lie with the governing body of the schools.

(Extract 37, MOE, 1987, p. v)

The report recommends that more autonomy be given to principals so that they would have sufficient scope to function effectively and plan good programmes for the development of their pupils. For example, greater autonomy and latitude should be given to principals to transfer pupils from one course to another as and when the principals think that their pupils would benefit by the move. The principal must be given authority to run his own school. Under such circumstances, great care has to be exercised in the selection and appointment of principals, to ensure that they use their authority in the interests of their pupils and teachers.

(Extract 38, MOE, 1987, p. 69)

Whilst devolution to 'principals' was made explicit in 1987 (Extract 38), it expanded to 'principals and teachers' in 1991 (Extracts 39 and 40 and even further to 'school leaders' in 2002 [Extract 41]). The increasing spatial 'nesting' of hierarchised surveillance/observation to understand the needs of pupils and therefore to put in place forms of tailored curriculum embeds layers of responsibility that function like a piece of machinery (cf. Foucault, 1995, pp. 171–172). Interestingly, in Extract 40, 'schools' as the nominalised agent 'will advise parents on the appropriate stream for their children' and in Extract 41, 'Schools are able to customise their programmes and initiatives to suit the needs of their students more flexibly and responsively.' The moral evaluation concerns the institutional authority's opinions about necessary improvements in the education system with respect to greater diffusion of responsibility.

Notably, here, using the words of Mulderrig (2009, p. 104), 'a double-layered rationalisation appeals in the first instance to the positive effects of this proposition to be legitimated, and secondly to the purpose of those effects'. Through the moral evaluations embedded in the discourse of interests, this legitimation strategy also adds to the texturing of the government's social identity: here it is both strategic and moral. There is another important assumption at work in this legitimation – that there is a logical either/or relationship that holds the provision of principals/programmes and pupils'/teachers' interests. Thus, an essentially arbitrary logic is being put to work in order to justify a policy for devolution that contradictorily reinforces state regulation and the exercise of power.

This contradiction is illustrated in Extract 38: '*great care* has to be *exercised* in the selection and appointment of principals, *to ensure* that they use their authority in the interests of their pupils and teachers'. The contradiction is further reiterated in Extract 37, with reference to independent schools: 'Should independent schools be established, the authority to appoint their principals should lie with the governing body of the schools.' These moralised activities illustrate the complex and often contradictory ideological principles at work. Although state de/regulation rests on individuals, its functioning is that of a network of relations from top to bottom: 'We r*ecommend*' (Extract 37), 'The report *recommends*' (Extract 38), but also from bottom to top and laterally: 'more autonomy be given to principals' (Extract 38), 'greater autonomy and latitude should be given to principals' (Extract 38), 'principal must be given authority' (Extract 38); this network 'holds' the whole education system together and traverses it in its entirety with effects of power that derive from one another (cf. Foucault, 1995, pp. 176–177) so that no one any longer possesses full responsibility (Nietzsche, 1967a, p. 383); that is, these relations of power, *co-regulate*, to borrow Thich Nhat Hanh's (2010, p. 62) term, they *inter-are*.

Summary

This chapter has examined how the metaphor of flexibility performs *ideologising* work to obscure the agent or agency involved in generating desirable outcomes. It explored how the lack of agency can serve to obfuscate state responsibility with respect to (hidden) policy trajectories. More importantly, the chapter has examined how the lack of (state) agency in discourse underplays the potential of active agents. It proposes that the devolution of responsibility to educators and transformation to a flexible system in no way entails relinquishing state control. Further, the work of this metaphor facilitates an orientation to a general depoliticisation of responsibilities in relation to decentralisation and within a frame of ethical practices.

A key finding of this chapter is that the contradictions between regulation and deregulation are held together by the metaphor of flexibility. One of the ways in which this was done was by drawing on the *implicit* use of the metaphor. That is to say, even though the metaphor is absent in the text, metaphorical relations built in other texts and throughout policy discourse embed its implicit meaning to drive the rationale of the policy. In the next chapter, this tendency will be made more obvious in the analysis of how a political economy of surrealism works.

Note

1 Although examining the construction of gendered subject positionings and terminology in policy discourse is not the focus of this chapter, attention must be drawn to the use of the pronoun 'his'. It is not gender-neutral and possibly inbuilds gender inequality and male dominance (cf. van Dijk, 1993, p. 255) by projecting that all heads of schools will be male and cannot be female.

7 Theme 3

Political economies of surrealism

Overview

This third micro movement highlights the notion of 'political economies of surrealism' as embedded in the continuing development of Singapore's education policy. This notion, then, places analytic emphasis on examining how metaphors perform *ideologising* work to bring together realities that appear to have limited logical relationship or rational link, to produce conditions of emerging political economies that permit new values (cf. Adonis, 2005, p. 41). This chapter ties previous analyses into a wider reflection on how metaphors sustain the ideology of economic growth as the only way forward by interweaving both realis and surrealis/irrealis states, the actual and the potential (Lemke, 1998, pp. 60–61). In doing so, the analysis demonstrates how the notion of necessity and the discursive construction of reality are bound together. That is, the analysis foregrounds a functional aspect of policy metaphors as divisive mechanisms of neo-liberalism through associating individuals with the appearance of discriminatory forms of economic materiality which does not in fact exist in reality. Specifically, this chapter calls the 'real' into question through the notion of 'surrealism'. Through this, the analysis presents an evolving, *ideological* context with which to show how ambiguous and impalpable the border between appearance and reality can be made to be, and to view the re-creation of the past and creation of the future as necessary to establish a moral obligation to put *particular* values into practice. This is done through the overarching examination of three micro-meso and meso-macro movements: 'Emergent discourses of "innovation-driven" future', 'Transitioning of economies and competition' and 'Diverse pathways to meet the needs of "our" people in the future'. This chapter relates neo-liberal values to distinctive organisational features of imagined political economies.

Policies of surrealism in time and space in policy texts

Although policy development involves the movement of time and action from what has been (Graham, 2005, pp. 120–122) to what should be (i.e., the future – an idea, an illusion, illusory pursuits, abstractions of perceived demands), time is often rendered unmeasurable, as the surrealistic discourse extends over the whole past, with implications for the whole future (cf. Bohm, 1980, p. 188). Within the modification of the future through propositions and proposals, there is, paradoxically, no physical measurement of the time element involved when these irrealis states exist; that is, time is fragmentary and spherical within this space-time dimension. There is only the projection of particular skills that are purported to be the necessary conditions to achieve *particular* ends (for example, skills and economic growth) in these states, what can be termed an orientation to 'reverse engineering' (Graham, 2005, p. 124). Through the discursive production and the dual juxtaposition of these unstable states, this chapter presents the illusory nature of time as an ideological cover-up of absolute and final realities (Medina & Wood, 2005, pp. 11–12). This illusory character of time brings to the fore the crucial interdependence of the discursive production of both relative states – realis and irrealis – by conferring perceived legitimacy onto specific practices and interests as *truth* (cf. Medina & Wood, 2005, p. 11). These effects, as this chapter argues, require analytic templates that begin from a synthetic view of the relationship between discourse and the continuous overlapping discursive (re)construction of political economies (Graham & Luke, 2011, p. 104). Here, the hegemony of macro values, based entirely on the logic of illusory economies, calls the 'real' into question through the notion of 'surrealism'.

The focus of this chapter is not so much on the metaphors themselves as on what is called the 'Political economies of surrealism'. The reified, apparently autonomous, systems of these imaginary economies take on a distorting and determining role in the prioritisation of resources. The extracts selected for analysis may not necessarily have the metaphors explicitly evident, because the analysis draws more on how economies are (re)constructed. Whilst Chapters 5 and 6 demonstrate the utilisation of metaphors, this chapter focuses on how the use of the metaphors of flexibility, diversity, and choice is not explicit but is implicit and embedded within the themes. As a development from the previous meso-macro analysis of de/regulation on the moving away from the metaphor as a central condition for inequality (see Chapter 6, in the section 'Meso-macro movement: Moving towards flexibility to raise performance'), this chapter demonstrates that the architectural grid constructed on the basis of thematic metaphors continues to be destabilised. That is, the principal axis of analysis that draws on metaphors no longer stands. One of the underlying assumptions in adopting this multi-level approach is that relationships that hold at the micro-meso level of analysis may be stronger or weaker at the meso-macro level of analysis, or may even reverse or provide a new direction (Ostroff, 1993 as cited in Klein & Kozlowski, 2000, p. 213).

This last type of mechanism supports the implicit work of the metaphors by alluding to surrealistic economic landscapes. This chapter ties the previous two together by illustrating how the circular, aggressive logic of meeting the *perceived* demands of imaginary economies is a recognisable and persistent feature of policy discourse. More visibly, in relation to value-forming labour within the *perceived* demands arising from the changing material conditions of political economies, this logic has a fully fungible relationship with the skills by which they are exchanged for economic growth.

In the development of the previous themes that were explicitly formulated by the utilisation of metaphors, a certain inflection can be observed in the analysis of this third key theme of 'Political economies of surrealism': an insistence on the ambiguity of the effects of metaphorical relations, an ambivalent extension of correlations attributed to them, and a valorisation of meeting the preconceived demands of future economies. So, whereas previously the analysis was based on word use, this chapter demonstrates that it does not have to be the word itself that forms the precursor of inequality, but a concept. The absence of the metaphors makes explicit another layer and depth of complexity. This demonstrates how the utilisation of metaphors is no longer needed to in-build structural inequality. Structural inequality is no longer directly contingent upon the deployment and use of metaphors, but is actually hidden by a focus on the construction and the purely perceived demands of irrealis industrial economies. As explicated in the previous thematic movements, the value system arises from the mutual influence of valuations and metaphors on one another. However, in the analysis of this chapter, it is revealed that the value system is neither located in the metaphors exclusively, nor subsumed under them as a whole. So, whereas the collisions of metaphorical relations with one another produce a self-valorising power standing above them previously, here the power expands and (re)produces independently of them. This destabilisation of the architectural grid indicates that policy texts can be *empty* of metaphors and yet can be dependent on their implicit existence through metaphorical relations built in other texts for inequality to transpire. In doing so, this chapter provides another layer of analytical dimension by opening possibilities for autonomous metaphorical relations.

To open up the possibility of overcoming the traditional dualism and false dichotomy of realis and irrealis states, the discussion proposes that policy discourse is surrealistic, characterised by the evocative bipolar juxtaposition and relativism of these incongruous states that create a tangible solidity of an elusive reality. A pure differentiation of the two states, however, is not possible as they are conditional upon, and being conditioned by, the presence of each other. Each state contains traces of its past within its present which, in turn, contains the seeds of all possible futures within its present form (cf. Graham, 2000, p. 149). It is surrealistic because the establishment of contradictory juxtaposition and interplay of states in policy discourse calls into question changing political economies as part of normal experience (cf. Foucault, 1982b, p. 47). Surrealism is that innermost essence of the real which reaches outward most fully and to the outermost limits of the imaginary, and so decisively that, rightly considered, the idea of irrealis and realis states does not arise. Following Foucault's (1982b, p. 47) analysis of Magritte's *This Is Not a Pipe*, 'each element of this (ir/realis states) could thus hold an apparently negative discourse – because it denies, along with resemblance, the assertion of reality it simultaneous conveys'. To overcome the porous juxtaposition of the contradictory conditions of actual (of *what is*) and potential (to *what should be*) realities, this chapter draws on the philosophical movement of surrealism. The 'sur' in 'surrealism' means both 'through' and 'beyond' the reality that can be seen; hence, 'surrealism' is the realism of superstructural hyperreality achieved through perceptive abstraction that is free from excessive mechanical rigidity. It arises through the free association of images and words, that is, the absence of any control exercised by reason. Within these two spatial frames, reason is excluded from the realm of the *games of truth*. Before turning to an analysis of the three key micro-meso-macro themes of this chapter, a clarification of the concept of surrealism is necessary.

Political economies of surrealism and the recourse to make-believe

As an abstract symbolisation of movement, *surrealism* represents the manipulation and juxtaposition of realis and irrealis spaces which can be seen as an extension to the multidimensional order of reality (cf. Graham, 2001a, p. 761). That is, since realis and irrealis spaces exist only as imaginary ideas and impressions, surrealism as a three-dimensional 'isness' is neither of these, but rather, it is something else, something that transcends this dualism and extends continuously (cf. Bohm, 1980, p. 238). That is to say, each of the realis and irrealis spaces in policy texts constitutes a system as a projection of a 'higher-dimensional' reality, rather than as a separate element, existing together in a common three-dimensional space (cf. Bohm, 1980, p. 238). The temporal aspect between both spaces is the primary focus of this chapter's analytical approach.

The analytic focus leading from this is, then, towards the hybridisation of spaces by means of fragmentation. By this, the games of truth, which constitute ir/realis policy narratives within the texts influence and direct unequal institutional practices while masquerading changing political economies as naturally independent entities that both precede and supersede our lived experience (McKerrow, n.d., p. 2). Further, changing surrealist imageries of political economies throughout the policies displaces the 'repetition' of a *singular* representation (a hyperreality). This dissolves a comfortable, naturalised impression of reality at the same time as constructing and confounding a particular *hyperreality* underpinning the policy as part of 'the real' (cf. Foucault, 1982b) through the *games of truth*. With the characterisation of this hyperreality, any other kind of reality is indemonstrable. Further, by embracing the principle of nonduality through the philosophical movement of surrealism, there is a sense of momentary 'fixedness' with respect to a particular ir/realis's state in space. As such, the analytical focus is not on reasons for the various changes in types of political economies, but on the *conditions* that make this construction of structural change possible. The constructed existence of these political economies creates a sense of necessity in relation to the need for re-skilling or the acquisition of skills which does not in fact exist in reality; that is, particular types of skills have been made contingent on the pre-existence of these economies. In relation to the desiring subject as discussed in Chapter 3, desire in this instance is the *movement* of the mind into the future; it is non-existential because whatever that is subject to change has no enduring reality. Without a logical foundation for their necessity, the existence of these economies is their justification. The analysis of three separate but interdependent movements in combination makes explicit how metaphors are ideological in so far as they contribute to the construction of a *hyperreality*, that is, the privilege of one understanding of reality over others (cf. Chilton, 1996, p. 74).

The political economies of sur/realism lay emphasis on the bringing together of realities that appear to have limited logical relationship or rational link, to produce conditions of emerging political economies that permit new knowledge and new truths (cf. Adonis, 2005, p. 41). The aim of this analytical chapter is to show how discourse analysis can play a significant role in understanding the reshaping of political economic relations and how this is closely associated with hierarchising and valuing particular types of knowledge (cf. Graham & Luke, 2011, p. 104). Within the broad context, the analyses here argue that political economy/ies emerge from the field of moral philosophy of 'care of the self' and its complex relationships with 'caring for others' (Foucault, 1997, p. 287; cf. Graham, 2005, p. 118; cf. Nietzsche, 1967a, p. 415[1]; cf. Smith, 1759 [2010], p. 99[2]).

Policies inevitably select from among the (economic) possibilities to which every person is susceptible. In doing so, the analysis illustrates how policies contextualise overarching abstractions, especially in how imagined economies are pushing the boundaries of conventional egalitarian-based morality through the use of metaphors. Embroiled in a complex web of interactions, jumping between the past and the future, the persistent tension in political rationality maintained during these years by juxtaposing the duality of reality and sur/reality is one of the profound strategies of constructing particular forms of morality. In this instance, neo-liberal discourse, beyond and within the exhortation of metaphors and human agency, 'focuses not on the players, but on the rules of the game, not the (inner) subjugation of individuals, but on defining and controlling their (outer) environment' (Lemke, 2001, p. 200). As an explicit evolution from the 1979 MOE report, the later policy discourses shift from characterising the individual to constructing the environment, more specifically in changing the social conditions. A prevalent major shift that will be explored in the analysis outlined in this chapter is how, historically, (human) agency fades and is replaced by the *hyperrealism* of global social structure. Hence, whilst Chapters 5 and 6 analyse how discursive movements in policies are enhanced or altered by large-scale global economic trends, the discussion here is concerned with examining the effects of the resulting global changes in education policies.

This marks the point at which the research orientation moves from a concern with construction of the subject to legitimise systemic restriction according to learner abilities, towards a perspective more grounded in the conceptions of objectification of subjects within the context of value-forming labour in relation to the *perceived* demands of political economies. In relation to the 'care of self', as discussed in Chapter 3, the analysis of policy propositions and proposals here alludes to the commodification of labour and is increasingly orientated towards what Foucault (1986, p. 353) argues as 'the way in which people are invited or incited to recognise their moral obligations' through the material pursuit of self and national interests.

More importantly, the use of the metaphors under analysis adds another dimension. The exhortation of these metaphors not only builds a structural contradiction between the rhetoric and practice of economic growth as the game of truth, but constitutes a neo-liberal *distortion* in the way that they contribute to the *construction* of global competition and certain core economic principles and models as inevitable. Within the broader argument of structural inequality, it is argued that within a meritocratic system, the parallel duality in *how* the use of these metaphors are exploited cannot be taken as an indicator of greater 'equality' within the system, and attention is drawn to the ways in which the use of these metaphors operate as moral discourses.

Emergent discourses of an 'innovation-driven' future

The analytic focus of the first theme is on how policy texts draw on and simultaneously reshape political economy/ies so as to incorporate fundamental shifts leading to an 'innovation-driven' future. The micro-meso movement builds on the previous chapter's theme of de/regulation by illustrating the importance of school leaders having greater autonomy within the advent of a 'more competitive and innovation-driven future' (Extract 42, line 2). The meso-macro movement traces the rhetoric of 'innovation-driven future' as an abstract challenge to be met and how this legitimises structural changes. The analysis of both sections illustrates how 'innovation-driven growth' as a strategic goal can be seen as moving through and between the micro, meso, and macro discourses of imagined realities that create the necessity for structural flexibility, diversity, and the provision of choice and opportunity.

Micro-meso movement: flexibility for an innovation-driven growth

In Extract 42 from the 2002 report, policymakers propose an *ability-driven* approach to education for an *innovation*-driven future. More importantly, building on the discussion in the section 'Flexibility to group pupils and decentralising state responsibilities' of Chapter 6, this analysis illustrates how school leaders are imbued with agency through greater autonomy in relation with the transition into this imagined reality: that is, '*school leaders* have been given *greater autonomy* in key areas such as personnel management and development, finance, use of resources and programme development' (lines 6–9), but within the broader context of an 'innovation-driven future' (line 2). 'Innovation-driven growth' as a strategic goal moves through and between the micro and meso discourses of imagined realities that create necessity for structural flexibility.

The first sentence frames the competitiveness agenda through an existential claim: 'TSLN[3] as a *vision* to prepare both our schools and our nation for a more competitive and *innovation*-driven future' (lines 1–2). This formulation exploits the positive semantic prosody (or connotations) of the word 'prepare' (line 1) in the textual context of an economic discourse. Of particular interest are the preferred model of economic growth and its implications for education's role in society (Mulderrig, 2008, p. 158). Here the adjective, 'ability-driven', serves to instil schools with an 'ability-driven approach to education' (line 3) as the agent-driven processes; it functions to embed the social relations of schooling with the global trading practices of an *innovation*-driven capitalism by drawing on the

Extract 42: 2002 MOE Report of the junior college/upper secondary education review committee

Lines	*Text*
1	In 1997, the Prime Minister unveiled TSLN as a vision to prepare both our
2	schools and our nation for a more competitive and *innovation-driven* future.
3	We adopted an ability-driven approach to education, where there is maximal
4	development and harnessing of different talents and abilities. We have moved
5	towards greater customisation within the education system as we seek to
6	maximise the full potential of our students. At the school level, *school*
7	*leaders* have been given *greater autonomy* in key areas such as personnel
8	management and development, finance, use of resources and programme
9	development. Schools are able to customise their programmes and initiatives
10	to suit the needs of their students more **flexibly** and responsively.

Source: MOE, 2002, p. 3.

abstract condition, *competitive* (line 2) (cf. Mulderrig, 2008, p. 158). Less clear, however, is what being competitive in an *innovation*-driven future entails. The *ability-driven* approach to education 'to suit the needs of their students more *flexibly* and responsively' (line 10) is then construed as a vital factor in preparing the nation for a more competitive and innovation-driven future through the 'harnessing of different talents and abilities' (line 4). It is in this context that the power of the rhetoric of 'an innovation-driven future' (line 2) lies in its representation as an abstract challenge to be met, rather than agent-driven processes. The analysis of the meso-macro movement is divided into two sections, indicating the progression of how structural changes are legitimised based on the need to meet the demands of changing political economies from the 2002–2019 policies. Level 1 traces the rhetoric of 'innovation-driven future' and 'innovation-driven growth' as abstract challenges to be met. While aligning education more closely with economic policy goals was projected as a key mechanism for achieving growth from the 2002–2008 policies, it was revealed in 2019 that 'growth driven by the knowledge-based industry' has deepened inequality (Extract 49). Level 2 thus illustrates how an 'enabling' mode of governance is employed as a strategy of persuasion to mitigate possible pushback through the provision of structural opportunities for education and skills training to enhance employability while continuing to contextualise growth as the strategic goal.

Level 1. Meso-macro movement: flexibility, diversity, choice, and opportunities to meet the demands of an innovation-driven future

The previous analysis of the micro-meso movement illustrates how policy texts are involved in drawing on and simultaneously reshaping political economy/ies so as to incorporate fundamental shifts leading to an 'innovation-driven' future. The following meso-macro movement continues to trace the rhetoric of 'innovation-driven future' as an abstract challenge to be met and how this legitimises structural changes through the 2002–2008 policies. In doing so this section highlights the way the theme of 'innovation-driven' future transits from the metaphorical relations of flexibility in the micro-meso movement and evolves in a policy discourse around the necessity for flexibility, diversity, choice, and opportunities to meet the requirements of imagined realities, particularly for junior college students.

Arguments for 'innovation-driven growth' as the strategic goal in policy texts are largely implicit (cf. Fairclough, 2005, p. 21). By contextualising 'innovation-driven growth' as the strategic goal, the following examines the construction of 'innovation-driven future' as an imagined reality. In this respect, the term *innovation* serves as an abstraction that seeks to grasp the totality of the policy shift and describe it all at once (Graham & Paulsen, 2002, p. 449).

In Extracts 43–48, the introduction of 'innovation-driven *growth*' as a strategic goal becomes established on the basis of idealised claims about an 'innovation-driven *future*' as a global-universal reality (cf. Fairclough, 2005, p. 22). Building on the initial micro-meso movement in which the economic imaginary of an 'innovation-driven' future legitimises structural change, the analysis here focuses on how policy texts construct the primary nodal discourse of an 'innovation-driven future' and a secondary nodal discourse of 'the innovation-driven growth' (see Fairclough, 2005, p. 19). According to Fairclough (2005, p. 14), 'nodal' discourses are 'discourses which subsume and articulate in a particular way a great many other discourses' and possess a predictive and descriptive quality. While framing the analysis through movements between, through, and within the meso-macro level, there seems to be no clear and stable relation between the two nodal discourses within the metaphoric relations of flexibility, diversity, choice, and opportunities, overall. However, while they are articulated together in different ways in different texts, there is a primary orientation of reverse engineering through which the predominant features of the rhetorical structure from Extracts 43–48 are arguments that involve a movement from problems to solutions and from *ends* to *means* (Fairclough, 2005, p. 19).

Extracts 43 and 44 are both arguments organised around moving from problem *to* solution. That is, from what 'is' happening to what 'must' be done in response to this imagined context of economic uncertainty and rapid change: from 'an *innovation-driven* future and one of *continuous* change' (Extract 43) and 'a globalised, innovation-driven future' (Extract 44), to the necessary response – that 'We should move towards greater *diversity* and *choice*' (Extract 43), which is what this future 'require[s]' (Extract 44).

Similarly, Extract 45 constructs an argument that involves a movement from ends ('innovation') to means ('require new structures and curricula'), while Extract 46 also involves a movement from ends to means: 'preparing students for a future of innovation-driven growth, and frequent and unpredictable changes in the economic and social environment' by 'equipping them for lifelong learning and creating their own *opportunities*'.

Extracts 43 to 48: Flexibility, diversity, choice, and opportunities through MOE policy texts 2002–2008

Need for greater **diversity**

We should move towards greater **diversity** and **choice** in the JC/Upper Secondary education landscape, in the form of different programmes, mix of schools and alternative qualifications. There is no single formula for preparing our young for an innovation-driven future and one of continuous change. We want students to leave our school system with a variety of educational experiences, and with **diverse** approaches to learning. A more **diverse** education system will also allow us to better cater to the different interests and talents of our students.

(Extract 43, MOE, 2002, p. 23)

The new JC curriculum will be more broad-based and better suited to nurturing the skills, spirit and values required for a globalised, innovation-driven future. The changes to the JC/Upper Secondary education landscape will inject greater **diversity**, vibrance and **choice** in the types of programmes and mix of schools, and will offer new pathways to a university education.

(Extract 44, MOE, 2002, p. vii)

We should build on the strengths of the current system, and transit to the next phase of development in our education system. The focus of education must shift from efficiency to **diversity**, from knowing to thinking, and from fitting people to specific jobs to equipping them for lifelong learning and creating their own **opportunities**.

Changes and improvements in recent years, including the 'Thinking Schools, Learning Nation' initiative, have set in motion new mindsets in schools and JCs, better oriented to innovation. However, further improvements in the quality of the JC and secondary school system will require new structures and curricula, not just new methods and technologies.

(Extract 45, MOE, 2002, p. i.)

Going forward, we face the challenge of preparing students for a future of innovation-driven growth, and frequent and unpredictable changes in the economic and social environment. We have to re-gear our secondary school and JC system, and align it with changes in the university system. The focus of education must shift from efficiency to **diversity**, from knowing to thinking, and from fitting people to specific jobs to equipping them for lifelong learning and creating their own **opportunities**.

(Extract 46, MOE, 2002, p. ii)

This is why **diversity** and **flexibility** has become the leitmotif of the education system. It is not a passing theme. The changes that we are making in education, step by step, are the way we are preparing young Singaporeans for the innovation-driven workplace. It is how we will make our living in the world.

(Extract 47, Shanmugaratnam, 2006 speech, n.p.)

The Government has accepted the recommendations set out in your Committee's Report. The review is timely as the Singapore economy forges ahead to create new knowledge and innovation-driven industries. The recommendations present bold moves that will enable Singapore's university sector to continue to meet the needs of our fast-changing economy, while also providing more **opportunities** for young Singaporeans who can benefit from tertiary education.

On behalf of the Government, I thank you and your Committee for your efforts in crafting a bold vision of our long-term university landscape that, when implemented, will allow more Singaporeans to benefit from a high-quality university education, as well as enhance Singapore's position as a vibrant education hub for the region.

(Extract 48, MOE, 2008a, n.p.)

The rhetorical structures in the texts constitute a frame within which diverse discourses of 'innovation-driven', 'diversity', 'choice', and 'opportunities' are articulated together in particular ways. Relations are textured (textually constituted) between these discourses. Of particular interest here, is the placing of expressions that are associated with different discourses in relations of 'equivalence' (Fairclough, 2003, p. 88). For instance, in Extract 46, the formulation of 'innovation-driven growth' sets up a relation of equivalence between 're-gear our secondary school and JC system and align it with changes in the university system', 'efficiency to *diversity*', 'knowing to thinking', 'lifelong learning' and 'creating their own *opportunities*'. More precisely: there is a what Fairclough (2005, p. 20) calls a 'comitative' structure which sets up a relation of equivalence between the first and other two sentences, all as attributes of 'a future of innovation-driven growth'.

Extract 47, on the other hand, involves a movement from a means to an end: '*diversity* and *flexibility* has become the leitmotif of the education system' in order to prepare 'young Singaporeans for the innovation-driven workplace. It is how we will make our living in the world.' In identifying flexibility as part of a global and globalising policy discourse, *flexibility* and *diversity*, 'the leitmotif of the education system' (Edwards, Nicoll & Tait 1999, p. 619), are largely positioned as a necessary response by individuals to meet the competitive demands of the 'innovation-driven workplace'. 'Flexibility' and 'diversity' as the means to this end are amongst the conditions, out of all possibilities, the system must meet. Within the logic of this prevailing political imaginary, it follows that the education system *must* be adequately *flexible* and *diverse* in order to be responsive to the changing conditions created by global competition. Here the inclusive 'we' assumes shared (neo-liberal) values and serves as the rationale for the government's policy decisions in ensuring the relevance of the workforce (Mulderrig, 2012, pp. 714–716): 'It is how we will make our living in the world' (Extract 47). The reference to the 'innovation economy' (Fairclough, 2003, p. 45) also assumes that there is an 'innovation-driven workplace' (Extract 47) and that 'young Singaporeans' must be prepared for jobs within it (Extract 47).

Extract 48 returns to an ends-to-means structure, moving from the need to 'meet the needs of our fast-changing economy, while also providing more opportunities for young Singaporeans who can benefit from tertiary education' and 'enhance Singapore's position as a vibrant education hub for the region' to the means of governance for achieving them. As part of a discourse of social change (Fairclough, 2005, pp. 21–22), 'innovation-driven industries' are then to be *implicitly* established as Singapore's strategic goal on essentially *extraneous* grounds. The grounds for this strategic goal are the benefits they bring as an existing reality while the commitment to this strategic goal is to '*create new knowledge* and innovation-driven industries' and 'allow more Singaporeans to benefit from a high-quality university education as well as enhance Singapore's position as a vibrant education hub for the region'. These claimed *potential* effects and benefits are presented as if they were *actual* effects and benefits to 'meet the needs of our fast-changing economy'.

In line with Fairclough's (2005, pp. 20–21) analysis of the role of discourse in processes of 'transition', the discourse forms around and argues that the formulation of problems, the strategic goal, and the strategies for achieving it, involve a process of articulating discourses which represent the economy ('innovation driven growth' as the strategic goal) with discourses which represent economic and social policies: 'equipping them for lifelong learning and creating their own opportunities' (Extract 46), 'how we will make our living in the world' (Extract 47), and 'enhance Singapore's position as a vibrant education hub for the region' (Extract 48).

Diverse policy areas and associated discourses (e.g., full employability, competitiveness) are articulated together in particular relations within the nodal discourse of an 'innovation-driven future' (cf. Fairclough, 2005, p. 20). That is, this is an argument towards a nodal discourse where various forms of discourse, intersecting with others in subtle ways, are employed and put to use in the omnirelevant discourse of 'innovation-driven future'. By subsuming various forms of configurations of economics under a single heading, possible intersections and shades with other discourses have been obfuscated. The general result of these metaphorical evaluative transfers as they move within and through the meso-macro levels is to focus attention on the 'possibilities arising from general claims about economic and social change and the strategies for realising them' (Fairclough, 2005, pp. 23–24).

Level 2. Meso-macro movement: 'enabling' as a strategy of persuasion

Building on the first two sections of analysis, the third section examines the recent emergence of the more devolved, 'enabling' mode of governance through two 2019 policy speeches made by Minister of Education Ong Ye Kung and Second Minister for Education Indranee Rajah. The analysis focuses on the extent to which the government acts as the instigator or controller of others' actions to achieve economic aims through education policy discourse. In particular, the analysis examines how the metaphor of 'opportunity' is used to build a rationale for systemic change within the education system through the ethical-political discourse of 'growth', and where the causal relation between the policy problem and policy solution is presented through the idea of the 'enabling state' (Mulderrig, 2014, p. 441). Framed in the rhetoric of reciprocity, the idea of an 'enabling' model of governance is a contractual relation between workers and state, in which the state provides structural opportunities for education and acquisition of skills which the individual is expected to utilise for achieving economic growth and to enhance employability (Mulderrig, 2014, p. 441).

Overcoming the skills divide: from problem of unemployment to vision plan

In line with Fairclough's (2006a, pp. 8–9) analysis on the relationship between economic activities and moral dispositions and norms, in Extract 49, 'growth' is here specified as 'driven by the knowledge-based industry', and is the best of all

Extracts 49 to 52: Opportunities and skills through MOE 2019 policy speeches

In an era where growth is driven by the knowledge-based industry in which the well-educated and exceptionally talented reap more rewards than others, economic and social benefits quickly accrue to those at the top. This is exacerbated by rapid technological advancement. The structure of our economy, like that of many others, is seeing rapid change driven by technology, automation and AI. Some of these changes have had the effect of worsening wage dispersion, threatening to deepen the divide between higher-skilled and lower-skilled workers. Lower-skilled workers risk being shut off from the new **opportunities** being created.

(Extract 49, Rajah, 2019 speech, n.p.)

This government will strive to ensure that no one, no matter the conditions of his or her birth, will be denied the **opportunities** to improve the conditions of their life. We will make sure that all are enabled to take advantage of the **opportunities** we provide in education, **skills** training, housing and other relevant areas. This is what we mean by an **enabling** meritocracy.

(Extract 50, Rajah, 2019 speech, n.p.)

But broadening meritocracy does not mean lowering of standards. We still take pride in working hard, excelling, and maintaining high standards in everything we do. That is what accords Singapore and Singaporeans the good reputation we enjoy internationally. What we want to ensure is that standards for something as complex as human capability and potential are not measured with one single ruler – academic excellence – there must be other rulers and other yardsticks.

(Extract 51, Ong, 2019 speech, n.p.)

That is why we are making comprehensive adjustments throughout the entire education system – from the PSLE[4] scoring system, the basis for Direct School Admission, and admission to polytechnics and universities. When we talk about the SkillsFuture movement, it is much more than just training programmes. Underlying it is the principle of valuing people of different aptitudes and strengths, and recognising diverse talents. It is an approach already used in many industries and companies. Many start-ups and technology companies mostly recruit based on **skills**, not academic results. Artificial Intelligence (AI) will in time help employers sieve out applicants with the right **skills**, which will make sorting solely by academic grades outdated and ineffective. When I speak to CEOs, almost everyone agrees that they have to hire based on **skills** and not just academic grades, so I think the impediments to better hiring policies today are largely operational in nature, and will be overcome with time.

(Extract 52, Ong, 2019 speech, n.p.)

assumed (or implied) goods for this economic system. What is never questioned is that 'growth' is the main objective of economic activity, and it is claimed or assumed that economic and social benefits come from 'growth'. Here is it assumed that economic activity which results in growth is ethical, with scant regard for consequences in terms of 'worsening wage dispersion' and 'lower-skilled workers being shut off from the new opportunities being created'. So the tension, or contradiction, is between the representation of 'knowledge-based industry' as the engine of endogenous growth which cannot, and should not be stopped, and as a set of policies which need to be argued for, especially given the risk of a backlash of 'lower-skilled workers being shut off' (cf. Fairclough, 2006a, p. 11). This contradiction can be seen as arising from the Singapore government's determination on the one hand to stick to its industrial positions while also minimising the damage to their credibility and risk lower-skilled workers being 'shut off'. These issues touch on an overarching and very delicate problem: the interplay between the dialogism of opportunity discourse.

'Enabling' model of governance

Extracts 49 to 52 illustrate the ubiquitous, centripetal movement of power towards an 'enabling' model in which the individual assumes the weight of the responsibility to improve their own social and economic conditions, and employability, while the government takes on a more managerial and devolved, centrifugal form of power through the provision of structural *opportunities* for others to act (Mulderrig, 2014, p. 450).

In Extract 49, Rajah narrates a tension in the state that requires radical change in the internal organisation of the state and its articulation with the economy. Having diagnosed the economic problem in terms of a 'deepen[ing] … divide between higher-skilled and lower-skilled workers' arising from the 'rapid change driven by technology, automation and AI', an opening was created for a new mode of educational management inspired by industrial practices (Extract 52). While she does not fully specify the economic imagery underpinning such a policy, it does indicate an uncertain, rapidly changing and competitive economy, which not only frames the proposals in education policy but also (re)produces a new economic regime and reinforces the legitimacy of 'new' educational practices in Extract 52. While such 'rapid change' necessarily produces losers and thus social divisions through 'worsening wage dispersion' (Extract 49), the neo-liberal argument would be that these are temporary; in the long run the government's intervention in 'making sure that all are enabled to take advantage of the opportunities' (Extract 50) would lift 'lower-skilled workers' as whole. This can be seen as a 'catch-all' and 'cure-all' concept – *enable everyone to take advantage of the opportunities* (Extract 50) to address the social divide and widening wage dispersion (Extract 49). This despite the paradox that, 'SkillsFuture *movement*' (Extract 52) suggests that the weight of the responsibility for securing continuing employment shifts to the individual. That is, in an era where the economy is driven by technology, the central role of governments is no longer in guaranteeing full employment but in enhancing employability (Mulderrig, 2014, p. 441). One of the main policy instruments to achieve this is through training programmes (Extract 52) where workers are expected to respond quickly to changing business needs. No other possibility is entertained. That is, it is saying that people need to take advantage of the opportunities in *specific ways* that the government 'provides' (Extract 50) for the desirable outcome of growth (Extract 49) or risk being unemployed (Extract 49).

Stemming from a management discourse (Mulderrig, 2008, pp. 153–162), in Extract 51, these specific ways are textured through the prominence of *standards* as a keyword fits with a 'narration of crisis' in state education, and indicate a managerialist concern with centralising controls over the outputs of education and the types of skills people should acquire. The example here is a proposal for an expansive performance management and assessment system to appraise human capability and potential. The managing action, *ensure*, constructs a steering role over educational practices, setting targets for excellence, and entails rendering measuring standards for 'human capability and potential' amenable to calculation and comparison as a condition of progress. Through this process of standardisation, human dimensions and potential become restricted and limited by the production of goods for economic gain, and is therefore intimately associated with the question of hegemony. However, the verb *want* is used to modalise the actions represented for *we*, thereby absolving the government from making a full commitment. That is, the government determines the target to be achieved and benchmarks progress – although exactly how to accomplish this is unclear – while ensuring conformity and compliance to normative *standards*.

In particular, in line with Mulderrig's (2014) analysis, rather than being the direct agent of processes, in this case, the government is the instigator or controller of others' actions. The government assumes a managing role X (make sure, all are enabled, provide) with the implied power relation and causal assumption that 'without X, Y could not do it' (p. 463). Thus, through the state 'managing actions', governmental power functions in a subtly hegemonic way, making assumptions about the desirability of the proposed policy actions and about the willingness of diverse actors to be managed in *particular ways* under predetermined conditions (p. 464). This is essentially a discursive process of hegemonic generalisation, whereby responsibility for fostering the ideal conditions aimed at continued economic value creation in the current phase of the knowledge-based industry is *spread to all of us*, in the form of a set of imperatives – to reinvent ourselves as highly-skilled workers as *lower-skilled workers risk being shut off from the new opportunities*. These *opportunities*, however, are overtly spatial in their constitution, in the sense that they are attributed to technological advances. This benefit appears from nowhere and we can only assume that they are causally related. They are presented metaphorically as the spatial aspects of surrealistic states; as the result of future ways of enacting hyperrealist spaces (cf. Fairclough, 2000, cited in Graham, 2001a, p. 771).

The discourse of skills as opportunities

In Extract 52, we come to the end of this evaluative chain with the necessity for institutional 'reform' to align education policy more closely with economic policy goals. The necessity of educational change, which has already been established based on the desirable effects of technology, is transferred to 'comprehensive adjustments' because 'hiring based on skills and not just academic grades' (Extract 52) is presented as an intrinsic property of *new opportunities* (Extract 49). To establish the organisational weight of *new opportunities* as an evaluation for the desirability and importance of comprehensive adjustments to the entire education system (Extract 52), it is helpful to trace out the elements that are most explicitly inscribed with evaluations in Extract 49 (cf. Graham, 2002, pp. 247–248).

Overall, *rapid technological advancement* is presented as having both positive and negative effects upon society. We are told that 'technology, automation and AI' have the 'effect of worsening wage dispersion' and threaten 'to deepen the divide between higher-skilled and lower-skilled workers'. But this undesirable effect is indirectly offset by 'new opportunities being created'. That is, negative outcomes are offset by new opportunities (cf. Graham, 2002, 248). Without this evaluator, there would be no solution to the problems of technological advancement identified by the speaker. Technology would otherwise appear solely as the cause of widening wage dispersion and social divide and would offer no mitigation. The desirability of *new opportunities* dominates the evaluation and propagates throughout Extracts 49–50. The desirability of *new opportunities* (Extract 49), counterposed to the undesirability of unemployment ('shut off') for *lower-skilled workers*, and the importance of acquiring new skills to adapt to the exogeneous effects of new technology, is translated into the necessity for policymakers to act on behalf of the whole country ('will strive to ensure', Extract 50).

Paradoxically, in this sense, desirable opportunities are problematised to bring forth an evaluated proposal: there needs to be 'comprehensive adjustments throughout the entire education system' (Extract 52) if the *new opportunities* of technology (previously presented as unmitigated 'effects') are to be realised (Extract 49) (Graham, 2002, p. 250). Thus, a policy framework that is designed to facilitate the positive effects of technology becomes necessary. So, what were construed as inevitable effects in Extract 49 now become *opportunities* for benefits to be realised. Hence, the use of the metaphor of 'opportunities' in conjunction with these conditions for employability and the individual pursuit of social and economic benefits (Extract 49) does not only entail individuals being responsive to change; it also means they have higher levels of responsibility about the ways in which they learn to stay adaptable and competitive. The provision of *new opportunities* is not, however, guaranteed, but rather is subject to 'being created' (Extract 49), though the processes that produce *new opportunities*, and the agents involved, are absent.

Despite not having a productive agent, *new opportunities* are seen as desirable (Extract 49) through counterpoising the undesirability of unemployment ('shut off') for *lower-skilled workers*. At this point, if we accept the major premises of evaluation, it becomes a matter of 'common sense' that education is oriented towards addressing the perceived needs of these industries, and that hiring policies become oriented towards re-education of the population if the Singapore economy is to reap the 'economic and social benefits' (Extract 49) of new technologies. This evaluative 'logic' elides the need for justification or to elaborate further on the desirability of skills training programmes, the undesirability of 'shutting off lower-skilled workers', or warrantability of the claim that new technologies will result in 'new opportunities being created' (Extract 49). All these are presupposed as facts.

Extract 52 illustrates a substantive shift in schools policy rhetoric towards the centrality of education and training strategies in shaping and securing responsive strategic policy action on the part of the government for a knowledge economy (*making comprehensive adjustments throughout the entire education system*). A key theme running through the text is education's central aim of producing a better skilled workforce, and in an escalating rhetoric about the links between an integrated system of education, training programmes, and the need to safeguard future 'employability' through the accumulation of skills and qualifications as assets (*almost everyone agrees that they have to hire based on skills and not just academic grades*).

The closer link forged between the worlds of schooling and of work is also evidenced in the invocation of CEOs in Extract 52 as key social actors as they set global strategies to be implemented by national governments (Mulderrig, 2008, p. 159). The vision of a state and society actively adjusting to the ephemeral and unstable phenomena of 'valuing people of different aptitudes and strengths, and recognising diverse talents' is informed by the policy paradigms that rest on 'many start-ups and technology companies'. This reverse-engineering approach of the industrial, commodity-based framework suggests that unless a particular form of knowledge labour is oriented towards what *already* exists in industrial commodity forms (Extract 52), it is unlikely to attract investment (Graham, 2005, p. 124). Shaped by the tenets of neo-liberalism and its technological biases, implicit in this conception is a dedication to the creation of a knowledge labour that is committed to the production of *particular* commodities, and that this activity must be oriented towards net economic gain (Extracts 49 and 52) (Graham, 2005, pp. 124–125).

Thus, in articulating 'hiring policies', the government acts as social agents for conformity to managerial models of organisation as they implement strategies heavily informed by the logic and needs of business, as articulated by the producers of business knowledge, the CEOs. This accords labour market subordination of education to economic policy, in which students from primary school to university represent a crucial object of intervention in eroding the distinction between education and work through the metaphor of opportunities.

Transitioning of economies and competition

To realise national strategies, the texturing of a relationship between the 'global' and 'national' in policy discourse takes on an important role (Fairclough, 2010, p. 285). In order to illuminate the nexus between the actual and potential processes and the representation of the political economies, this second theme aims to analyse the metaphor of flexibility in the micro-meso movement and the transliteration of this metaphor through other rhetorical strategies in the meso-macro movement. In doing so, the analysis in the micro-meso movement reveals the representations and discourses of political economies through the metaphor of flexibility. Here it is argued that the metaphor does not merely construe the processes and tendencies of the political economies; they are also closely linked to the creation of actual/potential processes of these economies in complex and contingent ways.

The second part of this theme demonstrates how the utilisation of the metaphor of flexibility in the micro-meso movement is made implicit in the meso-macro movement. In this movement, the metaphor of flexibility working at the micro-meso level is superseded by other rhetorical strategies at the meso-macro level. This discussion helps to understand how the architectural grid is destabilised as the principal axis of analysis that draws on metaphors no longer stands, in this case by defining them out of existence. Justification for structural changes is drawn from the use of rhetorical strategies instead. Overall, this meso-macro movement demonstrates the complexity of reframing how the metaphor is implicitly utilised.

Micro-meso movement: ability-driven system for innovation economy

The analysis below focuses on the construction of 'truth' (through evaluations) around the central ideas of the (neo-liberal) innovation economy and education. What can be observed initially is that rather than foregrounding *flexible* learning in an ability-driven system, increased flexibility within the education system is now pushed to the fore as a necessary response to future economic and global uncertainty (Nicoll, 2006, p. 29). What is clear is that such arguments construe education policy as subordinate to or even dialectically related to economic policy. This section presents a context in which the focus is on the analysis of the connections between education, ethical practice, and economics.

In the following extract from a 2006 speech by T. Shanmugaratnam, then Minister for Education and second Minister for Finance, the analysis examines how the metaphor of flexibility in the micro-meso movement is used to build a rationale for systemic change through the ethical-political discourse of 'progress' and the transliteration of this metaphor through other rhetorical strategies in the meso-macro movement to provide legitimacy for institutional changes. The general result of *metaphorical evaluative transfers* in these policy genres is to create evaluations for high degrees of necessity in re-skilling, which are almost invariably transferred – quite directly – from high degrees of importance in relation to changing types of (global) political economies.

Extract 53 illustrates the relationship between actual/potential *processes* of the innovation economy and *representations* of the innovation economy (i.e., '*flexible*, flatter and more agile organisations', line 6) (Fairclough, 2009, p. 318). In broad terms, the analysis argues that representations and discourses of the innovation economy through the metaphor of *flexible* do not merely construe processes and tendencies of the innovation economy that are happening independently; they also actively contribute to creating and shaping actual/potential processes of the innovation economy, though in 'complex and contingent ways' (Fairclough, 2009, p. 318). That is, in examining how the term has been appropriated, discourses of the 'innovation economy' (line 8) are situated within a complex of other discourses – the counter-discourse of the 'old economy' (line 4), for instance – that form their conditions of existence. The reduction of rational action to neat contrasts between both these economies will be scrutinised.

Extract 53: 2006 speech by T. Shanmugaratnam

Lines	*Text*
	The fluidity that we are injecting into our ability-driven system is not just a matter of educational philosophy. It mirrors the way the workplace is moving, in the innovation-driven industries that we must insert ourselves in. The organisational structures that were well suited to the old economy with strict hierarchies and distinctions between employees with different skills, are being replaced by more **flexible**, flatter and more agile organisations. Up and down the line, every worker has to deal with some complexity, learn to multi-task, and be willing to learn new skills quickly. That's how the innovation economy works. Stay agile, and work in teams, or you're out of the game.

Source: Shanmugaratnam, 2006, n.p.)

The text relates to the concerns of this chapter: the way in which the global and the national are constructed and how the relationship between them is characteristically neo-liberal. The term 'neo-liberal' here denotes the dominant political position within current *discontinuous*, impermanent transformations of capitalism, as they transition from one network to another (Fairclough, 2010, p. 285). Drawing on Fairclough's (2010, p. 285) approach, 'in using the term "texturing", the analysis highlights the "work" that is done textually, i.e. the textual "working up" of that relationship'. The text producer is writing about, and texturing a relationship between, 'the old economy' (line 4) and 'the innovation economy' (line 8), and between an 'ability-driven system' (line 1) and 'the workplace is moving, in the innovation-driven industries that we must insert ourselves in' (lines 2–3). This is akin to what Fairclough (2010, p. 285) refers to as two different 'space-times': the global space-time and the national space-time. The analysis illustrates how these space-times are constructed, and then on how they are textured together. More importantly, it explores how the text producer construes responsibilities to adapt to innovation-driven industries as 'caring for the self' (Foucault, 1997, p. 282) and sets up relations between private morality and education policy. As such, there are positive evaluations for the new-ness of the innovation economy, whereas the 'old' economy is associated with negative evaluations of doing things that are perceived as 'barriers' to individual and national progress (Graham, 2001a, p. 773).

In line with Fairclough's (2001, p. 100) analysis on the metaphorical representation of social problems, the metaphorical construction of organisations as 'flexible' suggests an ideological attachment to systemic efficiency. Notice it incorporates a metaphor for 'flexible' (line 6) itself, as a requirement for 'complexity' (line 7), 'multi-task' (line 7), and 'new skills' (line 8). This development of the educational institution as a 'system' (line 1) for 'innovation-driven industries' (line 3) insinuates that learners' learning capacities could be manufactured, together with educational practices that emphasise agility (i.e., 'stay agile', line 9). The argument for the discourse of flexibility concerns the relationships between institutional structure and learning capacity: that is, '*flexible*, flatter and more agile organisations' (line 6) and 'every worker has to deal with some complexity, learn to multi-task, and be willing to learn new skills quickly' (lines 7–8), respectively.

Both these issues touch on an overarching and very delicate problem: the interplay between the dialogism of flexibility discourse. The use of the term 'every worker' in relation to '*flexible*, flatter and more agile organisations' (line 6) thus attempts to solve the ideological dilemma of 'injecting fluidity' (line 1) into 'ability-driven' (line 1) systemic policies by a strategy of 'fluid' or '*flexible*' educational pathways, seeking the exclusion of those who are not able to 'insert' (line 3) themselves into the 'innovation economy' (line 8), that is: 'Stay agile, and work in teams or you're out of the game' (line 9). While couched as well-intentioned advice, it implies the opposite. This strategy serves to make up a kind of ideological background which can be regarded as mental representations of the public's 'common-sense' views in conceptualising parallel realities between students and workers who are not able to cope with the (flexible) system, constructed as not being able to deal 'with some complexity' (line 7), not being able to 'learn to multi-task' (line 7), and not be 'willing to learn new skills quickly' (line 8). In effect, this strategy reproduces discriminatory educational and social ideologies (Fairclough, 2001, pp. 73, 131; Fowler, 1991, pp. 122–124). Flexible accumulation within this context means greater flexibility in the workforce (extensive reskilling of workers) (Fairclough, 2010, p. 545). The discourse of flexible accumulation enters complex and shifting configurations of the political economy.

The representations of the global economy as 'innovation-driven industries' (line 3) are presented here as social actors in the representation of the innovation economy. The new innovation economy is represented as an arena of competition between workers; 'actually the claim goes rather further: it is that *successful* workers in an innovation economy depend on *fairness of the rule*' (Fairclough, 2000a, p. 43). This is illustrated by the direct assertion, 'Stay agile, and work in teams or you're out of the game' (line 9) in the sense that it is those workers who are highly skilled and enterprising that will succeed. This is an important step in the logic of the 'ability-driven system' (line 1): if Singapore is forced into an increasingly intensive competition in the innovation economy whose nature is unquestionable and unchangeable, then enabling/empowering future workers to 'deal with some complexity, learn to multi-task, and be willing to learn new skills quickly' (lines 7–8) becomes the primary task for the government. However, the agency is rather more complex. Drawing on Fairclough's (2000a, pp. 63–64) analysis of social exclusion as an effect of flexibility, it is up to the government to provide 'fluidity' (line 1) that 'mirrors the way the workplace is moving' (line 2) through an 'ability-driven system' (line 1). People have a 'right' to this education system; but they also have the 'responsibility' to 'Stay agile, and work in teams' (line 9), but only within the parameters set by the government through the innovation-driven industries that 'we must insert ourselves in' (line 3).

The use of the inclusive 'we' is significant here. In proposing that 'we must insert ourselves in' (line 3) provides a reduction that serves corporate ideologies which stress the unity of the people at the expense of recognition of divisions or conflicts of (self) interest. Within the inclusive use of 'we', it is significant that the verb *must* is used in line 3. It conveys the personal authority of the speaker and places the text producer in an authoritative position with respect to what must be done (Fairclough, 2001, p. 151), even though it is not made explicit whether this should be done by the government or by the addressee(s). This is again, as highlighted in the previous section, essentially a discursive process of hegemonic generalisation, whereby responsibility for surviving in an innovation economy is spread to *all of us*, in the form of a set of imperatives – to reinvent *ourselves* as *flexible* and competitive beings (Mulderrig, 2008, p. 158) within the innovation-driven industries.

The use of the metaphor *flexible*, in conjunction with these conditions for employability and individual pursuit of economic interests, does not only entail individuals being responsive to change; it also means they have more decisions about the ways in which they learn to stay adaptable and competitive, as the provision of labour opportunities itself becomes more flexible. To be an enterprising individual in the context of an 'innovation-driven industry', more flexible forms of self-learning within the work organisation need to take place. The text thus interweaves a moral discourse of 'care of the self' (Foucault, 1981b) and labour market participation. In the case of economic *necessity*, it then becomes a matter of *self-preservation* (cf. Nietzsche, 1909, p. 102). It is thus that the flexibility of mobile subjects becomes the ethical goal to be achieved through an ability-driven education system. The changes are coerced by a projection of new global imperatives (not just possibilities) for meeting the tasks of survival in the present finitude. And it is to this finitude and these sorts of tasks to which changes in the education system must relate (Olssen, 2006, p. 229).[5]

But the main point for present purposes is that 'change is represented as an unstructured list of effects' (Fairclough, 2001, p. 212). Significantly, the processes that produce these effects, and the agents involved in those processes from the 'old economy' to 'innovation economy', are absent (Fairclough, 2001, p. 212). In line with Fairclough's (2001, pp. 212–213) analysis on the tendency towards 'codification' in the globalisation of discourse, for instance, 'are being replaced by' (lines 5–6) represents insecurity of employment as a simple matter of fact (using what is probably best seen as an attribution process – although 'replaced' is a verb, it functions more like an attributive adjective), rather than as the result of decisions taken to serve particular interests.

Meso-macro movement: drawing on abstract actors and nominalisations as agents of the global economy to legitimise structural changes for talents

The micro-meso movement illustrates how the metaphor of flexibility does not merely construe processes and tendencies of the political economies, but how it is also closely linked to the creation of actual/potential processes of these economies in complex and contingent ways. By tracing this theme in the 2002–2012 policy documents, the meso-macro movement illustrates how the use of the metaphor is superseded by other rhetorical strategies. That is, justification for structural changes for the 'better able' students or talents (i.e., junior college and university students) is based on the use of rhetorical strategies instead. Overall, this meso-macro movement demonstrates the complexity of reframing how the metaphor is implicitly utilised. In doing so, this movement highlights the way the themes of transition and competition evolve in a policy discourse around the necessity of the acquisition of particular skills to meet the challenges of imagined realities.

Whilst the micro-meso movement demonstrates the utilisation of the metaphor of flexibility, the overall goal of this chapter is to demonstrate how the use of this metaphor is not explicit but implicit within the theme. In this movement, the metaphor of flexibility working at the micro-meso level is superseded by other rhetorical strategies at the meso-macro level. These strategies are, first, the cascade of change and the logic of appearances and, second, competition between nations. The architectural grid is then destabilised: as the principal axis of analysis that draws on metaphors no longer stands, in this case by (re)defining them as non-existent. In contrast to the term 'sub micro-meso-macro movements' used in the section 'Flexible system for VITB trainees' of Chapter 5, here the term 'rhetorical strategies' refers to the ways in which rationalities of policy discourse are not necessarily drawn on the explicit use of metaphors. In contrast, the term 'sub-movements' in Chapter 5 denotes the examination of justifications that are explicitly drawn on the use of the metaphor.

To further explore the complex and shifting configurations of *change*, this section examines how both the *actual* and *potential* are being prefigured in policy discourses, through abstract actors and nominalisations, to form the foundations of other emerging political economies.

The cascade of change and the logic of appearances

There are various processes and social actors represented in the texts below, which will be discussed later, but the following section will first focus on processes involving agents of a more abstract and impersonal character in the global economy (Fairclough, 2000a, p. 26). For example, in these extracts from the 2002, 2008, and 2012 policy documents:

Notice the metaphorical character of these processes: 'change' in Extracts 54 to 57 implies inevitability; as that which Singaporeans must be 'versatile' and 'resilient' (Extract 57) to; and as a place they can 'thrive' and 'support' (Extract 57) and 'compete' (Extract 57). Interestingly, the 'sophisticated economy' is positioned as an environment that Singaporeans 'must support' (Extract 57). The inevitability of change is also implicit in the representation of its consistency, 'frequent and unpredictable' (Extract 54) and 'continuous' (Extract 55).

Within these texts, the word 'change' is used not as a verb but as a noun and hence is represented not as a process but rather as a causal entity in other processes. The use of the noun serves to background the processes themselves, and backgrounds questions of agency and causality, of who or what causes change

Extracts 54 to 57: Agents of the global economy through MOE policy texts 2002–2012a

... a future of innovation-driven growth, and frequent and unpredictable **changes** in the economic and social environment.

(Extract 54, MOE, 2002, p. ii)

... innovation-driven future and one of continuous **change**.

(Extract 55, MOE, 2002, p. 23)

The last five years have seen significant **changes** in our economy.

(Extract 56, MOE, 2008a, p. 5)

In an increasingly dynamic and interconnected global environment, there is a need to review our higher education policies to ensure that they remain robust enough to respond to new global challenges of greater complexity.

Singaporeans must be more highly-skilled, versatile and resilient to **change**, to thrive in and support an increasingly sophisticated economy, and compete effectively with a highly-mobile international talent pool.

(Extract 57, MOE, 2012a, p. 16)

(Fairclough, 2000a, p. 26). Yet the changes listed were largely made by decisions on the part of business and economics.

The absence of responsible agents for these economic changes further contributes to the sense that change is inevitable. In line with Fairclough's (2000a, p. 27) analysis on abstract actors and 'nominalisations', one of the effects of nominalisation is that 'change' is construed as an external force, over which individuals have no control. This is evident in the four choices that are given for responding to change: to be 'versatile' and 'resilient' to change, to 'thrive in' and 'support' (Extract 57). These changes are objectivised, represented as generalised, intangible 'phenomena' that are inescapable quasi-natural processes of 'change' rather than actions by special social actors (cf. van Leeuwen, 1995, p. 82). At the same time, they are also represented as affecting Singaporeans. Thus, the change in economies themselves remains an unexamined and unexaminable given, while the reactions to them are represented through tangible structural proposals, as though they should be 'our' main focus of attention.

Competition between nations

In Extracts 56 and 57, again from the 2008a and 2012a policies, the global economy is pervasively represented in the language of policy discourse as an arena of competition between nation-states. The main social actors in global economic competition are represented as nation-states and individuals, rather than multinational corporations. This is an important step in the logic of education policy discourse: if Singapore and Singaporeans are forced into increasingly intensive competition in a global economy whose nature is unquestionable and unchangeable, then in the words of Extract 57, reviewing 'our higher education policies to ensure that they remain robust enough to respond to new global challenges of greater complexity' becomes the primary task of the government.

Extracts 56 and 57: Economic and business decision-making through MOE policy texts 2008 and 2012a

---

As Singapore's economy has grown and evolved, Singapore's publicly-funded university sector has continued to provide a large proportion of the graduate manpower needed to power our industries. It also serves to attract talented international students to study in Singapore, many of whom choose to stay and contribute to our country.

The last five years have seen significant changes in our economy and in the university sector. There is growing demand for highly-skilled graduate manpower as our economy moves increasingly into knowledge-based, high value-added activities such as research and development. At the same time, Singapore faces increasingly fierce competition from other countries for talented students and graduates.

(Extract 56, MOE, 2008a, p. 5)

To prepare Singaporeans and Singapore for the future economy.

In an increasingly dynamic and interconnected global environment, there is a need to review our higher education policies to ensure that they remain robust enough to respond to new global challenges of greater complexity. Singaporeans must be more highly-skilled, versatile and resilient to change, to thrive in and support an increasingly sophisticated economy, and compete effectively with a highly-mobile international talent pool. The review is thus in line with the recommendations of the 2010 Economic Strategies Committee (ESC), which stressed that 'Singapore's future rests on growing a deep pool of highly capable and entrepreneurial people'. To this end, the ESC recommended that tertiary institutions must develop professionals with 'T-shaped' competencies, so that they possess both the in-depth skills required of their particular disciplines, and broad-based knowledge of other related areas, in order to operate in different environments.

(Extract 57, MOE, 2012a, p. 16)

Although the above policy discourse represents competition and 're-skilling' as complementary aspects of the changing economies, there are apparent contradictions (Fairclough, 2000a, p. 32). Accounts of the global economy as a field of competition between nation-states, through the assertion that 'Singapore faces increasingly *fierce competition* from other countries for talented students and graduates' (Extract 56) construct both students and graduates as subject to abstract, threatening processes of 'change' which they cannot control. Further, the propositions that 'The last five years have seen significant changes in our economy' (Extract 56) and that 'our economy *moves increasingly* into knowledge-based, high-value added activities such as research and *development*' (Extract 56) presuppose that this movement is simply a matter of fact. As far as irrealis policies are concerned, changing economies are agents that are profoundly transformative, all-encompassing, and borrowing from the words of Graham (2002, p. 258, italics included) '*exogeneously acting* phenomena' that determine the skills we should acquire, 'seemingly regardless of *what* we do'. This limits the kinds of knowledge that attract investment in differed economies (Graham, 2005, p. 124). In this vision, global economies are the carriers of some rather vague attributes that not only exist independently of what people do (Graham, 2002, p. 762), but which also present imaginary phenomena as if they had already happened. The most likely outcome of this realis/irrealis orientation through the exhortation of multiple economies (that are not necessarily more 'developed' than its predecessors) is the constant 'reverse engineering' (Graham, 2005, p. 124) of what already exists in industrial commodity forms. Put more strongly, *economy* is presented as a substance rather than a process. It is defined by particular attributes. It is about the transformation of the education system through the types of skills people should acquire; there is only the possibility of emergent 'new' economies, and their temporal-relational aspect of 'new' skills (cf. Foucault, 1995, p. 151).

By contrast, in Extract 57, accounts of the graduate labour force construct Singaporeans as jointly managing and in control of the global economy: '*support* an increasingly sophisticated economy, and *compete effectively* with a highly-mobile international talent pool'. These evaluative dimensions become condensed for importance. Policymakers have a responsibility to 'review our higher education policies to ensure that they remain robust enough to respond to new global challenges of greater complexity'. Policymakers are constructed here as rational agents acting in moral ways. Actually, the claim goes further: for instance, success in a 'sophisticated economy' depends on the *fairness/equality of global competition* in the sense that it is those countries that *grow* 'a deep *pool* of highly capable and entrepreneurial people' that will succeed best (Fairclough, 2000a, p. 43).

Describing this necessity for agentless, nominalised action allows the exhortation to pose as a fact. After this proposal for action by unnamed agents (countries/nations are not agents), we are given an explicitly evaluative (axiological) justification for the proposition, which is also cast as a statement of fact: 'tertiary institutions *must* develop professionals with "T-shaped" competencies' (Extract 57). Here we see how evaluations for *importance* become translated *directly* into *necessity* in the policy genre (Graham, 2001a, p. 771, italics included). Evaluative meaning has been transferred metaphorically from *importance* to *necessity* and through the smuggling in of a second exhortation by what seems like a relational proposition: 'tertiary institutions must develop professionals *with* "T-shaped" competencies' (Extract 57). Thus, education and training will necessarily play a central role in 'an increasingly sophisticated economy'. Singaporeans have a right to expect this but, referring to the preceding analysis, also a (collective) responsibility in working together against the threat of 'increasingly *fierce competition* from other countries' (Extract 56) by paradoxically ensuring that they '*support* an increasingly sophisticated economy, and *compete effectively* with a highly-mobile international talent pool' (Extract 57). The contrast underscores the observation that was made above: that abstract and externally imposed 'change' is partly caused by the decisions made by governments as well as industries.

Two strands of arguments can be drawn from the language of policy discourse as an arena of competition between nation-states. First, discourses of changing, impermanent economies function to define and regulate what counts as 'useful', commodifiable knowledge as that which can be turned into economic gain (Graham, 2005, pp. 123–124). They regularise the circulation of these commodities and thus build up 'tables' that provide rational classifications for knowledge that might serve as the principle of the increase of economic growth (cf. Foucault, 1995, p. 148; 2002, p. 8). Second, neo-liberal and educational ethics is realised here in the pretence that human achievement is a function of (economic) competition through biased (talent) investment rather than cooperation (Graham, 2005, p. 125). In this case, the problematisation of desirable outcomes/neo-liberal imperatives did not grow out of a polygamous structure but out of a monogamous obligation to what has been construed as (common) 'national interests' within (global) competition.

Diverse pathways to meet the needs of 'our' people in the future

In relation to meeting the *perceived* demands of political economies as explicated in the second key theme, the third key theme investigates the nature, function, and uses of the metaphor of diversity in meeting the future needs of Singaporeans. The micro-meso movement examines the discursive positioning of the metaphorical expression 'diverse pathways' in meeting both the needs of the economies and Singaporeans and how this also relates to the ethical aspects of education policy. Such discursive strategies serve to strengthen the argument for structural reforms within the context of imagined realities. The meso-macro movement continues to examine the means by which diverse pathways are integral to meeting economic and global challenges confronting Singaporeans, which further imbues the value of this metaphor positively.

Micro-meso movement: diverse pathways in the university

The following analysis from the 2008 policy document on higher education examines the way the metaphor of diversity draws on notions of development through '*diverse* pathways' (line 3). In order to meet the future needs of Singaporeans, the discursive positioning of the metaphorical expression under examination – diverse pathways – illustrates how the metaphor moves through the micro and meso discourses in relation to the ethical aspects of education policy.

Drawing on Fairclough's (2001, pp. 99–100) examination of ideological attachments embedded in particular representations, Extract 58 involves the metaphorical construction of 'diverse pathways' (line 3) as attending to the needs of the nation, and is illustrated through the phrase, 'the rapidly changing global economy' (lines 1–2), and explicitly states the intended process and ideological attachments of changing demands and expectations. This recommendation, which is based on common-sense assumptions, gives coherence (Fairclough, 2001, p. 68) and social meaning to the metaphorical representation of 'diverse pathways' (line 3) and suggests the revision of the university sector so that it '*will* continue' (line 5) to support the nation's development. The adjectives 'rapidly changing global' (line 2) to describe the economy has been utilised to justify 'the need to provide diverse pathways' (lines 2–3). It is important to note that the definite article – 'the' – triggers the presupposition (Fairclough, 2006a, p. 2) that there exists a need. This presupposition, however, also has the characteristic that it holds under negation: diverse pathways 'will continue to support our development and meet the needs of our people in the future' (lines 5–6), suggesting a slippage between the potential and actual.

Extract 58: 2008 MOE report of the committee on the expansion of the university sector

Lines	*Text*
1	Singapore's university sector has served us well thus far. However, the
2	rapidly changing global economy, the evolving education landscape, the
3	need to provide **diverse** pathways, and the challenge of attracting and
4	retaining talent make it timely to review the university sector to ensure that
5	it will continue to support our development and meet the needs of our
6	people in the future.

Source: MOE, 2008a, p. 8.

Indeed, Graham (2002) observes that, in cases where a prediction representing (desirable) outcomes follows a verb like *ensure* – that is, 'the rapidly changing global economy, the evolving education landscape, the need to provide diverse pathways, and the challenge of attracting and retaining talent make it timely to review the university sector to *ensure* that it will continue to support our development and meet the needs of our people in the future' (lines 2–6) – it elides the future orientation of the predicate, thereby construing it as the unquestionable result of the government's (MOE) action, rather than a possible future effect. As a result, '***diverse*** pathways' (line 3) takes on the appearance of inevitability; 'the managed action is represented as if it were already accomplished, rather than being a possible future outcome, thereby reducing room for negotiation over the matter' (Mulderrig, 2011a, p. 55). Thus, in this case, the independence of the managed actor (people) is comparatively limited and the agency of the manager (the university) is made more prominent (Mulderrig, 2011a, p. 55).

Meso-macro movement: moving towards diversity for talents to meet the demands of irrealis economies

The analysis of the micro-meso movement examined the discursive positioning of the metaphorical expression 'diverse pathways' (Extract 58, line 3) in meeting both the needs of the economies and Singaporeans and how this also relates to the ethical aspects of education policy. Such an analysis demonstrates how policy discourse asserts the need for structural reforms within the context of imagined realities. The meso-macro movement continues to examine the means by which diverse pathways in the 2002, 2008, and 2012 policy documents are conceived as an ethical practice. That is, diverse pathways are integral to meet irrealis economic and global challenges confronting Singaporeans, which further imbues the value of this metaphor as positive. This further reinforces the key role of the metaphor of diversity in providing a rationale for structural inequality as an ethical form of practice.

Graham draws attention to Halliday's (1994) understanding of Substances: Substances are described within propositions through the deployment of relational processes (Graham, 2002, pp. 230–232). In Extract 59 the Substances, 'skills,

Extracts 59, 60, and 61: Diversity to meet the demands of irrealis economics through MOE policy texts 2002–2012a

The new JC curriculum will be more broad-based and better suited to nurturing the skills, spirit and values required for a globalised, innovation-driven future. The changes to the JC/Upper Secondary education landscape will inject greater **diversity**, vibrance and choice in the types of programmes and mix of schools, and will offer new pathways to a university education.

(Extract 59, MOE, 2002, p. vii)

The Committee began its work by exploring the university landscape of developed countries, which have evolved to provide more **diversity** to support their economies and to cater to a wider range of student interests and abilities. Between September and October 2007, members of the Committee and Working Groups (the New University Working Group and the Liberal Arts College Working Group) visited countries in Europe and the United States to learn about different university models and systems. Successful features of these well-established systems were distilled as learning points for Singapore's own long-term vision.

(Extract 60, MOE, 2008a, p. 6)

As our fifth AU, SIT[6] will need to develop itself into a distinctive institution, different from the existing AUs and polytechnics. The value proposition of SIT will lie in the coherence in which the applied elements permeate the character, curriculum and pedagogy of the institution to benefit its students. In doing so, SIT can add **diversity** to the higher education landscape by offering a distinct degree education that caters to a wider spectrum of student abilities and preferences, and produce a different type of graduate to meet the **diverse** needs of our economy. SIT must also provide value-added, higher-order training to polytechnic graduates, so that both students and the labour market recognise the value that SIT can create.

(Extract 61, MOE, 2012a, pp. 45–46)

spirit and values' are attributed as valuable characteristics at a particular time-space; they are given a particular type of economic value within 'a globalised, innovation-driven future'. The construal is organised around a relational-attributive process ('required') in what Halliday (1994, as cited in Graham, 2002, pp. 230–231) calls a 'Token^Value' (Tok^Val) construction. Within this construction, the Token, 'skills, spirit and values' is explicitly evaluated and identified as fitting within a certain hierarchical space, that is, 'a globalised, innovation-driven future'.

Different 'types' and methods of evaluation are foregrounded in these texts. They are operationalised in different ways and at different levels of abstraction. In Extract 59, a direct evaluation is being made for 'skills, spirit and values' within a particular socio-historic circumstance. We see that 'skills, spirit and values' nurtured through 'greater *diversity*, vibrance and *choice*' are desirable commodities in 'a globalised, innovation-driven future'. In Extract 60, an abstract agent ('The Committee') has done something that will supposedly lead to all sorts of desirable outcomes: 'exploring the university landscape of developed countries, which have evolved to provide more diversity to support their economies and to cater to a wider range of student interests and abilities'. In the first instance, the authors explicitly evaluate particular Substances ('skills, spirit and values') required for an irrealis economy; in the second, the evaluation is propagated for the outcomes of a particular Process (provision of more diversity in the university landscape to support the economy and cater to a wide range of students interests and abilities), the value of which needs to be inferred textually.

Graham (2002, pp. 231–232) highlights that 'in Process language, evaluations are generally propagated at different levels of abstraction … Unlike language that defines Substances, evaluations made in Process language must often be inferred (unless the action is explicitly evaluated)'. In Extract 60, the Committee has done something with particular outcomes in mind. The authors rely on assumptions that whatever 'supports economies' and 'cater[s] to a wide range of student interests and abilities' will be perceived as desirable and important (perhaps necessary) outcomes for any action on the part of government: 'Successful features of these well-established systems were distilled as learning points for Singapore's own long-term vision.' In other words, the interrelated evaluations for desirability, necessity, and importance are 'propagated for and from' within the main value system 'upon which the authors intertextually draw when they construe action and its outcomes' (cf. Graham, 2002, p. 231). In Extract 61, the value of diversity in relation to the economy is being reproduced: 'SIT can add *diversity* to the higher education landscape by offering a distinct degree education that *caters to a wider spectrum of student abilities and preferences*, and produce a different type of graduate to *meet the diverse needs of our economy*'.

Another aspect worth noting is the mixture of proposal and proposition operationalised in Extract 60 of the 2008 MOE report and in Extract 61 of the 2012 MOE report, especially in terms of the time and tense elements (Graham, 2002, p. 232). First, there is a description of something the Committee has already done: it has 'began its work by exploring the university landscape of developed countries' (Extract 60). Then we are told *why* the Committee has done what it has done. These reasons are future-oriented: 'to provide' certain desirable outcomes for 'Singapore's own long-term vision'. In Extract 61, the future orientation is elided where the outcomes are concerned: 'SIT must also provide value-added, higher-order training to polytechnic graduates, so that both students and the labour market *recognise* the value that SIT *can create*'. Again, the reasons for the provision of 'value-added, higher-order training' are *future*-oriented: '*recognise* the value that SIT *can* create'. Paradoxically, where the modal verb 'can' suggests a possibility, the absence of the modal verb before 'recognise' suggests a level of certainty. This gives the impression that the stated desirable outcomes are inevitable, which in turn elides the need for explicit evaluation for warrantability: *recognise* the outcomes as if they were already the unquestionable result of the government's action.

Summary

The analysis within this chapter has illustrated that policy texts are involved in reshaping political economy/ies so as to incorporate a fundamental acceptance of shifts leading to an 'innovation-driven' future. Perceived economic imperatives in relation to this future have been employed to make moral values, translated into micro and macro values, appear permanent and inextricable conditions for the existence of a successful society (cf. Nietzsche, 1967a, p. 155) in permeable, imagined futures. Beyond the spherical time frame, the theme of political economies of surrealism is seen to extend to the multidimensional order of reality, the dimensionality of which is effectively infinite as the data unfolds. This means that economic success of self and the nation is dictated by the advent of changing political economies (Fairclough, 2000b, p. 147).

Through drawing on the illusory images built and sustained by society and education, subjects are conditioned to act towards some future state of being and are caught in a constant endeavour to *become* something psychologically through time (cf. Krishnamurti & Bohm, 2014, pp. 251–256, 451). It is within this time-binding context and movement of becoming that an entire ethics revolving around the care of the self is formulated. First, by linking together national economic goals with individual well-being, the form of ethics that is complicit within neo-liberalism in relation to the Singapore government meant ensuring full-employability of the self. In relation to labour market flexibility, the value of an individual resides reductively in their utility. To this end they must be (re)equipped with particular skills of changing political economies such that within the realm of imagined realities, the human being is in a state of becoming. Second, it meant having subjects fulfilling their (citizenry and moral) obligations so as to enable state talent investment for the (common) interests of increasing employment opportunities 'for all'.

In tying the analysis in this chapter to previous analytical chapters, this is the point at which discursive practices that formulate and sustain power-relations dovetail with ethics. This interplay of truths and values through the exhortation of metaphors frames the discourse of educational ethics and practice. The analysis of Chapters 5 to 7 highlights how these values act as *desirable outcomes* underpinned by a moral imperative that interweaves disruptive, *shifting* modes of de/regulation-de/valuation (cf. Foucault, 1981b; 1981c). This moral imperative involves the political need to find a whole calculated practice of individual and collective actions and attitudes. Through examining what and how desirable outcomes are presented and configured in the policy texts, it is possible to highlight how specific macro (neo-liberal) values are made desirable through supporting, and being supported by, micro valuations. Through the analysis, the main value that unifies contradictions is: It is in the interests of the Singapore people that 'talents' should get privileged access to knowledge as it is through this that more opportunities for the rest of the population are created. As Foucault (2005, p. 328) points out, it is in the principle of discontinuity – and within this study, that discontinuity relates to the absence of rational or logical links between propositions and proposals – that 'the events of discourse find the principle of their regularity'.

Drawing on Foucault's conceptualisation of ethics, the analytical Chapters 5 to 7 have made explicit how the transvaluation of values is consequent upon the emergence of neo-liberal ethics. Through the same laws of discursive formation (Foucault, 2002, p. 83) using metaphors, new concepts appear and new value systems of regularity can be built. This 'neo-liberal–ethical' complex reveals a paradox that situates the morality constructed in these texts as problematic. Further, the value system threading through all the analytical chapters orients political thought and action towards the reproduction and reinforcement of unequal outcomes, rather than the transformation of inequality. Within this argument, the concluding Chapter 8 will discuss how the analytical chapters highlight a fundamental and irreconcilable tension and a sharp disconnect within the streaming policy's dual commitment to both 'customisation' and 'opportunity' agendas in the context of educational meritocracy that proclaims 'equal opportunities'. Cogently, the research demonstrates that the *untruth* of meritocracy must derive from the essence of the Truth (Heidegger, 1961, n.p.) that economic growth is the only way forward. That this untruth and Truth belong together makes it 'possible for a true proposition to enter into a pointed opposition to the corresponding untrue proposition' (Heidegger, 1961, n.p.).

Notes

1 'One must *vivre, pour vivre pour autrui*: Live to live for others' (Nietzsche, 1967a, p. 415).
2 Although this argument is a sidebar to this chapter, Smith's (1759 [2010], p. 99) *Theory of Moral Sentiments* provides the ethical and philosophical underpinnings for political-economic morality and the sense of duty: 'All the rich do is to select from the heap the most precious and agreeable portions. They consume little more than the poor, and in spite of their natural selfishness and greed, and despite the fact that they are guided by their own convenience, and all they want to get from the labourers of their thousands of employees is the gratification of their own empty and insatiable desires, they do share with the poor the produce of all their improvements [meaning: their well-cultivated land, their up-to-date ploughs, their state of the art milking sheds, etc.]. They are *led by an invisible hand* to share out life's necessities in just about the same way that they would have been shared out if the earth been divided into equal portions among all its inhabitants. And so without intending it, without knowing it, they advance the interests of the society as a whole and provide means for the survival of the species.'
3 Thinking Schools, Learning Nation.
4 Primary School Leaving Examination.
5 It also evokes the traditional capitalist and classical economics assumption of the infinitely flexible perfectly 'supply' of labour (labour market flexibility) able to move effortlessly to adjust to changes in demand in particular industries, and thereby relegating the possibility and problem of unemployment.
6 Singapore Institute of Technology.

8 Inequality as meritocracy

Overview

This final chapter highlights the contributions of the philosophical-analytical methodology with a commitment to a systematic interdisciplinary investigation of educational discourse in interpreting empirical material. The discussion here relates the material presented in previous chapters to the theoretical and operational objectives of the study in explicating more general trends in policy discourse. This is followed by a critical reflection on the broader philosophical-analytical considerations and implications of this research. The multiple approaches developed through the analyses pay off as the discussion here highlights the way in which this combination of approaches may be of utility to researchers in examining the relationships between evaluative propagation in policy discourse, political economy, and inequality. The chapter concludes with an explication on how meritocracy in Singapore has conditions which are unequal, and raises questions about the moral and social objectives of education, seeing this as an opportunity for the emergence of a 'Singapore model' to lead education policies for advanced economies.

On the specific aims of the research

The specific aim of the research was to examine *how* an ability-driven system can function as a major mechanism through which inequality of educational opportunities is transmitted and maintained. In doing so, the study made both methodological and theoretical contributions simultaneously, by means of historical research, and by critically analysing metaphors as apparatuses of knowledge production and the power relations that they maintain to reproduce and sustain inequality (cf. Anais, 2013, p. 133).

The underlying theme of the analysis was the unbroken wholeness of the totality of being and becoming of the ideology of economic growth as an undivided, flowing movement between three broad key micro movements: 'Metaphorical realism', 'De/regulation', and 'Political economies of surrealism'. The analysis illustrates that these metaphors have supported systemic discrimination within the education system and that this inequality is given legitimacy as necessary through various moral discourses. In making and sustaining propositions for explicit institutional segregation to meet national and economic demands, policymakers persistently use these metaphors as the ideological foundation for inequitable opportunities. In tracing the discursive developments or shifts of these three metaphors as they *move between values* – that is, their transforming possibilities through evaluative propagation, within and between texts in the micro-meso and meso-macro movements – the study involved a combination of Foucault's and Nietzsche's perspectives with approaches to critical discourse analysis (CDA). This philosophical-analytical approach provided a way to understand both the philosophic relevance of the 'games of truth' (Foucault, 1984b, n.p.) and valuation as the (primordial) essence of truth (Nietzsche, 1967a, p. 275). Their perspectives *constituted* and *were constituted by* various critical discourse analytical approaches to enable an analysis of how morality, understood as achieving *desirable* individual and national economic outcomes within surrealistic economies, is central to legitimising inequality.

In doing so the study has attempted to contribute to the analytic tools of critical analysis by showing how genealogy and CDA can be combined as a methodological basis to highlight further levels of analysis for the sociological investigation of historical texts. In doing this the analysis places emphasis on the ability of the framework not only to take account of, but to locate the framework's analytic strength in, the constantly shifting superfluidity of interrelated elements of texts. Through this, the analysis evidences both the temporal evolution of discourse(s) and the layered and reflexive interconnection between micro texts and macro ideologies. Here, then, Chapters 5 to 7 have utilised the micro-meso-macro grid to show how *metaphors, movements,* and *valuations* are made necessary as conditions to attain comprehensive forms of dominion that support inequality, and where, as a form of power, valuation plays at once a conditioning and conditioned role for inequality.

The analysis emphasised that value judgments are continually at work in these policy discourses, and that institutional change has to be driven exclusively by changing political economies as a simple and certain way forward, despite the strong discourse of meritocracy that the Singapore education system promotes. The relationship between the meritocratic education system and the reproduction of inequality was made explicit through an examination of the way in which the esoteric dimensions of the metaphors of flexibility, diversity, choice, and opportunity provide a sustainable tool from which to deploy a contractual-ethical discourse for inequality. Through the notion of metaphorical superfluidity – where each metaphorical transfer converges and presses forward to a system of value regularity, the analysis made explicit the policy's main argument that it was in the interests of Singaporeans that 'talents' should get privileged access to knowledge to create opportunities for all and strengthen Singapore's international economic position, even if, as Graham (2001a, p. 772) argues, *opportunities* as pre-evaluated desirable potentialities are not available or equal for all, that is, independent of the distributive consequences generated. The implicit ethics and moral philosophy of desirability underpinning this value system is the object of criticism. That is, the findings demonstrate that although the underlying assumptions of this 'logic' that has been constructed in policies are unsubstantiated, the logic is efficaciously legitimated through forms of e/valuations. Thus, in providing the internal coherence of policy discourse, the metaphors illustrate how the education system has reached the limits of its own meritocratic logic. Through the desire for economic growth, one is precluded from desiring equality of access.

As such, if the opportunities open to the 'less academically inclined' in a competitive society are much more restricted than those open to 'talents' (cf. Hayek, 2007, p. 135) in a society that has been conditioned to (want) more, is the meritocratic promise of equal opportunity then merely providing legitimacy and cover to further the interests of a particular segment of the population (cf. Hayek, 2007, p. 146)? Herein also lies the possibility of an unsubstantiated and arbitrary relational assumption between the discourses of opportunity and meeting the demands of changing political economies. Even where it was proposed that something should be done in relation to increasing importance in a globalised economy, by whom or how opportunities would grow is not made explicit. This tension generates a paradox within a meritocratic educational policy discourse that actually threatens to undermine the very opportunistic mentality that it purportedly seeks to promote through the principle of meritocracy. The idea of a meritocratic education system must then be questioned for possibly entrenching structural limits on upward mobility as not everyone has the *same* opportunity to be educated and to openly compete. If this is true, meritocracy can exist only as an idea, an idea which can never be realised in practical life. Before delving into the implications of this concern, the next section discusses the theoretical-methodological approach and the innovativeness and contribution of the research.

On the twin theoretical-methodological objectives of the research

To go beyond commentary and critique in examining educational inequality, and more importantly, to challenge the 'ideological' premises of government policies, a critique of the language of policy was necessary. Towards this end, the guiding principles and methodological framework for the analytical work proper were established.

This monograph shows how abstract philosophical concepts work not as a theory but in actuality; that is, they are not asserted as a basis for analytical work but they are an evolving, *ongoing* conceptualisation as the analytical work proceeds through a historical analysis (Foucault, 1982a, p. 778). Due to the rigorous analytical examination demanded of CDA, it is not possible to provide this level of analysis to entire policy texts but, as is the disciplinary convention, to focus in detail on particular features using extracts from the texts which, it is argued, are central elements of the internal coherence of the overall text. The analysis does not offer nor argue that this is all that is going on in the texts or that the analysis is a comprehensive examination of Singapore's education policies, but that metaphors, as textual devices, are utilised to argue for particular ways in which the education system in Singapore is conceived and developed over the course of 40 years.

Although analytical and theoretical differentiations were made, they are ultimately entangled in each other in the discourse analytical process because of the immediacy and pervasiveness of the philosophical-analytical domains within which they operate, and because of their intimate involvement with language and *being*. Thus, theory and methodology have become analytically inseparable. Consequently, the theory and methodology are mediated, and operationalised, as a unitary phenomenon in language. This phenomenon is thus not autonomous in-itself, but only an in-itself-in-relation-to discourse analysis. That is, rather than relying on any one pre-existing approach being applied to the exclusion of others, the analysis of policies should be able to demonstrate sensitivity to the data as it unfolds. As such, an amalgamation of CDA approaches that sought to examine e/valuations was developed in this study to enhance the level of multiple, nuanced interpretations of discursive strategies possible and make sense of how they manage institutional practices and processes. This methodology worked in a framework that was open to improvisations at every analytical level in order to provide for a 'bottom-up' methodological, data-driven CDA approach sensitive to discursive vicissitudes produced within a policy text. In constructing this 'working' methodology for policy analysis, the study has strengthened discourse analytical work by bringing the tools and perspectives of the philosophical study of valuation to bear on concrete problems that arose in addressing questions of inequality. This 'working' methodology did not attempt to construct and impose *a priori* dispositions but allowed the phenomenon to reveal itself through the data. It was developed with an understanding that analytical approaches are not unique to a particular discourse, but are available as resources that can flexibly be drawn upon at various junctures, with a view to understand the 'rhetorical effect of evaluative lexis as texts unfold' (Martin, 2000, p. 148). It is through this process that the interplay of valuations and their relations in the institutional structures could be made obvious. It is, then, the particular assemblage of analytical approaches that is unique to this study.

The philosophical-analytical model built was then applied to an initial analysis of some data from the 1979 MOE report. This framework combined Foucault's philosophical perspectives and CDA to critically examine the 'regime of truth' (Foucault, 1980, p. 131) that made possible capability-based identity constructs. This approach was significant in providing multifaceted perspectives to unravel complex, implicit relationships between language, identity construction, and systemic unequal opportunities. In doing so, the first analytical stage examined how the changing policy discourses on these particular learners are used to maintain the legitimacy of divisive practices through the streaming 'mechanism'. As a methodological development of the first stage of research, the analytical apparatus is developed to include a critical analysis of language as part of the contemporary critique of morality through the philosophical study of valuation.

The aim of the second stage was to model how CDA and philosophy can be usefully synthesised to analyse systemic changes in education policies. The application of Foucault's work on power-knowledge-truth enabled a level of abstraction that made the use of CDA less susceptible to an ideological predisposition.

This approach did not look for particular forms of discourse that makes a phenomenon what it is. Further, by using CDA, Foucault's abstract concepts took concrete form in relation to Singapore's education system, and revealed underlying 'obscured' workings of the institution in rationalising (above and beyond neo-liberal discourses, as suggested by Fairclough [2002, 2006b, 2010], for instance) or/and legitimising certain practices. This consisted of analysing policy as an activity which functions as the principle and method for the specific rationalities of governmental practices (Foucault, 1982a, pp. 779–780; Foucault, 1989 as cited in Burchell, 2006, p. 269). Consequently, this research's method for analysing evaluations in language cannot separate itself from theory-building efforts to conceptualise how the value system is produced and reproduced through a set of connected parts. Towards this end, the guiding principles and framework for subsequent analytical work was established.

Expanding the boundaries: rupturing the stability of established frameworks

One of the objectives of this research was to provide a flexible philosophical-analytical model in which to employ CDA. The interpretations and approximations of forms of valuations, using CDA, adhere to the non-deterministic, philosophical orientation of the micro-meso-macro framework. The research was designed to show that it was possible to add and analyse data to a living framework.

Rather than a simple sedimentary process, a framework was constructed to convey a sense of historical 'weaving' (cf. Graham, 2001b, p. 389). In setting out to explore how e/valuations were foregrounded in policy texts, the three-layered analysis provided a methodological frame by which to bridge the complexity of contradictions that were constantly on the borders of the arbitrary in policy discourse, and to examine how the policy texts cohere by drawing on the same value system that is connected throughout these levels. By framing the analysis through movements between, through, and within the micro-meso-macro levels, this study retained the essential point that temporal *metaphorical transfers* continued throughout all stages where they contributed to the constant *becoming* and *being* – conceptualised as a continual flux of discursive formations to bring the ideology of economic growth as the only way forward into immanent existence, and to project a constant anticipatory state of potential becoming of *surrealistic* economies. In this process of becoming, of changing, there is the duality and conflict between meritocracy as the discourse of equal opportunities and the privileging of economic imperatives through the rationalist discourse of past/future, regulation/deregulation, centralisation/decentralisation, realis/irrealis/surrealis[1] states, and actual/potential.

Here, then, the architectural grid ruptured particular ways of functioning in established, systematic, analytical frameworks. One of the best ways to accomplish this goal is to include what might be termed as the philosophical study of valuation in shaping the research design. This philosophical dimension provided the knowledge and ways to understand how policies form the necessary links between the principles of political ethics, economic structures, and the aesthetics, or conditions of our existence. In making such an assertion, the grid displayed philosophical-analytical sensitivity to the context of analysis. Employing the benefits of philosophical inquiry, the research design gained a new ability to account for and incorporate the dynamics of discourse and representation into truths or the overarching Truth narrative of policy discourse that enhanced existing methods of analysis (Bridges, 1997; Fisher, 1998; Madison, 1988; McCarthy, 1997; all as cited in Kincheloe, 2001, p. 688).

Thus, while the approach allowed for an analysis where a 'movement' is self-contained as a distinct part in each of the micro-meso-macro analytical sections, it also provided a constant reminder that these three movements are inextricably entwined such that individual movements exerted a cumulative effect. This did not mean that they are or are not related causally, but rather that causal sequence and linear determinism are replaced by the notion of *metaphorical superfluidity*. This notion illuminates the concept of conditionality where each metaphor exists in an intrinsic movement of its own but that which also gives way and converges in ways amenable to description and analysis. This fluid interplay of games of truths and values, through the pervasive use of metaphors, frames the discourse of educational ethics and practice analysed in this study. By constantly alluding to and postulating the Truth of economic growth, the metaphorical relations of policy discourse orientate political thought and action towards the reproduction and reinforcement, rather than the transformation, of inequality.

By combining a genealogical approach with the micro-meso-macro framework, the analytic sophistication of CDA was extended and improved by embracing historical analyses that take the problematisation (of truth) as a point of departure instead of pre-determined parameters (Anais, 2013, pp. 127–133). The capacity of this philosophical position to cross (and sometimes question, even destabilise) established identity boundaries by demonstrating how they are discursively constructed and progressed through language analysis, was precisely the inspiration and motivation for the development of this project; and it is reflected in the construction of its CDA methodology.

Using this framework, the second stage of analysis made explicit how policy discourse circumscribes, extends, and limits the way metaphors are (re)conceptualised and constantly and successively imbued with particular, narrowed, positive valuations in creating distinctive visions of economic realities. The analytic chapters demonstrate that both micro techniques and macro strategies are neither a false dichotomy, nor is one a mere inversion of the other. They are marked by porous distinctions and therefore permeable and interchangeable. But for the purposes of investigation, artificial separation – that is, the appropriation of certain types of metaphorical relations to certain themes – is necessary and must be assumed, even though they are thematically interrelated.

The discursive formations and transformations traced through the analytic framework highlight how specific values and outcomes are *made* desirable, where *desirability* is valued in creating historical conditions for economic growth, and where economic growth is constructed as the (only) way forward (cf. Nietzsche, 1967a, p. 194–195). Through mapping the framework, the aim was to extend this approach to examine how genealogy and CDA can be combined as a methodological basis for further levels of analysis of the sociological investigation of historical texts. While here the research examined policy texts, this framework can be useful for other series of texts; that is, an historical analysis using this framework is not exclusively tied to policy texts.

By expounding schemas of valuation, the analytical chapters made explicit the processes through which metaphors function as the prodigious machinery of the will to truth, with its vocation of exclusion (cf. Foucault, 2005, p. 319). Through this, the framework examined neo-liberalism as a system of principles, and how metaphors as its existing mechanisms flow from this system by making analytically observable how changes associated with new modes of value determination serve to legitimise structural inequality through recursive themes and time. In this respect, the theoretical objective of making a contribution to policy analysis more broadly, one that puts philosophy to work – in terms of its integration and application with multiple CDA approaches in analysing policies – had been met. Through tracing the evolution of Singapore's education policy, the findings clearly suggest that structural reforms supporting the neo-liberal ideology of economic growth have gained ascendency.

Metaphors and neo-liberalism

This analytic framework is also developed to examine the way metaphors are put to work as part of the neo-liberal economic discourse and which legitimate inequality and differential access to resources. Metaphors are used to bridge, connect, and smooth over those tensions between meeting perceived demands of surrealistic industries in the pursuit of economic growth and the provision of equal opportunities which had to be aligned with economic priorities by means of state action, to translate one for the other, and provided the appearance of logical cohesion. The work of policy was most perspicuous through the use of metaphors.

The movement of metaphors traced across 40 years of policy discourse is discontinuous, in the sense that they are eventually defined out of existence. In terms of the value system and the esoteric dimensions of the metaphor, one may thus say that metaphorical relations are enfolded into everything. To make explicit the value system means, however, that the mechanistic order of interpreting data must be dropped. That is, the unfolding of discourse elements as the analysis proceeds must be free of conditioning to previously existing patterns and frameworks, otherwise it will ultimately be just an extension of mechanical and reductive reaction (cf. Bohm, 2004a, pp. 74, 127). The analysis of texts that do not explicitly draw on the existence of the metaphor suggests that there is nothing that cannot also be conceived as constituted of metaphorical elements. That is to say, the form and structure of the value system may be said to be enfolded within each policy extract. By using CDA on a particular text and by considering the analogy of a moving fluid, this form and structure were unfolded, to give a recognisable image of the notion of metaphorical fluidity through thematic condensation that pressed forward to unity.

The analysis demonstrated that competition, and the desirable acquisition of specific skills, elements of neo-liberal values (of competition, deregulation, and market economies) and rules, go hand in hand, and that unfettered technological change, driven by industries, is rendered desirable (Rooney, 2005, p. 418). Specifically, the analysis highlighted that these metaphors, as apparatuses of power, promote the development of productive forces characteristic of capitalism, which advocate support for macro neo-liberal values that propagate inequality (cf. Foucault, 1980, p. 158). Micro and macro values have been crystallised around this ideal. The analytical chapters traced the metamorphoses of desirability as the supreme value, its disguise beneath the cloak of growth, and its transfiguration through morality. By this, equal consideration for all may demand very unequal treatment in favour of the 'talents'. But inequality is justified on economic grounds. The economic valuation of ideals – that is, the selection of certain actions that privileged 'talents' at the expense of others – suggests an operation that ensures the regularity of economic performance and growth. This is the condition under which such an elevation is possible.

Within this argument, borrowing Foucault's (1997, p. 287) words: 'the care of the self' is ethical in itself; but it implies complex relationships with others' through contractual discourse. The master narrative of Singapore's education policy holds that the pursuit of economic growth means inequality of knowledge access through this *contractual relationship* (cf. Nietzsche, 1967b, p. 64). This neo-liberal value system privileges talent investment and provides coherence for a policy discourse that constantly borders on the arbitrary. The regimen of early streaming as the primary prescriptive system assumes economic stability through education in the management of one's life. This assumption is linked to the fundamental principle of the care of the self. With this economic valuation ideal comes an *economic* justification of virtue. This involves a general conditioning of man designed to produce or maintain the individual qualities that ensure economic growth. The task of policymakers is to make individuals as useful as possible and as far as possible, to make them 'compatible' with an infallible streaming mechanism: to this end they must be (re)equipped with particular skills of changing political economies. This mechanism constitutes people's intrinsic nature and associates them with discriminatory forms of economic materiality. A particular form of discursive practice that juxtaposes desirable outcomes with caring for the self is the condition for the insertion of the subject in this type of truth game. This insertion is explained by drawing on the interactions between the workings of power-knowledge-truth that not only legitimise but *necessitate* dividing practices in relation to learner representation.

Power-knowledge-truth: the subject and power

The social function of the education policy analysed here is to transmit a neo-liberal system of principles by which different categories of learners are produced, and the kind of knowledge and structural access they are permitted. A corollary to this is that 'truth' and 'power' function as a kind of double-sided, applied epistemology – it not only attempts to define the legal limits and principles of structural access, but also produces 'knowledge' on how the world is organised according to policies and how we should live in it, or, in other words, the examination of what we are (Foucault, 1982a, p. 785).

As a development of the first stage of analysis, the second analytical stage concluded that objectification is a fundamental part of the valorisation process in increasing the *relative* value of subjects through upskilling and modes of valuation within the perceived demands arising from the living *movement* of, and changing material conditions of, surrealistic political economies. The acquisition of differentiated skills as the basis of ethical practice that drive national and individual interests merits a consideration of whether it was in the interests of the Singaporean people that 'talents' should get privileged access to knowledge. This is especially so as Singapore has one of the highest levels of income inequality among developed countries (Chan, 2014, n.p.). Structural inequality has been legitimised on ethical grounds, in the presumed best interests of both 'talents' and 'non-talented' pupils. The assumption underlying this legitimisation is that better opportunities for talents will entail a more productive economy while assigning the 'non-talented' to the vocational stream is a benevolent act – that is, the system 'tries to seek ways of giving half a loaf when a whole loaf would choke' (MOE, 1979a, p. 6-4, lines 10–11). A vocational, or a 'less demanding' stream will provide them with the necessary skills for inclusion in the labour market (see Teo, 2002a, n.p.). Further, it was argued that a standard, albeit relatively 'more-demanding', curriculum could potentially cause students who consistently fail to suffer from low self-esteem (Teo, 2002a, n.p.).

Hence, the other aspect of this research was in all essentials a critique of morality. The most important and determining phenomena for moral reflection are related to the dynamic changes observed in the multifarious conditions – translated as developing thematic movements – of the exercise of power through the exhortation of policy metaphors. This could be seen in how, for instance, the existence of 'diversity' of capabilities necessarily demands 'flexibility' and 'choice' in institutional practices so as to cater to specific interests and inclinations. Thus, the use of metaphors is used to justify inequality as a *desirable* form of ethical practice.

The use of philosophy in policy

To transcend a purely linguistic dimension in the analysis and interpretation of policy discourse, philosophical dimensions were included. The research drew on Nietzsche's genealogical account of the 'will to truth' in order to show that truth has been put to the service of a neo-liberal ideology or constellation of values, and how this truth had been posited as the highest (unquestionable) value (cf. Medina & Wood, 2005, p. 3). By calling attention to the taken-for-grantedness aspects of truth, Nietzsche's works helped to bring the problematic aspects of the value of truth into sharper focus (Medina & Wood, 2005, p. 3). Further, Foucault's work on schemas of valuations in *The History of Sexuality* (1981a, 1981b, 1981c) emphasises the relation of truth to agency and its ethical dimension. Specifically, this research has made explicit the games of truth by which subjects are constituted as both desiring-desirable individuals (Foucault, 1981b, p. 7) in relation to the pursuit of economic growth. However, as Graham (2001b, p. 405) argues, 'it is presumptuous to claim that which is perceived to be necessary, desirable, and important in any given context will unquestionably motivate (and reduce) human behaviour and create the desiring (and desirable) subject'. Arguably, there is always the possibility for (opposing) agency (Walshaw, 2007, p. 43). This is especially so given that the ideology of economic growth in policy discourse requires the continuous support of discursive formations and transformations throughout the years to remain the dominant, legitimate, focus of unequal structural reforms. But it is through the process of synthesising this philosophical dimension with CDA that we, as subjects, can be made conscious of the movement of our desire and aware of the conditions by which the desire for economic growth, as the supreme valuable state, are determined.

Further, within Foucault's work on power lie three fundamental elements: 'a game of truth, relations of power, and forms of relation to oneself and to others' (1997, p. 117). In order to examine how these three elements are interrelated, archaeology, genealogy, and ethics were employed as methods to explicate how these elements are present in policy discourse, what roles they play, and how each conditions and is being conditioned by the transformation(s) of the other (Foucault, 1997, p. 117).

The policy discourse analysed here appealed to truth as 'an end in itself'; that is, it 'turned truth into an arbitrary point of explanation and justification, that explained nothing and was supported by nothing' (Medina & Wood, 2005, p. 9). To analyse how it is possible for truth to be spoken in a void, the analysis determined the conditions under which the rules of discursive 'policy' concerning the principles of classification, ordering, and distribution of knowledge access policy discourse may be employed (Foucault, 2005, pp. 320, 324). These rules, conceptualised as a system of principles of valuation and evaluation, serve to hold both policy propositions and proposals to truth logical and reasonable. As such, the analysis examined and made explicit the external conditions of existence. These conditions gave rise to the chance series of categorical and recurring events that fix the limits of the ultimately objectifying terms for learners (cf. Foucault, 2005, p. 328).

On the essence of truth

The question of truth is central to philosophy (Medina & Wood, 2005, p. 1). By examining the *value* of truth in policy discourse, the philosophical debate on truth may have taken a distinctive turn in contemporary philosophy: an evaluative turn. What unifies Nietzsche's and Foucault's philosophical concepts is the normativity of valuation as the essence of truth. This concept was brought to centre-stage in exposing the underlying assumptions that guide institutional practices. Further, it framed the constellation of questions concerning the formulation of truth that constitutes the focus of policymaking. This study of the question of truth afforded two benefits. In the first place, the philosophical concepts provided an excellent point of access to a wide set of fundamental issues in ethics, morality, political philosophy, and philosophy of language; they provided opportunities to examine the interrelations between them and the multiplying pathways that could be created among them (Medina & Wood, 2005, p. 1). More importantly, truth covered questions concerning how the possibilities available in each moment of an imagined reality become imbricated within constructed identities. That is, it was argued that propositional truths within discursive policy practices are intimately bound up with structuring conditions (Medina & Wood, 2005, p. 5). In relation to different categories of learners, the games of truth operate 'as a mechanism of inclusion and exclusion which empowered some and disempowered others' (Medina & Wood, 2005, pp. 4–5). As such, 'truth could not simply be said to serve power, it would be power (or a power) itself' (Medina & Wood, 2005, p. 6).

This philosophical-analytical apparatus was necessary as it served as an indicator of possible directions in which political economy might move so as to comprehend the nature of the neo-liberal system and for grasping changes in human objectification. However, abstract philosophical concepts must be rendered explicit through a linguistic pursuit to go beyond commentary and critique. As such, the research drew on a theoretical framing from Foucault, and the augmentation of Nietzsche's views on valuation, to link evaluative semantic categories with these sociological theories in order to bring out their relevance for the purpose of CDA. Further, it provided a flexible philosophical-analytical model through which to apply the analytic principles of CDA. As this model was formulated through this research, a consideration and e/valuation of the usefulness and the expediency of the philosophical-analytical apparatus are warranted, if only to understand how it can progress the field of CDA.

Evaluating the philosophical-analytical model

The task of this research was to start from policy extracts themselves by taking the problematisation of truth as a point of departure and to derive the analytical framework through abstraction. That is, the framework was based on the interactions of constitutive parts of the extracts which make up relatively autonomous movements. Further, in order to move beyond the mechanistic approach, the method for analysing evaluations in language in this research cannot separate itself from theory-building efforts to conceptualise how the value system was produced and reproduced through a set of connected parts.

The laws of the micro-meso-macro movement grid established in this study were not mechanical. Through thematic metaphors, the ideology of economic growth is sustained through the rapid recurrence of similar themes which intermingle and interpenetrate each other. In the same vein, values intermingle and interpenetrate to form a flowing movement. Paradoxically, through the principles of thematic condensation and continuous movement, even though this ideology is sustained throughout, the meaning of these metaphors evolves in dis/continuous ways. The preservation and promulgation of these metaphors are of central importance for the (full) transmission of inequality to occur. This observation was made possible by drawing on philosophical perspectives that deal largely with epistemological questions of truth and language.

The establishment of the guiding principles in the form of valuations for the construction of the micro-meso-macro movement is a form of conditioning. This conditioning may only serve us if it is not too rigid. Hence, what is important, necessary, and desirable, as *moral* valuations, can get conditioned in themselves and become too rigid, to the extent that they have to be perpetually conceived as contingent and as interacting simultaneously within a tripartite, mechanistic important-necessary-desirable system. To interpret policy discourse according to a 'fore-structure' – that which consists of a 'definite conceptuality' (Heidegger, 2003b, pp. 244–245), would suggest that there is only one set of systemic rules governing the whole of the reality which surrounds us and of which we are part. That is to say, the notion of valuation and the being and becoming of the world are completely wedded. Further, the underlying interpretations of what is important, necessary, and desirable are inherently assumptions, and abstractions in themselves. They can be conceived as broad notions, and notions are not realities. But they are three notions which ought to permit us to link the history of how the world is organised to the practical work of discourse analysis – three directions to be followed in the work of theoretical elaboration (cf. Foucault, 2005, p. 330).

Further, it is argued that forms of desirability point to a particular *holistic* conception that goes beyond a mechanistic response. Desirability is *sensed immediately* as the presence together of many different but interrelated, overlapping degrees of valuations that condition and are being conditioned by an implicit value system. Evidently this value system is *active* in the sense that it continually flows into the games of truth, each involving a compound set of valuations that are inseparable from the structural transformations out of which it is essentially constituted (cf. Bohm, 1980, pp. 198–200).

The study hence proposed that incorporating philosophical considerations might not only be fruitful but necessary for achieving explanations and understandings in highlighting the ways in which an argument for inequality permeates policy from within a frame of meritocracy. The policy texts examined in this research provided rich material for philosophical reflection, and philosophical reasoning is necessary if research is to inform the discursive phenomena of *what is*. There are major theoretical and intellectual gains and prospects opened up for policy analysis by the application of philosophical perspectives. Foucault provided the perspective of a micro-macro analysis which is here translated into micro-meso-(meso)-meso-macro movements. Drawing on both Foucault's and Nietzsche's works provided the impetus for the conceptualisation of an analytical framework. This framework constituted an image of philosophical-contemporary thought that executed ideas to realign the workings of policy discourse, and thereby confront the political contradictions of the present. The philosophical dimension was considered in relation to the question of truth, using aspects of CDA approaches to be articulated in terms of e/valuations. This not only captured the most distinctive aspects of the educational debates on meritocracy and ethical practices through formulation of truths, but also advanced the philosophical discussion of truth in policy discourse. Values are neither absolute nor self-evident (Medina & Wood, 2005, p. 9) and the way to call them into question is to expose the assumptions underpinning these claims for truth that are rationalised by propositional content.

This research's programme was to use philosophy as a tool for examining the rational discourse employed by policies to justify moral and ethical obligations. But it is also here that the analysis poses some philosophical or theoretical problems. This process raises the question of whether employing and being faithful to the philosophical concepts and principles – primarily discourse as the will to truth – have restricted the formulation of truth through valuation and even to reinforce it (cf. Foucault, 2005, p. 326). Nevertheless, this journey has not just been about contemplating these philosophical concepts but to show how they work in actuality. That is, the task of the micro-meso-macro movement was then to start from the analytical parts and to derive the value system through abstraction, explaining this system as the result of interactions of the micro-macro valuations (cf. Bohm, 1980, p. 179). The next section identifies possible problematic dimensions that are foregrounded in the philosophical-analytical model by acknowledging the underlying methodological assumptions of this study.

Methodological assumptions

There were three key assumptions underpinning this study. First, in examining the discursive construction of identities, the assumption was made that identities are a construction. However, *how* identities were a construction was made explicit through the policy analysis, and hence this assumption was substantiated. Even so, the circularity of drawing intertextually on Foucault's work on subjection and objectification and examining identities as discursive constructions boiled down to this: all forms of categorisations are constructions. But it must be acknowledged that despite the circularity of this analytical exercise, the findings were obtained through a reflexive methodology of e/valuations, and that they repeatedly point to *how* conceptual learner categories remain a pervasive, recognisable influence in structural reforms; that is, they were causally circular in the way that they reinforced as well as constituted institutional coordination and change. Through forms of objectification, discourse plays a role in embedding systematic inequality into the education system. The unearthing of relationships between forms of objectification and structural reforms were not an assumption of the methodology, but a consequence of it. As abstract forms of value objectify subjects, corresponding structural reforms that allude to different learner identities develop to meet the *perceived* demands of political economies. Forms of learner objectification are fundamental to the development and inculcation of new, more unequal structures.

This leads to the second assumption. The conditions for the objectification of learners were examined as a focal point based on the principle of the genealogical approach which iterates the importance of examining what is pervasive and recursive. However, why this principle was a significant consideration is not clear in Foucault's work. But this presupposition itself was not left without demonstrating how it is justified; that is, it is by taking the problematisation of truth as a point of departure first of all, rather than counting various aspects of the content of policy texts. By problematising truth, the analysis makes explicit the necessary conditions (of possibility) for the disclosure of what is pervasive and recurring, which in the case of this research, is the objectification of learners. But why do the understandings of 'being' and 'becoming' of learner identities solely anticipated and predicated upon *conditions of possibility* for truth formulation? (cf. Heidegger, 2003b, p. 241). Does this (provisional, *a priori*) perception suggest the simplicity of circumspect discourse interpretation (cf. Heidegger, 2003b, pp. 242–244)? It should thus be asserted that truth formulations and conditions as an interdependent phenomenon should not be conceived of as a finality in understanding the primordial constitution, or *being(s)*, of human identities. However, it can be argued that the conceptualisation of 'conditions' involves complex processes, that is, what can be conceived of as conditions, or correspondingly, truths, are not confined within known boundaries, that they can be multifarious, simultaneous, interacting, elements that can also change quite drastically. Thus, conditions can be appropriated depending on what the data unfolds through the employment of CDA.

The third assumption underlying policy analysis is that policy discourse makes a difference or has an impact on people's lives, that is, that it has identifiable material force in everyday life (Graham, 2001b, p. 403). That is to say that language frames the world that we live in; that language controls us instead of us controlling language. How policy is perceived, translated, and imbricated in everyday lives is not known. That is to say, discursive differences make material differences (Graham & Luke, 2011, p. 105). These 'events' – these policy proposals and propositions – are 'certainly not immaterial; they take effect, become effect, always on the level of materiality' (Foucault, 2005, p. 329). It was argued that policies have a certain material inevitability in Singapore. That is, in relation to the hortatory function of policies in Singapore, they are inevitably given material force with funding and corresponding actions by the state (Quah, 1984, p. 119). Nonetheless, how policies are discussed, translated, and implemented at the concrete level was neither the focus nor the concern of this study.

This project demonstrated that critical discourse analysis, political economy as a composite formulation of values, and the philosophical study of valuation can usefully inform each other to explicate the dynamics of discursive strategies, their histories, and the transference of metaphorical relations. Graham (2002, p. 253), however, points out the problematic aspects of analysing the 'complex interplay of evaluative dimensions': given that the social function of policies is hortatory, how does this get translated into understanding which evaluative semantics are propagated from most strongly within intricate and overlapping, interdependent networks of proposals, propositions, and their corresponding valuations? Because of the complex interplay of evaluative semantics and dimensions that can overlap or be interpreted differently over repeated readings of the whole course of a text, any analysis of these findings must therefore be seen as a partially informed interpretation of the data. The semantics of evaluation and the values placed on various phenomena within policy discourse involves complex operational processes which must be made explicit through CDA. Further, we have different assumptions as to what is important, necessary, desirable, and these assumptions can change depending on the methodological approach being drawn upon. Although this process calls attention to the relativistic elements in our assessments of truth and argues the case that (the essence of) truths are not of limited value – that is, they are neither stable nor final, that they can neither be confined nor defined – employing a transparent and rigorous form of analytical examination can make room for a strong claim to objectivity.

Concerning a possible issue of establishing an objective standpoint, being objective should not be equated to being value free. Being critical involves making judgments, and to 'make a judgment about something is to evaluate it according to some standard or other' (Graham, 2018, p. 187). It is hence incumbent on the analyst to make explicit the standards under which their value judgements are devised, or in this case, illustrating the relevance of the analytical approaches adopted (Graham, 2018, pp. 187, 201). In using CDA, a very considerable degree of attention is required to be cognizant of the subtle implications of one's own assumptions or assumptive/reactive tendencies, while also sensing similar discursive patterns within policy texts as a whole (cf. Lee, 2004, p. ix).

Implications of the research

The study set out to employ CDA to analyse policy texts in order to make explicit and provide critical evidence as to *how* inequality is inbuilt into the education system. This final section provides an overview of the empirical findings of this objective in relation to the broad overarching conceptualisation of meritocracy and its relations with metaphors, and the sole pursuit of economic growth. Further, it highlights the way the multiple approaches that have been developed may be of utility to researchers in examining the relationships between discourse, political economy, and inequality.

Meritocracy in Singapore has conditions which are unequal. Within the context of a meritocracy, inegalitarian access to privileged knowledge immediately abolishes privilege as a category on the basis of a particular value system. By exposing the assumptions that guide this ideology, the analysis demonstrated that the consequence of adhering to the value system is increasing structural inequality. This process which takes the problematisation of truth as a point of departure to examine *what is*, rather than drawing on the historical, social, and political contexts to understand the object under investigation, provides a practical anchorage to the normative dimension of ideological critique. In doing so, the philosophical foundations of policy discourse are made explicit and taken as problematic. Thus, this research offers an opportunity to view some of the most fundamental contradictions inherent in the logic of meritocracy – the basic, seemingly objective, seemingly immutable advent of changing economies. The paradox of 'self-interest' played out by these policies entails a moral imperative to relinquish one's own self-interested claim to access more valued forms of knowledge, now reserved for 'talents', for the sake of self and the nation's economic interests.

Paradoxically, the education policies claim to implement 'flexibility', 'diversity', and 'choice' as necessary responses to cater to different learner capabilities and the drive for economic growth. Yet, the analysis suggests that the *systematic-eternal recurrence* of these policy metaphors, and their complex metaphorical relations, enables systematic discrimination within the education system. As the analysis in the monograph demonstrates, the transliteration of meritocratic discourse into the metaphors of flexibility, diversity, choice, and opportunity pinpoints how the appeal of *development for all* necessarily also demands the advance of inequity for the sake of the whole. Further, through the process of valuation, these metaphors contribute to the *construction* of global competition and comparative advantage as inevitable. Neo-liberalism in this sense is strongly marked by the willingness to place ethical values on par with the desirability of economic growth. That is to say, neo-liberalism is a moral system. This study has argued that within a meritocratic system, *how* these metaphors are exploited cannot be taken as an indicator of greater 'equality' within the system, and attention was drawn to the ways in which the use of these metaphors operates as moral discourses. The educational inequality generated by the policies undermines any effort to realise the equality necessary to make meritocracy credible.

In order to allow incisive critique and to question prevailing structural reforms so as to improve the education system, it would help if policymakers mark their distance from the rhetoric of 'meritocracy' by first dropping it from public vocabulary, or at least admit to its downside. Refusing to question policy assumptions and the belief in the system as being fair on the basis that it is meritocratic and that every child has the *same* opportunity to succeed would mean that we will try to solve the problem of inequality at every level except the level at which the problems exist (cf. Walsh, 2005, pp. 73, 141). If the assumptions made about the system are accepted without problematisation, the difficulties in understanding the conditions underpinning their emergence become analogous to reinforcing issues facing the current problem of (educational) inequality. Using the analogy of a river that is being polluted continuously at its source, Bohm (2004b, p. 57) points out that attempts to eradicate pollution 'downstream' merely diverts attention away from solving the problem. In order to get the community past the sterility of such discourse, the real solution, he proposes, lies in addressing what is generating the pollution at the source, i.e. it means to see things as they really are, the 'what is' in order to see the source of what we believe as necessary has come to be. The purpose here is to raise critical self-awareness of how policy discourse supports this ideological framework that has established an order of *meritocratic inequality* as *necessary*, as 'what cannot be otherwise' (Bohm, 1994, p. 286), i.e., why this order and not any other?

The purpose here is not to transform the order of society into something else, to create a new belief system, or to think of alternate systems. To do so without being clear about 'what is going on' would only suggest a change from one form to another without examining the source of structural disadvantages. The deeper intention is to be aware of discrepancies or disharmonies between the intention of fulfilling the twin imperatives of equal opportunity and economic growth, and the actual consequences that flow out of this intention or purpose, and to allow the whole structural organisation to change if necessary (cf. Bohm, 1987, p. 82). For as Bohm (2004a, pp. 141–142) points out, if we are unconsciously in our practice doing the opposite of what we claim we want to do, we simultaneously create all of the activities which make the problem in the first place and then we create another set of activities to try to overcome it. We cannot see that we are creating a problem and are then apparently trying to solve it. He stresses, therefore, that 'the important point is to be aware of what we are actually doing.' Without discrediting their benefits, support from self-help groups and boosting financial assistance schemes for students can have limited effectiveness at remedying underachievement as long as these services or schemes are layered on a system that provides differential access to knowledge. Current initiatives to create special labels and programmes for 'at-risk' children and youth are unlikely to succeed if they do not attend to the structural conditions of schools that place children at risk. Students can be *placed* 'at risk' when fundamental institutional conditions fail to satisfy their needs (Ismail & Tan, 2005). Research that develops strategies to improve the core systemic practices of schooling, rather than layering additional programmes on systemic conditions that may be incompatible with the needs and aspirations of students, is hence fundamental.

The problem is with the prescriptive model

Further, drawing on the ethics-morality philosophical dimension elucidated the conditionings which are part of the subject. Understanding these conditions provides the possibility of freeing ourselves from neo-liberal capitalism. Neo-liberal capitalism is conceived as a machine designed to create a sense of *necessity* especially through the provision of *opportunities* that will arise only by meeting the *perceived* demands of political economies which do not in fact exist in reality. This *necessity* is a form of marketing strategy generated by a business-run society. Illustrating how truths are (re)produced exposes the arbitrary value of economic growth as the only way forward. This ideology is not a preordained logic. Rather, a (hidden) system of values extracted from policy discourse can explain the parameters of our current existence. This system of values gives rise to a particular model of the world which continually recreates our conditions of existence.

How the surrealist movement shaped the course of political economy and our lives

The notion and operation of necessity, as that which cannot be otherwise and that which limits the contingency of what can be otherwise (Bohm, 2006, p. 43), and the construction of hypperreality, can be argued as being inextricably bound together. Through the valuation of necessity, meeting the *perceived* demands of surrealistic economies is taken as a mere fact of life. The assumption of necessity entails powerful discursive effects. It is through this deterministic assumption that arbitrary propositions and proposals are able to hold themselves as true and produce the appearance of non-arbitrariness. Further, the being and becoming of the world is based on the notion of desire. Metaphorical movement in policy discourse is the movement of desire and its capacity to create the illusion of the notion of desire, or of the desiring subject, through juxtaposing ir/realis spaces.

Using a multi-level micro-meso-macro CDA framework, the transliteration of meritocratic discourse into these metaphors within the context of a wholly orchestrated and engineered economic regime is made explicit. This framework would be useful where part of the analytical task is to describe the field of dispersal of other sets of independently existent but interacting concepts of 'flexibility', 'diversity', and 'choice' in symbiotic relationships with educational-economic discourse in order to pursue and extend the neo-liberal economic order. Further, it provides a theoretical base for future archaeological-genealogical discourse analysis. This is an important undertaking, as this field of dispersal actualises ascending forms of global inequality where the narrative of progress and growth (Fairclough, 2000b, p. 148) is subsumed under the arbitrary logic of creating opportunities for all through the investment of a selected few.

Through the inception of the micro-meso-macro framework, the value system that is presented can be conceived of as a living system. That is, in order to make genealogy and CDA work together, the system is understood as 'living' in the sense that more data can be, and should be, added in the examination of evolving discursive change (Anais, 2013, p. 131). This value system works by a set of conditions that are potentially unlimited, as more and more data can be added, thus further modifying the conditions for structural changes. Hence, elementary conditions, as that which were determined by the micro-meso movement, may take the form of several modifications through and within the meso-macro movement. In order to delineate the subtle complexity of a metaphor and how its work is threaded through policy texts, the nature of metaphorical relations as contingent possibilities for structural conditions needs to be established through analysis.

The endeavour for political economies to constantly *become*, that is, this surrealist movement of becoming, is potentially divisive: it creates an illusion of our existence as humans as distinct and separate within the context of labour appropriation. To borrow Foucault's (1982a, pp. 777–778) words, 'the subject is either divided inside himself or divided from others' through human objectification. Further, this movement of becoming disconnects, through the projection of irrealis states as real, with our present, unique, existence – from *what is* to *becoming what should be*. That is, we have to constantly endeavour to *become* something ourselves, and caught in the trap of becoming, we are conditioned as slaves to the verb *to be* (Krishnamurti, 2005, p. 9), to respond to the model of realities that has been prescribed for us – that which meets the *perceived* demands of irrealis industrial economies. It is within this prescribed model that 'people are isolated from each other, and the participation is very limited' as 'we treat other people as objects, and eventually we must treat ourselves as an object, thus losing connection to the essence of who we really are, saying "I must fit in here, and I must do this and be that and become better", or whatever' (Bohm, 2004b, p. 101). As Maté (2012; 2019) points out, the more divorced people are from an essential part of themselves and from others, the more they can fit mechanistically into the neo-liberal economy which prioritises profitability and production through fabricating the human mind and human behaviour.

Fabricated versions of the world have been employed to ensure capital gains within the sphere of moral values under which the phenomenon of 'life' comes to be (cf. Nietzsche, 1989, p. 27). The very nature of capital accumulation brings about human division and can create conflict within oneself and with others (cf. Krishnamurti & Bohm, 2014, p. 325). As such, the twin imperatives of meritocracy and economic growth as mechanistic ideals of *what should be* that seems to dominate society can lead to a state of increasing fragmentation, both within the experience of individual human beings and in society as a whole through preventing us from examining the phenomenon of 'What is (really going on here)?' (cf. Krishnamurti, 2005, p. 11). That is, we have to see the truth of what is actually happening rather than following particular value systems without clarity. The policies' focus on the future without examining the present denies the possibility of deriving *what should be* from *what is*. That is, a reason should be given instead in policy for inferring *what should be* the case, from *what is* the case (Hume, 1739, pp. 244–245).

Government as a kind of civil service for corporations?

The economic success of self and nation are dictated by the advent of changing political economies (Fairclough, 2000b, p. 147). Educational programmes are hence tailored to the perceived demands of irrealis industries. Through policies, corporate sectors' interests are strengthened because policies privilege their demands over equality of the people. If this is indeed the case, how do governments of different political complexions come to accept the arbitrary logic of the global economy as an institutional imperative and its consequential role in society? Why are their policies designed to prioritise and meet the demands and terms of industries and corporations unquestioningly? That is, how did they become loyal adherents to, and under the control of, the neo-liberal economic order (Fairclough, 2000b, p. 147)? How have corporations been appointed to impose their choice and their conception of man on humanity, thus reducing him to an object (cf. Sartre, 1985, pp. 20, 37)? Within this context, can meritocracy which is defined as 'equal opportunities for each student to learn and to achieve his or her potential' (Wong, 2000, n.p.) exist if human dimensions and potential must conform to capitalist standards of labour and maintain profitability for corporations? Privileging an economic system that is motivated by profit through inequality can stand in the way of progress through accelerating established and problematic patterns of global industrial development that objectify and separate human beings one from another.

The endeavour for political economies to constantly *become*, that is, this movement of becoming, is potentially divisive: it disconnects, through the projection of irrealis states as real, with our present, unique, existence – from *what is* to *what should be*. That is, we as subjects, have to constantly endeavour to *become* something ourselves, to respond to the model of realities that has been prescribed for us – that which meets the *perceived* demands of irrealis industrial economies. In relation to the desiring subject, desire in this instance is the *movement* of the mind into the future; it is non-existential. Significantly, the desire to *become* for the changing unknowable, of constantly having to engage in shifting narratives of an uncertain world, that which is beyond all daily life would mean that desires are never really fulfilled. Would it be possible then to be free from this necessity, that is, to be released from this immediate recourse to make-believe from which emerges the compulsion to acquire particular skills that inevitably limit the range of choice for all of us, although for some very much more than for others (Hayek, 2007, p.77)?

Can Singapore's SkillsFuture policy initiative work to reduce income inequality and help upward mobility when streaming is an instrument for determining one's precise place in a school hierarchy, ostensibly in return for greater economic successes? Rather than viewing schools as environments to transmit to children 'knowledge' resulting from the need to meet the demands of industrial economies which could be obsolete given that these economies are continuously changing, there is a need to build democratic schools that *draw wisdom out* of children, 'in which they have as much to say about what they are to learn and how they will learn it as teachers' (Walsh, 2013, p. 366, italics included). An autonomous curriculum that focuses on demonstrating this co-creation with an ethos of unity and cooperation can give children the opportunity to find their own truth, value, and purpose, and the tools to conceive of a world that is distinct from the material realm and systems of separation (Walsh, 2013, pp. 378, 380, 382). Such a curriculum can create the conditions to reshape the economy around new values and behaviours leading to the dissolution of the worker–capitalist division. The following sections raises questions about the moral and social objectives of education.

Become seekers of truth rather than believers: the need to overcome the conditioning of belief

Streaming is underpinned by the 'fundamental ***belief*** that students had varying learning ability, and would therefore be *better off* being grouped together to learn at their appropriate pace. Put simply, streaming allows each child to better fulfil his inherent potential' (Ng, 2008a, n.p.). Progress can be blocked by a set of rigidly held assumptions that are taken for granted by society as a whole but must nevertheless be defended (cf. Bohm & Peat, 2010, p. 246). Bohm and Peat (2010) argue that 'Any belief in some definable form of the absolute entails the notion of absolute *necessity*, which leads to an unyielding attitude in which basic assumptions are nonnegotiable' (p. 266). There is thus a need to examine the implicit assumptions underpinning policy discourse if we are to overcome our conditioning in how the world should be organised. Out of this kind of conditioning has arisen what is perhaps the principal problem that Singapore's education system has to face in the domain of inequality – i.e., the difficulty of entertaining new concepts which clash with older ones that we have held habitually since its the inception of streaming in such a way that to go beyond such an idea seems inconceivable.

This problem of conditioning is serious. Despite the 1979 MOE report being produced over 40 years ago, its recommendations to move away from a uniform curriculum and instead to allow students to study at different paces that 'suited them' continues to be a major and central influence. The MOE recently introduced subject-based banding system in secondary schools. As reported in a *Straits Times* article titled 'Subject-based Banding to Replace Streaming in Schools', dated 6 March 2019:

> All Secondary 1 students in the 2024 batch will take subjects at three levels – G1, G2 or G3, with G standing for 'General'. G1 will roughly correspond to today's N(T) standard, G2 to N(A) standard and G3 to Express standard. ... MOE will develop new admission criteria for students going to junior college, polytechnic, and ITE. These will take effect in 2028.
>
> (Davie, 2019, n.p.)

However, *how* subject-based banding comprising a tripartite system of G1, G2 or G3, is a different system from the current institutionalised form of streaming remains to be seen, as it may still be underpinned by the 'belief that students would be better off being grouped together to learn at their appropriate pace' (Ng, 2008, n.p.). If this is the case, subject-based banding can be conceived as a superficial change of streaming. It is not a radical replacement, but merely a modified continuity of what has been, as students are still fundamentally grouped according to their 'learning ability'. Why this form of grouping is adopted, however, is not made clear. The burden of proof in choosing this approach rests with those who propose the idea (cf. Watts, 1951, p. 18). Have we taken for granted the assumption or perhaps, and more importantly, how have we been conditioned to accept that we *should* adapt our curriculum according to seemingly self-evident notions about the 'learning ability' of our students – a judgment made based on the students' standardised test scores or performance? Under what conditions was this value judgment devised? Asking fundamental questions that problematise or challenge this often taken-for-granted or 'naturalised' idea are thus crucial in disrupting its continuum. If we continue to focus on programmes to reduce inequality, without addressing the real underlying concerns that led to its production in the first place, and to its retention, we will advance neither the cause of meritocracy nor social equality. If we seek to advance right away a new profile or formula for the future of the education system without thoroughly examining all the assumptions underpinning historical policy discourse, we run the risk of letting unexamined assumptions be reproduced and sustained in subsequent policies. Isn't there a risk that we may be led into error?

Currently, the assumptions behind the 1979 MOE report need examining, as the assertions or causal link of factors linked to students' performance are mostly assumed rather than supported by empirical evidence. For instance, the analysis of the 1979 MOE report revealed the way a deficit view of students as failures was constructed and where the segregation from other children is framed as necessary to avoid exposing them to 'competition from brighter children'. But to assume that there is 'less danger of loss of self-esteem' since they are not 'exposed to competition from brighter children' needs to be examined. Important questions regarding the assumption on which streaming is said to be based is that 'slow learners' develop more positive attitudes about themselves when they do not have to face daily a classroom populated by those who are judged to be brighter must be raised (cf. Oakes, 2005, p. 196). Whether this pessimism is justified remains to be seen.

The crucial criteria underlying the judgments about students' educability are still unexplored, and this is disconcerting given that Oakes (2005, p. 191) argues that

> tracking does not appear to be related to either increasing academic achievement or promoting positive attitudes and behaviours. Poor and minority students seem to have suffered most from tracking – and these are the very students on whom so many educational hopes are pinned.

The decision made in the 1979 MOE report that a reduced academic load is appropriate for students deemed 'less academically inclined'[2] may not be a result of critical and compassionate inquiry of the human condition and of how students learn – the *what is*, but rather would most often result from unquestioned responses (cf. Oakes, 2005, p. 193) and a fragmentary approach to viewing reality. This fragmentation arises when an attempt is made to impose human subdivisions in an arbitrary fashion, according to the perceived demands of surrealistic political economies. These structural demands call for close scrutiny, especially given the hold they have on the organisation of society.

The novel synthesis of analytic approaches presented in this investigation demonstrates a model for researchers of discourse that takes a more dynamic approach to the analysis of policy. Taken together, the current investigation adds an incremental understanding of how inequality is built in to education policy discourse, and forges a path for further investigations to employ similar approaches in other policy-related studies focused on unpacking the discursive phenomenon of inequality. Through the examination of Singapore's policy discourse, one could find hope in recognising the real capacity of dismantling the logic of neo-liberalism. Today, subdued economic growth and widening income inequality (Goh, 2016) are undermining the education policies that were traditionally associated with economic growth and promising 'opportunities for all' through talent investment (Shanmugaratnam, 2003). Through a rigorous analytical examination, this research argues that neo-liberalism, as a system of principles of valuation and evaluation, in practice, translates into an ideology of inequality in the guise of economic growth.

What is the moral purpose of education?

The assumption here is that schools function as the basic institutional structure of a society, and that unless the framework for equity and the moral imperative to maximise each child's potential is fair, the society cannot be just. To ameliorate possible tensions and yield a patently just solution, what the situation here then demands is a respect for attaining equality of structural conditions, with priority given to the disadvantaged. This justice of an arrangement that takes note of a person's difficulties – naturally or socially generated – could potentially enable everyone to have the *same* opportunity to be educated and to openly compete (Sen, 1992, pp. 147–148).

Through examining the assumptions that underpin education policy discourse and demonstrating how they might possibly undermine and contradict meritocratic principles, we will then be able to examine the source of structural disadvantages. If we want the best for all our population, then we need to have a flexible, critically examined education system to make progressive improvements. If 'inequality' serves the purpose of high international evaluation assessments[3] then there needs to be professed transparency in communicating that the ideology of meritocracy fosters structural reforms that disadvantage a certain segment of the population. If we accept the operational objective of the system that everyone is not going to succeed in the same way, should that disproportionately affect a certain group of people? This contingent nature of meritocracy or reward system indicates that its relationship with inequality should be clearly demarcated in the objective function of the Singapore society (cf. Sen, 2000, p. 14), including making explicit whose interests are being served from the phenomenon of meritocratic inequality remaining unchanged. The contributions made in this study will hopefully be of some use to future research in policy analysis and illuminate how establishing societies with low inequality is not a desirable – even a *necessary* goal.

Spearheading a world-class education system

Since the underlying assumptions that drive the practice of neo-liberalism are, in essence, unveiled as unsubstantiated and arbitrary, current policies are susceptible to being systematically dismantled and rebuilt (Chomsky, 2013, p. 110). More importantly, in seeing how education policies are unfounded and unsupported through the idea of meritocracy, lies also an opportunity for the creation and evolution of the 'Singapore model'. Through letting go of the idea that the system is meritocratic, which is in effect allowing incisive critique through questioning prevailing notions and prior assumptions within the system by which to improve it and innovate, Singapore can move forward and become a pioneer in addressing challenges associated with inequality pertaining to advanced economies.

The Singapore education system is seen as being one that is internationally successful, and perhaps now, from a position of strength and maturity, is the time to take the lead in education policies. An honest approach is not to assume that everyone starts from the same point, and to recognise that identifying and allowing 'opportunity' would mean that the government will need to create the conditions for joinedup thinking in terms of policymaking and development. If the results desired have a strong distributive component, in which equitable knowledge access is seen as valuable in leading a worthwhile life, concerns about the resource distribution and learning conditions would need to enter the evaluation, as they can be directly influential in determining a person's well-being (cf. Sen, 2000, p. 13).

Is it time to equalise conditions across schools?

On 27 January 2016, Member of Parliament Denise Phua told Parliament that Singapore should 're-dream and slay the sacred cow of physically separating people who learn differently'. She called on the government to 'rethink the concept of Arts School, Sports School, Normal Tech School, SAP Schools, Special Schools'. She suggested that 'programmes – including those for the gifted – should be made available across more schools so that students of different abilities and talents can grow together' (Channel NewsAsia, 2016).

It can be deemed a huge waste of society's reserves if only those who are identified as 'talent' early in life are given the opportunity to fully develop. Attempts to invest in a small minority of talents identified through the streaming system can lead to severe curtailment of the capabilities that people can altogether have within the context of contending claims of economic efficiency (cf. Sen, 1992, p. 8). Is it time to realise the possibility of making programmes for the gifted and the conditions of specialised schools available across schools so that students of different abilities and talents can be given the *same* opportunities to grow together? The principal aim can be to provide and support our students with more control over what, when and how they study, with access to greater global exchange, mentoring and research opportunities. This will provide an avenue to illustrate Singapore's commitment to maintaining its reputation as a champion of institutional and knowledge leadership for a better world, through developing scalable pedagogical interventions to enable systemic improvement in the education system. Concerted efforts to ask new research questions that examine the assumptions underpinning the current economic model, which prioritises reforms primarily on industrial demands, are worthwhile.

Notes

1 The surrealis state is the juxtaposition of both realis and irrealis spaces (cf. Graham, 2000, p. 761).
2 This term was used by Minister for Education, Ong Ye Kung at the Schools Work Plan Seminar on 28 September 2018 in relation to the current school curriculum which 'caters to students of different learning paces and learning needs' (Ong, 2018, n.p.).
3 Singapore tops the world PISA (the OECD's Programme for International Student Assessment) scores in mathematics, science, reading, and collaborative problem solving, and in TIMSS (Trends in International Mathematics and Science Study). Singapore is number two in the world in PIRLS (Progress in International Reading Literacy Study), and has one of the smallest proportions of low performers in PISA, TIMSS, and PIRLS (Rajah, 2018, n.p.).

Policy reports and speeches

Note: The following texts have been taken directly from the reports and speeches.

1 Curriculum Development in Singapore. A Brief Review 1979

This report of 25 numbered pages (MOE, 1979b) consists of addresses to the Deputy Prime Minister and Minister of Education by Robert W. Morris and Gerald P. Thompson, and seven sections: Background to the visit; Working procedures; The curriculum – some general considerations; The curriculum – some particular aspects; Conclusions and recommendations; Acknowledgements; Annexes.

Following the publication of the 1979 report and the appointment of Dr Goh Keng Swee as Minister of Education, discussions took place between the British Council and the Ministry on the possibility of acquiring British expertise to assist with developments of the curriculum needed to meet the demands of the new system (p. 4). The terms of reference required the team to (p. 4):

- explore the existing mechanisms through which curriculum development is carried out;
- investigate the qualifications and experience of those involved in curriculum development;
- examine the constraints on curriculum development in Singapore;
- assess the support services for implementing new curriculum materials in schools;
- visit schools, teacher training institutions and other resources available to improve the quality of education in schools;
- make recommendations to the Ministry and to the British Council for continued cooperation.

2 *Towards Excellence in Schools*, 1987

This report of 85 numbered pages (MOE, 1987) consists of: Address to Dr Tony Tan Keng Yam Minister for Education by the principals in the study team; Address to the principals by Dr Tan; Key findings and recommendations;

Executive summary; Introduction; Chapter 1 – The schools in perspective; Chapter 2 – School philosophy and policy; Chapter 3 – Organisation and school structure; Chapter 4 – The headmaster; Chapter 5 – The staff; Chapter 6 – The school community; Chapter 7 – The curriculum; Chapter 8 – Finance; Chapter 9 – Physical resources; Chapter 10 – Conclusions and recommendations; Appendices and acknowledgements.

The 1987 report was based on the report by principals on the schools that they had studied during their visit to the United States of America and the United Kingdom in November/December 1986 that identified the factors which go to make a good and effective school, and considered how such factors could be developed in Singapore's schools (n.p.). While the reference is mainly to secondary schools, some of the issues are relevant to primary schools and junior colleges as well (n.p.).

3 *Improving Primary School Education: Report of the Review Committee*, 1991

The report of 29 numbered pages (MOE, 1991a) consists of: Address by Dr Tony Tan Keng Yam, Minister for Education, at the conclusion of the schools council meeting held on 9 March 1991 to discuss the Review Committee's report; Executive summary; Chapter 1 – Introduction; Chapter 2 – Review of present system; Chapter 3 – Proposed improvements to primary education; Chapter 4 – Consequential changes; and Chapter 5 – Conclusion.

This report provides recommendations that will give more children at least ten years of general education before they proceed to junior colleges or vocational or technical training in polytechnics and technical institutes. It was proposed that a new secondary level Normal (Technical) course will be introduced for pupils who are not academically inclined to better orientate and prepare them for vocational training (n.p.). The Minister for Education set up a Review Committee in July 1990 to review the system and take measures to ensure that it continues to meet the nation's needs in the 1990s and beyond, as Singapore becomes a developed nation (p. i). In its review, the Committee was guided by the curriculum needs of pupils. It considered the demands and expectations of the school system, streaming of pupils, and vocational education and training. In addition, it studied the primary school systems in Germany and Japan, which are models of successful modern economies, to consider features and practices which could be adopted or adapted for implementation in Singapore's system (p. i) as well as the provision of streaming and vocational education in Germany as practised in the state of Baden-Württemberg (p. 2).

4 *Upgrading Vocational Training* (Vocational and Industrial Training Board, 1991)

The report of 43 numbered pages (MOE, 1991b) consists of: Executive summary; Chapter 1 – Introduction; Chapter II – Review of present vocational training system; Chapter III – Proposed changes to upgrade vocational training; Chapter IV – Implementation plan and interim arrangements; Chapter V – Conclusions.

This report formulates plans to upgrade vocational training for a new secondary level Normal (Technical) course that will be introduced for pupils who are not academically inclined to better orientate and prepare them for vocational training. The review was guided by the following aims:

1 a system which enables secondary school leavers to achieve higher-level skills;
2 wider options in occupational choices;
3 more opportunities for progression to further education and training;
4 the upgraded vocational training system should be more attractive to school leavers and employers.

It should help produce a better educated and skilled workforce to meet the skilled manpower needs of Singapore in the 1990s and beyond (p. v). The committee took into consideration views expressed by employers, unionists, government officials, the strength of the 'dual system' of apprenticeship training in Germany, and findings established in previous relevant reports which include the Perception Study on Vocational Training and the annual VITB Graduate Employment Surveys (p. 2).

5 *Report of the Junior College/Upper Secondary Education Review Committee*, 2002

This report of 98 numbered pages (MOE, 2002) consists of: Aaddress to Radm Teo Chee Hean Minister for Education by Mr Tharman Shanmugaratnam, chairman of the review committee; Address to Mr Tharman Shanmugaratnam Senior Minister of State for Trade & Industry and Education, and Chairman, Junior College/Upper Secondary Education Review Committee; Executive summary; Chapter 1 – Introduction; Chapter 2 – Evolving the junior college/upper secondary education system; Chapter 3 – A broader and more flexible JC curriculum; Chapter 4 – A more diverse junior college/upper secondary education landscape; Annexes.

The 2002 report developed a revised junior college curriculum framework and set out a vision for the JC/upper secondary education system, including the appropriate structures, types of programmes to be offered, and the mix of schools to deliver the programmes. Their recommendations have two main thrusts. First, to introduce a revised JC curriculum to better develop students' thinking skills and engage them in greater breadth of learning. The revised curriculum should also provide the flexibility to take subjects at different levels, and provide space for students with exceptional aptitude and passion for a subject to pursue it to greater depth beyond the regular curriculum. Second, they proposed to free up the system to allow for new pathways in education. It was argued that Singapore will need more diverse talents in future, nurtured and trained along different routes. This can be enabled by allowing integrated programmes that combine upper secondary and JC education seamlessly; specialised schools for special talents in the arts, sports and mathematics and science; alternative, internationally-recognised curricula; and a few privately run schools. These new programmes will provide a valuable complement to the continuing innovation within the mainstream of the JC/upper secondary system (n.p.).

The Committee drew insights from visits and study of school systems in United Kingdom and United States, and top schools in Hong Kong and China (p. i).

6 *Report of the Polytechnic-School Review Committee*, 2006

This report of 45 numbered pages (MOE, 2006) consists of: Address to Mr Tharman Shanmugaratnam, Minister for Education, by the chairman of the review committee, Mr Gan Kim Yong; Address to Mr Gan Kim Yong Minister of State for Manpower and Education and Chairman of the Polytechnic-School Review Committee; Executive Summary; Chapter 1 – Introduction; Chapter 2 – Enriching our secondary school curriculum through advanced elective modules; Chapter 3 – Enriching our secondary school curriculum through applied graded subjects; Chapter 4 – Direct polytechnic admission exercise; Chapter 5 – Implementation; Annexes.

The Committee explored ways to enhance the learning experience of secondary school students through a more applied approach. There are three main thrusts to their recommendations. First, they propose greater curriculum flexibility and choice for students by introducing more applied modules as an enrichment to the upper secondary curriculum. Second, they will introduce more applied subjects that can replace existing 'O' Level subjects. Third, they want to recognise student achievements and talent beyond the academic areas and broaden measures of success. To do so, they propose to introduce a Direct Polytechnic Admissions (DPA) exercise similar to the Direct School Admission system available for entry to secondary schools and junior colleges (n.p.). The study drew insights from visits and study of school systems in Sweden, Switzerland, France and the United States (p. 8).

Annex B: Terms of reference (p. 25)

The terms of reference for the Polytechnic-School Review Committee are:

a To study the value and feasibility of putting in place a new applied and practice-oriented pathway in secondary education catering to the needs of the students with appropriate interest and ability.

b In the context of (a), to consider the feasibility of the following two options:

  i Offering relevant applied and practice-oriented subjects and elective modules, mounted in the secondary schools or the polytechnics, to enrich the secondary school curriculum; and

  ii Establishing a closer link between selected secondary schools and polytechnics so that students with suitable abilities can progress to these polytechnics without having to sit for the GCE 'O' level examinations.

  iii To study other local and foreign models that can contribute to an applied and practice-oriented pathway in secondary education, and provide a value proposition for secondary students to opt for a polytechnic education, which will better engage our students and offer them more choices.

7 Speech, 'The next phase in education: Innovation and enterprise', 2003

The 2003 policy speech (Shanmugaratnam, 2003) by Tharman Shanmugaratnam, Acting Minister for Education, with the theme, 'The next phase in education: Innovation and Enterprise' highlights that the key focus for MOE in the coming years is to nurture a spirit of innovation and enterprise among students and teachers in schools.

8 Speech, 'More support for school-based initiatives', 2006

The 2006 policy speech (Shanmugaratnam, 2006) by Tharman Shanmugaratnam, Minister for Education, with the theme, 'More support for school-based initiatives: Ground-up initiatives, top-down support', emphasises on how quality improvements will not come in top-down form, but from initiatives taken by teachers on the ground – whether it is a change in the school curriculum, or a new way of teaching the existing curriculum, or a new way of organising students for learning (n.p.).

9 *Report of the Committee on the Expansion of the University Sector: Greater Choice, More Room to Excel: Final Report*, 2008

This report of 48 numbered pages (MOE, 2008a) consists of: Address to Dr Ng Eng Hen Minister for Education and Second Minister for Defence by Lui Tuck Yew, Chairman of the committee; Aaddress to RAdm (NS) Lui Tuck Yew, Senior Minister of State for Education and Chairman, Committee on the Expansion of the University Sector by Dr Ng Eng Hen; Executive summary; Chapter 1 – Introduction; Chapter 2 – Singapore's current university landscape; Chapter 3 – Producing graduates for the future; Chapter 4 – Evolution and enhancement of the existing universities; Chapter 5 – A new publicly-funded university; Chapter 6 – Liberal arts education in Singapore; Chapter 7 – Niche degree programmes; Chapter 8 – Conclusion; Chapter 9 – Annexes.

The 2008 report recommends the best approach to expanding the university sector. This expansion aims to increase the university cohort participation rate from 25% to 30% of each primary one cohort by 2015, while maintaining the high standards of Singapore's tertiary sector and producing graduates who are well equipped to drive the country's economy. The Committee recommends the establishment of a new publicly-funded university. It was argued that a new university will offer the opportunity to create an institution with its own unique identity, character and model of education and add further diversity to Singapore's university sector. It will also provide more university places while upholding the quality of education and standard of excellence expected of Singapore's publicly-funded universities (n.p.). Between September and October 2007, members of the Committee and Working Groups (the New University Working Group and the Liberal Arts College Working Group) visited countries in Europe and the United States to learn about different university models and systems. Successful features of these well-established systems were distilled as learning points for Singapore's own long-term vision (p. 6).

10 *Report of the Committee on University Education Pathways Beyond 2015 (CUEP). Greater Diversity, More Opportunities,* 2012

This report of 78 numbered pages (MOE, 2012a) consists of: Address to Mr Heng Swee Keat, Minister for Education by Lawrence Wong Chairman of the committee; Address to Mr Lawrence Wong, Senior Minister of State (Education and Information, Communications and the Arts) and Chairman, Committee on University Education Pathways beyond 2015) by Mr Heng Swee Keat; Executive summary. Followed by Part 1: Considerations behind the committee's recommendations, consisting of Chapter 1 – Introduction to the Committee On University Education Pathways Beyond 2015 (CUEP); and Chapter 2 – Rationale and key considerations for the review of university education pathways beyond 2015. Part 2: Room to grow the university sector – quantitatively and qualitatively, consists of Chapter 3 – Increasing the publicly-funded university cohort participation rate (CPR); and Chapter 4 – A more diversified university landscape. Part 3: Diversifying the university sector, consists of Chapter 5 – A new applied degree pathway, with strong nexus with the economy; Chapter 6 – Leveraging on the private education (PE) sector; and Chapter 7 – Developing continuing education and training (CET) as a viable degree pathway. Part 4: Enablers, consists of Chapter 8 – Ensuring the continued affordability of a degree education; and Chapter 9 – Education and career guidance. This is followed by Chapter 10 – Conclusion; Acknowledgements; and Annexes.

The report examines how the university sector can better provide opportunities for Singaporeans to obtain a university education. This includes studies of feasible models and strategies, international trends, and Singapore's own unique context. The Committee recommends raising the publicly-funded, pre-employment training (PET) university cohort participation rate (CPR) to 40% by 2020, thereby creating about 3,000 additional places, compared to today. In order to diversify the current university landscape and create differentiated options for Singaporeans, the Committee also proposes that this increase should be through a new applied degree pathway, which would have a close nexus with the economy and produce graduates equipped with a strong theoretical foundation and a keen understanding of its real-life implications (n.p.). During its study trip overseas to the United States, Hong Kong, Canada, France, Germany, and Finland, the Committee encountered different university systems with varying compositions of public and private universities (pp. 8–9), and studied the university landscape and experiences of those countries and economies (p. 15).

11 Speech by Minister for Education Ong Ye Kung, at the Raffles Institution Founder's Day, 2019

The 2019 policy speech by Ong Ye Kung (Ong, 2019) presents three suggestions that can contribute to overcoming the limitations of meritocracy and fight against the ossification of social classes. They are: (1) calibrate expectations of meritocracy, (2) broaden the definition of meritocracy, and (3) to put in a strong effort to actively reach out and provide greater support to students from humbler backgrounds.

12 Speech, 'Working with low-income families through the life course: Challenges to social services', 2019

This policy speech by Minister for Education and Finance Indranee Rajah (Rajah, 2019) outlines how the fourth generation of Singapore's political leaders plan to approach the issue of inequality and social mobility through not just strengthening support for those who have less, but also striving to create opportunities for all citizens at every stage of life. The main concern highlighted is on how advancements in technology threaten to deepen the divide between higher-skilled and lower-skilled workers, who risk being shut off from new opportunities. The 4G's team approach is not to do away with meritocracy, or cap the top, but to uplift the bottom by improving access to opportunities among the less advantaged, in order to bridge the gaps of inequality and create an enabling meritocracy.

References

Adonis. (2005). *Sufism and surrealism*. London: Saqi.

Alvesson, M. & Karreman, D. (2000). Varieties of discourse: On the study of organizations through discourse analysis. *Human Relations*, 53(9), 1125–1149.

Anais, S. (2013). Genealogy and critical discourse analysis in conversation: Texts, discourse, critique. *Critical Discourse Studies*, 10(2), 123–135.

Anderson, N.A. (2003). *Discursive analytical strategies: Understanding Foucault, Koselleck, Laclau, Luhmann*. Bristol: The Policy Press.

Archer, L. (2007). Diversity, equality and higher education: A critical reflection on the ab/uses of equity discourse within widening participation. *Teaching in Higher Education*, 12 (5–6), 635–653.

Asher, N.Benamara, F. & Mathieu, Y.Y. (2009). Appraisal of opinion expressions in discourse. *Lingvisticae Investigationes*, 32(2), 279–292.

Astiz, M.F., Wiseman, A.W. & Baker, D.P. (2002). Slouching towards decentralization: Consequences of globalization for curricular control in national education systems. *Comparative Education Review*, 46(1), 66–88.

Ball, S. (1997). Policy sociology and critical social research: A personal review of recent education policy and policy research. *British Educational Research Journal*, 23(3), 257–274.

Barr, M. & Skrbiš, Z. (2008). *Constructing Singapore: Elitism, ethnicity and the nation-building project*. Copenhagen: NIAS.

Betts, R.H. (1975). Multiracialism, meritocracy and the Malays of Singapore (doctoral dissertation). Massachusetts Institute of Technology, U.S.A. Retrieved from http://search.proquest.com.ezproxy.library.uq.edu.au/docview/302759626

Bevir, M. (1999). Foucault and critique: Deploying agency against autonomy. *Political Theory*, 27(1), 65–84.

Bohm, D. (1980). *Wholeness and the implicate order* (2nd edn). London: Routledge & Kegan Paul.

Bohm, D. (1987). *Unfolding meaning: A weekend of dialogue*. London: Routledge.

Bohm, D. (1994). *Thought as a system*. London: Routledge. Retrieved fromhttps://s3.amazonaws.com/arena-attachments/2223192/ee192aafe12e541be6b3262b5f1939a1.pdf

Bohm, D. (2004a). *On creativity*. Routledge Classics: London & New York.

Bohm, D. (2004b). *On dialogue*. Routledge Classics: London & New York.

Bohm, D. (2005). *The essential David Bohm*. L. Nichol (Ed.). Taylor & Francis e-Library. Retrieved from http://cspeech.ucd.ie/Fred/docs/Bohm_2005_.pdf

Bohm, D. (2006). *Unfolding meaning: A weekend of dialogue*. London: Routledge.

Bohm, D. & Peat, F.D. (2010). *Science, order, and creativity*. Taylor & Francis e-Library. Retrieved from file: ///C:/Users/nadir/Downloads/epdf.pub_complete-series-bundle-rc-science-order-and-creati.pdf

Brown, B. & Cousins, M. (1986). The linguistic fault: The case of Foucault's archaeology. In M. Gane (Ed.), *Towards a critique of Foucault* (pp. 33–60). London: Routledge.

Bucholtz, M. (2001). Reflexivity and critique in discourse analysis. *Critique of Anthropology*, 21(2), 165–183.

Burchell, G. (2006). Liberal government and techniques of the self. *Economy and Society*, 22(3), 267–282.

Carruthers, B.G. & Stinchcombe, A.L. (1999). The social structure of liquidity: Flexibility markets and states. *Theory and Society*, 28(3), 353–382.

Chan, R. (2014, 11 February). Income + wealth inequality = More trouble for society. *The Straits Times*. Retrieved from www.straitstimes.com/singapore/income-wealth-inequality-more-trouble-for-society

Channel NewsAsia. (2016, 27 January). MPs call for rethink of streaming, specialist schools, emphasis on exams. Retrieved from: https://www.channelnewsasia.com/news/singapore/mps-call-for-rethink-of-streaming-specialist-schools-emphasis-on-8209648

Chia, Y.T. (2011). The loss of the 'World-Soul'? Education, culture and the making of the Singapore developmental state, 1955–2004 (doctoral dissertation). University of Toronto, Canada. Retrieved from http://search.proquest.com.ezproxy.library.uq.edu.au/docview/919571969

Chilton, P. (1996). *Security metaphors: Cold war discourse from containment to common house*. New York: Peter Lang.

Chomsky, N. (2013). *On anarchism*. New York: New Press.

Collins, J. (2000). Bernstein, Bourdieu and the new literacy studies. *Linguistics and Education*, 11(1), 65–78.

Davidson, A.I. (1986). Archaeology, genealogy, ethics. In D.C. Hoy (Ed.), *Foucault: A critical reader* (pp. 221–233). Oxford: Blackwell.

Davidson, A.I. (2005). Ethics as ascetics: Foucault, the history of ethics, and ancient thought. In G. Gutting (Ed.), *The Cambridge companion to Foucault*. 2nd edn (pp. 115–140). Cambridge: Cambridge University Press.

Davie, S. (2019, 6 March). Subject-based banding to replace streaming in schools. *The Straits Times*. Retrieved from https://www.straitstimes.com/singapore/education/subject-based-banding-to-replace-streaming-in-schools

Dopfer, K., Foster, J. & Potts, J. (2004). Micro-meso-macro. *Journal of Evolutionary Economics*, 14(3), 263–279.

Dr Goh pinpoints the three real causes of trouble in the system. (1979, 28 March). *The Straits Times*. Retrieved from http://eresources.nlb.gov.sg/newspapers/Digitised/Article/straitstimes19790328-1.2.43.aspx

Dreyfus, H.L. & Rabinow, P. (1983). *Michel Foucault: Beyond structuralism and hermeneutics. Second edition with an afterword by and an interview with Michel Foucault*. Chicago: University of Chicago Press.

Edelman, M. (1995). *From art to politics: How artistic creations shape political conceptions*. Chicago: University of Chicago Press.

Edwards, R., Nicoll, K. & Tait, A. (1999). Migrating metaphors: The globalization of flexibility in policy. *Education Policy*, 14(6), 619–630.

Fairclough, I. & Fairclough, N. (2012). *Political discourse analysis: A method for advanced students*. London: Routledge.

Fairclough, N. (1992). *Discourse and social change*. Cambridge: Polity Press.

Fairclough, N. (1993). Critical discourse analysis and the marketization of public discourse: The universities. *Discourse and Society*, 4(2), 133–168.

Fairclough, N. (1995). *Critical discourse analysis: Papers in the critical study of language*. Harlow: Longman.

Fairclough, N. (1999). Global capitalism and critical awareness of language. *Language Awareness*, 8(2), 71–83.

Fairclough, N. (2000a). *New Labour, new language?*London: Routledge.

Fairclough, N. (2000b). Language and neo-liberalism. *Discourse and Society*, 11(2), 147–148.

Fairclough, N. (2001). *Language and power* (2nd edn). Harlow: Longman.

Fairclough, N. (2003). *Analysing discourse: Textual analysis for social research*. London: Routledge.

Fairclough, N. (2005). Discourse in processes of social change: 'Transition' in Central and Eastern Europe. *British and American Studies*, 11, 9–34.

Fairclough, N. (2006a). *Metapragmatics, hidden assumptions, and moral economy*. Retrieved from www.academia.edu/3778294/Metapragmatics_hidden_assumptions_and_moral_economy_2006_

Fairclough, N. (2006b). *Language and globalization*. New York: Routledge.

Fairclough, N. (2009). Language and globalization. *Semiotica 2009* (173), 317–342.

Fairclough, N. (2010). *Critical discourse analysis: Critical study of language* (2nd edn). Harlow: Longman.

Fairclough, N. (2014). What is CDA? Language and power twenty-five years on. Retrieved from https://www.academia.edu/8429277/What_is_CDA_Language_and_Power_twenty-five_years_on

Fairclough, N. & Graham, P. (2002). Marx as a critical discourse analyst: The genesis of a critical method and its relevance to the critique of global capital. *Sociolinguistics Studies*, 3(1), 1–56. Retrieved from file: ///C:/Users/nadir/Downloads/graham__29764%20(1).pdf

Fairclough, N., Graham, P., Lemke, J.L. & Wodak, R. (2004). Introduction. *Critical Discourse Studies*, 1(1), 1–6.

Falk, I. (1994). The making of policy: Media discourse conversations. *Discourse: Studies in the Cultural Politics of Education*, 15(2), 1–12.

Feder, E.K. (2011). Power/knowledge. In D. Taylor (Ed.), *Michel Foucault: Key concepts* (pp. 55–68). Durham: Acumen.

Fong, L. (1979, 31 March). All 'ayes' for Goh report: Two amendments accepted. *The Straits Times*. Retrieved from http://eresources.nlb.gov.sg/newspapers/Digitised/Article/straitstimes19790331-1.2.5.aspx

Foucault, M. (1967). *Madness and civilization: A history of insanity in the Age of Reason* (R. Howard, Trans.). London: Tavistock.

Foucault, M. (1972). *The archaeology of knowledge; and The discourse on language*. New York: Pantheon Monographs.

Foucault, M. (1973). *The order of things: An archaeology of the human sciences*. New York: Vintage Monographs.

Foucault, M. (1977). *Discipline and punish: The birth of the prison* (A. Sheridan, Trans.). London: Allen Lane.

Foucault, M. (1980). *Power/knowledge: Selected interviews and other writings 1972–1977*. C. Gordon, Ed. (C. Gordon, L. Marshall, J.K. Mepham & K. Soper, Trans.). Brighton: Harvester Press.

Foucault, M. (1981a). *The history of sexuality. An introduction* (Vol. 1). (R. Hurley, Trans.). Harmondsworth: Penguin.

Foucault, M. (1981b). *The history of sexuality. The use of pleasure* (Vol. 2). (R. Hurley, Trans.). Harmondsworth: Penguin.

Foucault, M. (1981c). *The history of sexuality: The care of the self* (Vol. 3). (R. Hurley, Trans.). Harmondsworth: Penguin.

Foucault, M. (1982a). The subject and power. *Critical Inquiry*, 8(4), 777–795.

Foucault, M. (1982b). *This is not a pipe* (J. Harkness, Trans. and Ed.). Berkeley: University of California Press. Retrieved from http://monoskop.org/images/9/99/Foucault_Michel_This_Is_Not_a_Pipe.pdf

Foucault, M. (1984a). The ethic of the care for the self as a practice of freedom. An interview with Michael Foucault. (J.D. Gauthier, Trans.). *Philosophy and Social Criticism*, 12 (2–3), 112–131.

Foucault, M. (1984b). Foucault. Retrieved from http://foucault.info/foucault/biography.html

Foucault, M. (1986). *The Foucault reader*. P. Rabinow (Ed.). Harmondsworth: Penguin.

Foucault, M. (1991a). Questions of method. In G. Burchell, C. Gordon & P. Miller (Eds.), *The Foucault effect: Studies in governmentality: With two lectures and an interview with Michel Foucault* (pp. 73–86). Chicago: University of Chicago Press.

Foucault, M. (1991b). Politics and the study of discourse. In G. Burchell, C. Gordon & P. Miller (Eds.), *The Foucault effect: Studies in governmentality: With two lectures and an interview with Michel Foucault* (pp. 53–72). Chicago: University of Chicago Press.

Foucault, M. (1991c). Governmentality. In G. Burchell, C. Gordon & P. Miller (Eds.), *The Foucault effect: Studies in governmentality: With two lectures and an interview with Michel Foucault* (pp. 87–104). Chicago: University of Chicago Press.

Foucault, M. (1994). On the genealogy of ethics: An overview of work in progress. In H. Dreyfus & P. Rabinow (Eds.), *Michel Foucault: Beyond structuralism and hermeneutics* (pp. 253–280). Chicago: University of Chicago Press.

Foucault, M. (1995). *Discipline and punish: The birth of the prison* (2nd edn). (A. Sheridan, Trans.). New York: Vintage.

Foucault, M. (1997). *Ethics: Subjectivity and truth*. New York: New Press.

Foucault, M. (1998). *Essential works of Foucault, 1959–1989, Volume 1: Ethics: Subjectivity and truth*. New York: New Press.

Foucault, M. (2001). *The hermeneutics of the subject: Lectures at the Collège de France, 1981–1982*. [L'hermeneutique du sujet. Cours au Collège de France, 1981–1982]. Paris: Gallimard Seuil.

Foucault, M. (2002). *Archaeology of knowledge*. New York: Routledge.

Foucault, M. (2003). *The essential Foucault: Selections from essential works of Foucault, 1954–1984*. P. Rabinow & N. Rose (Eds.). New York: New Press.

Foucault, M. (2005). The discourse on language and 'Truth and Power'. In J. Medina & W. David (Eds.), *Truth: Engagements across philosophical traditions. Introduction* (pp. 315–335). Oxford: Blackwell.

Fox, M. (2002, 25 January). Michael Young, 86, scholar, coined, mocked 'meritocracy'. *New York Times*. Retrieved from https://www.nytimes.com/2002/01/25/world/michael-young-86-scholar-coined-mocked-meritocracy.html

Fowler, R. (1991). *Language in the news: Discourse and ideology in the press*. London: Routledge.

Fraser, N. (1981). Foucault on modern power: Empirical insights and normative conclusions. *PRAXIS International* (3), 272–287.

Fraser, N. (1995). From redistribution to recognition? Dilemmas of justice in a 'post-socialist' age. *New Left Review* (212), 68–93.

Gale, T. (2001). Critical policy sociology: Historiography, archaeology and genealogy as methods of policy analysis. *Journal of Education policy*, 16(5), 379–393.

Garcia-Perez, D. (2012). Dismantling contemporary deficit thinking: Educational thought and practice [Review of R.R. Valencia, *Dismantling contemporary deficit thinking: Educational thought and practice*], *International Journal of Educational Psychology*, 1(3), 278–279.

Garrity, Z. (2010). Discourse analysis, Foucault and social work research: Identifying some methodological complexities. *Journal of Social Work*, 10(2), 193–210.

Gaventa, J. (2003). Foucault: Power is everywhere. Retrieved from www.powercube.net/other-forms-of-power/foucault-power-is-everywhere/

General information. (n.d.). Retrieved from https://www.seab.gov.sg/pages/nationalExaminations/PSLE/general_information.asp

Goh and his team get down to the task. (1978, 20 August). *The Straits Times*. Retrieved from http://eresources.nlb.gov.sg/newspapers/Digitised/Article/straitstimes19780820-1.2.3.aspx

Goh, C.T. (2016). Singapore faces income inequality, social cohesion challenges. *Channel NewsAsia*, 21 April 2015. Accessed 15 June 2016. www.channelnewsasia.com/news/singapore/singapore-faces-income/2718188.html

Goh, C.B. & Gopinathan, S. (2008). The development of education in Singapore since 1965. In S.K. Lee, C.B. Goh, B. Fredriksen & J.P. Tan (Eds.), *Toward a better future: Education and training for economic development in Singapore since 1965* (pp. 12–39). Washington, DC: The World Bank.

Gopinathan, S. (1996). Globalisation, the state and education policy in Singapore. *Asia Pacific Journal of Education*, 16(1), 74–87.

Gopinathan, S. (1999). Preparing for the next rung: Economic restructuring and educational reform in Singapore. *Journal of Education and Work*, 12(3), 295–308.

Gopinathan, S. (2006). Preparing for the next rung: Economic restructuring and educational reform in Singapore. *Journal of Education and Work*, 12(3), 296–308.

Gopinathan, S. (2007). Globalisation, the Singapore developmental state and education policy: A thesis revisited. *Globalisation, Societies and Education*, 5(1), 53–70.

Graham, L.J. (2011). The product of text and 'Other' statements: Discourse analysis and the critical use of Foucault. *Educational Philosophy and Theory*, 43(6), 663–674.

Graham, P. & Paulsen, N. (2002). Third-sector discourses and the future of (un)employment: Skilled labour, new technologies and the meaning of work. *Text*, 22(3), 443–467.

Graham, P. (1999). Critical systems theory: A political economy of language, thought, and technology. *Communication Research*, 26(4), 482–507.

Graham, P. (2000). Hypercapitalism: A political economy of informational idealism. *New media and Society*, 2(2), 131–156.

Graham, P. (2001a). Space: Irrealis objects in technology policy and their role in a new political economy. *Discourse and Society*, 12(6), 761–788.

Graham, P. (2001b). Hypercapitalism: An investigation into the relationship between language, new media, and social perceptions of value (doctoral dissertation). Queensland University of Technology. Australia.

Graham, P. (2002). Predication and propagation: A method for analysing evaluative meanings in technology policy. *Text* 22(2), 227–268.

Graham, P. (2005). Analysing policy values in a knowledge economy. In D. Rooney, G. Hearn & A. Ninan (Eds.), *Handmonograph on the knowledge economy* (pp. 118–128). Northampton: Edward Elgar.

Graham, P. (2007). Critical discourse analysis and evaluative meaning: Interdisciplinary as a critical turn. In R. Wodak & W. Gilbert (Eds.), *Critical discourse analysis: Theory and interdisciplinarity* (pp. 110–129). London: Palgrave Macmillan.

Graham, P. & Luke, A. (2011). Critical discourse analysis and political economy of communication: Understanding the new corporate order. *Cultural Politics*, 7(1), 103–132.

Graham, P. (2018). Ethics in critical discourse analysis. *Critical Discourse Studies*, 15(2), 186–203.

Hall, S. (2001). The work of representation. In M. Wetherell, S. Taylor & S.J. Yates (Eds.), *Discourse theory and practice: A reader* (pp. 72–81). London: Sage.

Halliday, M.A.K. (1994). *An introduction to functional grammar* (2nd edn). London: Arnold.

Hamilton, M. & Pitt, K. (2011). Changing policy discourses: Constructing literacy inequalities. *International Journal of Educational Development*, 31(6), 596–605.

Hao, X. (1996). The press and public trust: The case of Singapore. *Asian Journal of Communication*, 6(1), 111–123.

Hayek, F.A. (2007). *The road to serfdom*. London: University of Chicago Press.

Hegel, G.W.F. (1970). *On art, religion, philosophy: Introductory lectures to the realm of the absolute spirit*. J.G. Gray (Ed.). New York: Harper and Row.

Heidegger, M. (1961). On the essence of truth. Retrieved from http://aphelis.net/wp-content/uploads/2011/02/Martin-Heidegger-On-the-Essence-of-Truth.pdf

Heidegger, M. (2003a). The phenomenological method of the investigation (1972). (J. Stambaugh, Trans.). In Manfred Stassen (Ed.), *Philosophical and political writings* (pp. 57–69). New York: Continuum.

Heidegger, M. (2003b). Philosophy of language and poetry: Understanding, interpretation, discourse, language, idle talk (1927) . (J. Stambaugh, Trans.). In Manfred Stassen (Ed.), *Philosophical and political writings* (pp. 236–264). New York: Continuum.

Heidegger, M. (2003c). The question of being. (Letter to Ernst Junger 'Concerning "The Line"') (1955). (W. Kluback & J.T. Wilde, Trans.). In Manfred Stassen (Ed.), *Philosophical and political writings* (pp 120–151). New York: Continuum.

Heidegger, M. (2005). On the essence of truth. In J. Medina & W. David (Eds.), *Truth: Engagements across philosophical traditions. Introduction* (pp. 235–260). Oxford: Blackwell.

Heng, S.K. (2012). Prepared remarks for Mr Heng Swee Keat, Minister for Education, on "Education for competitiveness and growth" at the Singapore conference in Washington D.C., USA, on Wednesday, 8 February 2012. Retrieved from www.moe.gov.sg/media/speeches/2012/02/08/speech-by-mr-heng-swee-keat-at-the-singapore-conference-washington-dc-usa.php.

Heng, S.K. (2014). FY 2014 Committee of Supply debate: 1st reply by Mr Heng Swee Keat, Minister for Education: Bringing out the best in every child. Retrieved from www.moe.gov.sg/media/speeches/2014/03/07/first-reply-by-mr-heng-swee-keat-bringing-out-the-best-in-every-child.php

Hume, D. (1739). *A treatise of human nature: Being An attempt to introduce the experimental method of reasoning into moral subjects*. Retrieved from https://people.rit.edu/wlrgsh/HumeTreatise.pdf

Ismail, M. & Tan, A.L. (2005). *Voices from the normal technical world: An ethnographic study of low-track students in Singapore*. Proceedings of the Redesigning Pedagogy: Research, Policy, Practice conference, Singapore, May–June 2005. https://repository.nie.edu.sg/bitstream/10497/214/1/2005v4.pdf

Jessop, B. (2004). Critical semiotic analysis and cultural political economy. *Critical Discourse Studies*, 1(2), 159–174.

Kincheloe, J.L. (2001). Describing the bricolage: Conceptualizing a new rigour in qualitative research. *Qualitative Inquiry*, 7(6), 679–692.

Klein, K.J. & Kozlowski, S.W.J. (2000). From micro to meso: Critical steps in conceptualizing and conducting multilevel research. *Organizational Research Methods*, 3(3), 211–236.

Krishnamurti, J. (1978a). *The impossible question*. New York: Penguin.

Krishnamurti, J. (1978b). *Truth and actuality*. San Francisco: Harper & Row.

Krishnamurti, J. (2005). *Inward revolution: Bringing about radical change in the world*. R. Mckoy (Ed.). Boston: Shambhala.

Krishnamurti, J. & Bohm, D. (2014). *The ending of time: Where philosophy and physics meet*. New York: HarperCollins.

Lamont, Michèle (2012). Toward a comparative sociology of valuation and evaluation. *Annual Review of Sociology*, 38(21), 201–221.

Lee, K.Y. (2011). *Hard truths to keep Singapore going*. Singapore: Singapore Press Holdings.

Lee, N. (2004). Foreword. In D. Bohm, *On dialogue* (pp. xv–xxvii). Routledge Classics. London and New York: Routledge.

Lee, S.K., Goh, C.B., Fredriksen, B. & Tan, J.P. (Eds.) (2008). *Toward a better future: Education and training for economic development in Singapore since 1965* (pp. 39–68). Washington DC: The World Bank.

Lemke, J.L. (1995). *Textual politics: Discourse and social dynamics*. London: Taylor & Francis.

Lemke, J.L. (1998). Resources for attitudinal meaning: Evaluative orientations in text semantics. *Functions of Language*, 5(1), 33–56.

Lemke, T. (2001). The birth of 'bio-politics': Michel Foucault's lecture at the Collège de France on neo-liberal governmentality. *Economy and Society*, 30(2), 190–207.

Liasidou, A. (2008). Critical discourse analysis and inclusive educational policies: The power to exclude. *Journal of Education Policy*, 23(5), 483–500.

Lim, L. (2013). Meritocracy, elitism, and egalitarianism: A preliminary and provisional assessment of Singapore's primary education review. *Asia Pacific Journal of Education*, 33(1), 1–14.

Loy, D.R. (1997). The religion of the market. *Journal of the American Academy of Religion*, 65(2), 275–290.

Luke, A. (1997). Critical discourse analysis. In L. Saha (Ed.), *International encyclopaedia of the sociology of education* (pp. 50–57). Oxford: Elsevier.

Luke, A. (2002). Beyond science and ideology critique: Developments in critical discourse analysis. *Annual Review of Applied Linguistics*, 22, 96–110.

Luke, A. (2009). Critical realism, policy, and educational research. In K. Ercikan & W.M. Roth (Eds.), *Generalizing from educational research: Beyond qualitative and quantitative polarization* (pp. 173–200). New York: Routledge.

Markula, P. (2004). 'Tuning into one's self': Foucault's technologies of the self and mindful fitness. *Sociology of Sport Journal*, 21(3), 302–321.

Marshall, J. (1996). *Michel Foucault: Personal autonomy and education*. London: Kluwer.

Martin, J.R. & Rose, D. (2007). *Working with discourse: Meaning beyond the class* (2nd edn). New York: Continuum.

Martin, J.T. (2000). Beyond exchange: Appraisal systems in English. In S. Hunston & G. Thompson (Eds.), *Evaluation in text: Authorial stance and the construction of discourse* (pp. 142–175). New York: Oxford University Press.

Marx, K. (1976). *Capital: A critique of political economy*. Vol. I (B. Fowkes, Trans.). London: Penguin.

Maté, G. (2012, 12 August). What promotes positive health. Retrieved from https://www.youtube.com/watch?v=rYbeyU3pQvI

Maté, G. (2019, 14 June). *Dr Gabor Maté on childhood trauma, the real cause of anxiety, our 'insane' culture and Ayahuasca*. Retrieved from https://www.youtube.com/watch?v=e7pV0IPWUlI

Mautner, G. (2009). Checks and balances: How corpus linguistics can contribute to CDA. In R. Wodak and M. Meyer (Eds.), *Methods of critical discourse analysis* (2nd edn) (pp. 122–143). Los Angeles: Sage.

Mauzy, D.K. & Milne, R.S. (2002). *Singapore politics under the People's Action Party*. London: Routledge.

May, T. (1993). *Between genealogy and epistemology: Psychology, politics, and knowledge in the thought of Michel Foucault*. University Park PA: Pennsylvania State University Press.

Mckee, K. (2009). Post-Foucauldian governmentality: What does it offer critical social policy analysis? *Critical Social Policy*, 29(3), 465–486.

McKerrow, R. (n.d.). *Foucault and surrealism of truth*. Retrieved from www.ohio.edu/People/mckerrow/foucault.pdf

Medina, J. & Wood, D. (Eds.) (2005). *Truth: Engagements across philosophical traditions. Introduction*. Oxford: Blackwell.

MOE (Ministry of Education). (1987). *Towards excellence in schools. A report submitted to the Ministry for Education*. Singapore: Ministry of Education.

MOE (Ministry of Education). (1979a). *Report on the Ministry of Education 1978, prepared by Goh Keng Swee and the Education Study Team*. Singapore: Singapore National Printers.

MOE (Ministry of Education). (1979b). *Curriculum development in Singapore. A Brief Review 1979*, created by Robert W. Morris. Singapore: Ministry of Education.

MOE (Ministry of Education). (1991a). *Improving primary school education: Report of the Review Committee*. Singapore: Ministry of Education.

MOE (Ministry of Education). (1991b). *Upgrading vocational training/Vocational and Industrial Training Board*. Singapore: The Board.

MOE (Ministry of Education). (1997). *Performance by ethnic group*. Retrieved from www.moe.gov.sg/media/press/1997/pr02397.htm

MOE (Ministry of Education). (2002). *Report of the Junior College/Upper Secondary Education Review Committee*. Retrieved from http://www3.moe.edu.sg/jcreview/JC_Upp_Sec_Review_Report.pdf

MOE (Ministry of Education). (2006). *Report of the Polytechnic-School Review Committee*. Retrieved from http://www3.moe.edu.sg/corporate/pdf/psrc-report.pdf

MOE (Ministry of Education). (2008a). *Report of the Committee on the Expansion of the University Sector. Greater choice, more room to excel: Final report*. Retrieved from www.moe.gov.sg/media/press/files/2008/08/ceus-final-report-and-exec-summary.pdf

MOE (Ministry of Education). (2008b). Enhanced programmes by Special Assistance Plan schools to enrich students' learning of Chinese language and values. Retrieved from www.moe.gov.sg/media/press/2008/02/enhanced-programmes-by-special.php#annex-b.

MOE (Ministry of Education). (2012a). *Report of the Committee on University Education Pathways Beyond 2015 (CUEP). Greater diversity, more opportunities: Final report. August 2012*. Retrieved from www.moe.gov.sg/media/press/files/2012/08/cuep-report-greater-diversity-more-opportunities.pdf.

MOE (Ministry of Education). (2012b). Education in Singapore. Retrieved from www.moe.edu.sg/about/files/moe-corporate-brochure.pdf

MOE (Ministry of Education). (2012c). Press Release: Performance by ethnic group in national examinations 2002–2011. Retrieved from www.moe.gov.sg/media/press/2012/10/performance-by-ethnic-group-in.php

Normal course curriculum (n.d.). Retrieved from www.moe.gov.sg/education/secondary/normal/

Mulderrig, J. (2003). Consuming education: A critical discourse analysis of social actors in New Labour's education policy. *Journal of Critical Education Policy Studies*, 1(1), 96–123.

Mulderrig, J. (2007). Textual strategies of representation and legitimation in New Labour policy discourse. In A. Green, G. Rikowski & H. Raduntz (Eds.), *Renewing dialogues in Marxism and education: Openings* (pp. 135–150). Basingstoke: Palgrave Macmillan.

Mulderrig, J. (2008). Using keywords analysis in CDA: Evolving discourses of the knowledge economy in education. In B. Jessop, N. Fairclough & R. Wodak (Eds.), *Education and the knowledge-based economy in Europe* (pp. 149–170). Rotterdam: Sense Publishers.

Mulderrig, J. (2009). *The language of education policy: From Thatcher to Blair*. Saarbrucken, Germany: VDM Verlag.

Mulderrig, J. (2011a). The grammar of governance. *Critical Discourse Studies*, 8(1), 45–68.

Mulderrig, J. (2011b). Manufacturing consent: A corpus-based critical discourse analysis of New Labour's educational governance. *Educational Philosophy and Theory*, 43(6), 562–578.

Mulderrig, J. (2012). The hegemony of inclusion: A corpus-based critical discourse analysis of deixis in education policy. *Discourse and Society*, 23(6), 701–728.

Mulderrig, J. (2014). 'Enabling' participatory governance in education: A corpus-based critical analysis of policy in the United Kingdom. In P. Smyers, D. Bridges, N. Burbules & M. Griffiths (Eds.), *International handbook of interpretation in educational research*. Springer International Handbooks of Education, 1 (pp. 441–470). Dordrecht: Springer. ISBN ISBN: 9789401792813.

Nasr, S.H. (1996). Mulla Sadra: His teachings. In S.H. Nasr & O. Leaman (Eds.), *History of Islamic philosophy* (pp. 643–662). London: Routledge.

Ng, D.F.S. (2008c). Strategic management of educational development in Singapore (1965–2005). In S.K. Lee, C.B. Goh, B. Fredriksen & J.P. Tan (Eds.), *Toward a better future: Education and training for economic development in Singapore since 1965* (pp. 39–68). Washington DC: The World Bank.

Ng, E.H. (2008). Educating the next generation. Speech by Dr Ng Eng Hen, Minister for Education and Second Minister for Defence, at the 4th Anniversary Public Lecture at the Lee Kuan Yew School of Public Policy, 14 August. Retrieved from www.moe.gov.sg/media/speeches/2008/08/14/speech-by-dr-ng-eng-hen-at-the-10.php

Ng, I.Y.H. (2011). Growing worry of social mobility. *The Straits Times Review*, p. A25. Retrieved from http://newshub.nus.edu.sg/news/1102/PDF/IMMOBILITY-st-16feb-pA25.pdf

Ng, I.Y.H. (2013). The political economy of intergenerational income mobility in Singapore. *International Journal of Social Welfare*, 22, 207–218.

Ng, P.T. (2008b). The phases and paradoxes of educational quality assurance. *Quality Assurance in Education*, 16(2), 112–125.

Nicoll, K. (1998). 'Fixing' the 'Facts': Flexible learning as policy intervention. *Higher Education Research and Development*, 17(3), 291–304.

Nicoll, K. (2006). *Flexibility and lifelong learning: Policy, discourse and politics*. New York: Routledge.

Nietzsche, F. (1909). *Human, all too human: A monograph for free spirits*. (H. Zimmern, Trans.). London: Allen & Unwin.

Nietzsche, F. (1924). *The antichrist.* (H.L. Mencken, Trans.). New York: Vail-Ballou Press.

Nietzsche, F. (1967a). *The will to power.* (W. Kaufmann & R.J. Hollingdale, Trans.). New York: Random House.

Nietzsche, F. (1967b). *On the genealogy of morals.* [and] *Ecce homo.* (W. Kaufmann & R.J. Hollingdale, Trans.). New York: Vintage.

Nietzsche, F. (1974). *The gay science: With a prelude in rhymes and an appendix of songs.* (W. Kaufmann, Trans.). New York: Random House.

Nietzsche, F. (1979). On truth and lies in the nonmoral sense. In D. Breazeale (Ed.), *Philosophy and truth: Selections from Nietzsche's notemonographs of the early 1870s* (pp. 79–97). Atlantic Highlands, NJ: Humanities Press.

Nietzsche, F. (1989). *Beyond good and evil.* New York: Random House.

Oakes, J. (2005). *Keeping track: How schools structure inequality.* New Haven, CT: Yale University Press.

OECD. (2011). *Perspectives on Global Development 2012: Social cohesion in a shifting world.* Paris: OECD Publishing. doi:10.1787/persp_glob_dev-2012-en

Olssen, M. (2006). Understanding the mechanisms of neo-liberal control: Lifelong learning, flexibility and knowledge capitalism. *International Journal of Lifelong Education*, 25 (3), 213–230.

Ong, Y.K. (2018a). *MOE FY2018 Committee of Supply debate response by Minister for Education (Higher Education and Skills) on 5 March 2018.* Retrieved from https://www.moe.gov.sg/news/speeches/moe-fy2018-committee-of-supply-debate-response-by-minister-for-education-higher-education-and-skills–mr-ong-ye-kung

Ong, Y.K. (2018b). Opening address by Mr Ong Ye Kung, Minister for Education, at the Schools Work Plan Seminar on 28 September 2018. Retrieved from https://www.moe.gov. sg/news/speeches/opening-address-by-mr-ong-ye-kung-minister-for-education-at-the-schools-work-plan-seminar

Ong, Y.K. (2019). Speech by Minister for Education Mr Ong Ye Kung, at the 2019 Raffles Institution Founder's Day, on 27 July 2019. Retrieved 20 August 2019 from https://www.moe.gov.sg/news/speeches/speech-by-minister-for-education-mr-ong-ye-kung-at-the-2019-raffles-institution-founders-day

Pennycook, A. (2001). *Critical applied linguistics: A critical introduction.* Mahwah, NJ: Lawrence Erlbaum.

Peters, S.J. (2007). 'Education for all?' A historical analysis of international inclusive education policy and individuals with disabilities. *Journal of Disability Policy Studies*, 18(2), 98–108.

Poole, B. (2010). Commitment and criticality: Fairclough's Critical Discourse Analysis evaluated. *International Journal of Applied Linguistics*, 20(2), 137–155.

Quah, J.S.T. (1984). The public policy-making process in Singapore. *Asian Journal of Public Administration*, 6(2), 108–126.

Rahim, L.Z. (1998). *The Singapore dilemma: The political and educational marginality of the Malay community.* New York: Oxford University Press.

Rajah, I. (2018). Parliamentary motion 'Education For Our Future' response by 2nd Minister for Education, Ms Indranee Rajah on 11 July 2018. Retrieved 14 October 2019 from https://www.moe.gov.sg/news/speeches/parliamentary-motion-education-for-our-future-response-by-2nd-minister-for-education-ms-indranee-rajah

Rajah, I. (2019). NUS Social Service Research Centre conference 'Working with Low-Income Families through the Life Course: Challenges to Social Services'. Keynote speech by second Minister for Education, Ms Indranee Rajah, on 18 July 2019. Retrieved 20 August 2019 from https://www.moe.gov.sg/news/speeches/nus-social-service-research-centre-confer

ence-working-with-low-income-families-through-the-life-course-challenges-to-social-services-keynote-speech-by-second-minister-for-education-ms-indranee-rajah

Raman, P.M. (1978, 17 August). New team to study education. Group to be led by Dr. Goh. *The Straits Times*. Retrieved from http://eresources.nlb.gov.sg/newspapers/Digitised/Article/straitstimes19780817-1.2.3.aspx

Rawlinson, M.C. (1987). Foucault's strategy: Knowledge, power, and the specificity of truth. *Journal of Medicine and Philosophy*, 12(4), 371–395.

Rogers, R. (2004a). Critical approaches to discourse analysis in educational research. In R. Rogers (Ed.), *An introduction to critical discourse analysis in education* (pp. 1–20). Mahwah, NJ: Lawrence Erlbaum Associates.

Rogers, R. (2004b). A critical discourse analysis of literate identities across contexts: Alignment and conflict. In R. Rogers (Ed.), *An introduction to critical discourse analysis in education* (pp. 51–78). Mahwah, NJ: Lawrence Erlbaum Associates.

Rogers, R., Malancharuvil-Berkes, E.; Mosley, M., Hui, D. & Joseph, G.O. (2005). Critical discourse analysis in education: A review of the literature. *Review of Educational Research*, 75(3), 365–416.

Rooney, D. (2005). Knowledge, economy, technology and society: The politics of discourse . *Telematics and Informatics*, 22(4), 405–422.

Rouse, J. (2005). Power/knowledge. In G. Gutting (Ed.), *The Cambridge companion to Foucault* (2nd edn) (pp. 95–122). New York and Cambridge: Cambridge University Press.

Saarinen, T. (2008). Position of text and discourse analysis in higher education policy research. *Studies in Higher Education*, 33(6), 719–728.

Sandberg, J. & Alvesson, M. (2011). Ways of constructing research questions: Gap-spotting or problematization? *Oragnization*, 18(1), 23–44.

Sartre, J-P. (1985). *Existentialism and human emotions*. New York: Citadel Press.

Satz, D. (2007). Equality, adequacy, and education for citizenship. *Ethics*, 117(4), 623–648.

Scheurich, J.J. (1997). *Research method in the postmodern*. Brighton: Falmer Press.

Schopenhauer, A. (1907). *The world as will and idea* (Vol. 2). (R.B. Haldane & J. Kemp, Trans.). London: Kegan Paul, Trench, Trubner.

Secondary education (n.d.) Retrieved from www.moe.gov.sg/education/secondary/

Sen, A. (1992). *Inequality reexamined*. New York: Russell Sage Foundation.

Sen, A. (2000). Merit and justice. In K. Arrow, S. Bowles & S. Durlauf (Eds.), *Meritocracy and economic inequality* (pp. 5–16). Princeton, NJ: Princeton University Press. Retrieved 8 August from http://assets.press.princeton.edu/chapters/s6818.pdf

Shanmugaratnam, T. (2003). Speech by Mr Tharman Shanmugaratnam. Acting Minister for Education, at the MOE work plan seminar at Ngee Ann Polytechnic on Thursday, 2 October 2003: The next phase in education: Innovation and Enterprise. Retrieved from www.moe.gov.sg/media/speeches/2003/sp20031002.htm

Shanmugaratnam, T. (2004). Schools: Refinements to primary school streaming; The Normal Course. Retrieved from www.moe.gov.sg/media/speeches/2004/sp20040318.htm

Shanmugaratnam, T. (2006). Speech by Mr Tharman Shanmugaratnam. Minister for Education, at the MOE work plan seminar 2006, on Thursday, 28 September 2006 at 10.00 am at the Ngee Ann Polytechnic convention centre: More support for school-based initiatives. Ground-up initiatives, top-down support. Retrieved from www.moe.gov.sg/media/speeches/2006/sp20060928_print.htm

Sharpe, L. & Gopinathan, S. (2002). After effectiveness: New directions in the Singapore school system? *Journal of Education Policy, 17*(2), 151–166.

Smith, A. (1759 [2010]). *The theory of moral sentiments.* Retrieved from www.earlymoderntexts.com/authors/smith

Soon, T.W. (1988). *Singapore's new education system. Education reform for national development.* Singapore: Institute of Southeast Asian Studies.

Springer, S. (2012). Neoliberalism as discourse: Between Foucauldian political economy and Marxian poststructuralism. *Critical Discourse Studies*, 9(2), 133–147.

Tan, K.P. (2008). Meritocracy and elitism in a global city: Ideological shifts in Singapore. *International Political Science Review*, 29(1), 7–27.

Taylor, S. (2004). Researching educational policy and change in 'new times': Using critical discourse analysis. *Journal of Education Policy*, 19(4), 433–451.

Teo, C.H. (2002a). Education system caters to all abilities. *The Straits Times*, 22 May 2002. Retrieved from http://global.factiva.com.ezproxy.library.uq.edu.au/ha/default.aspx

Teo, C.H. (2002b). Meeting different needs. *The Straits Times*, 26 November 2002. Retrieved from http://global.factiva.com.ezproxy.library.uq.edu.au/ha/default.aspx

Thich Nhat Hanh. (2010). *Together we are one: Honouring our diversity, celebrating our connection.* California: Parallax Press.

Thomas, S. (2005). The construction of teacher identities in educational policy documents: A critical discourse analysis. *Melbourne Studies in Education*, 46(2), 25–44.

Thomas, S. (2009). Newspapers on education policy: Constructing an authoritative public voice on education. In R. Fitzgerald & W. Housley (Eds.), *Media policy and interaction* (pp. 205–223). Burlington, VT: Ashgate Publishing.

Thompson, G. & Hunston, S. (2000). *Evaluation: An introduction.* In G. Thompson & S. Hunston (Eds.), *Evaluation in text: Authorial stance and the construction of discourse* (pp. 1–27). Oxford: Oxford University Press.

Trew, T. (1979). 'What the papers say': Linguistic variation and ideological difference. In R. Fowler, B. Hodge, G. Kress & T. Trew (Eds.), *Language and control* (pp. 117–156). London: Routledge.

Valencia, R.R. (2010). *Dismantling contemporary deficit thinking: Educational thought and practice*], *International Journal of Educational Psychology*, 1(3), 278–279.

van Dijk, T.A. (1993). Principles of critical discourse analysis. *Discourse and Society*, 4(2), 249–283.

van Dijk, T.A. (2001). Multidisciplinary CDA: A plea for diversity. In R. Wodak & M. Meyer (Eds.), *Methods of critical discourse analysis* (1st edn) (pp. 95–121). London: Sage.

van Dijk, T.A. (2003). Critical discourse analysis. In D. Schiffrin, D. Tannen & H.E. Hamilton (Eds.), *The handbook of critical discourse analysis* (pp. 352–371). Oxford: Blackwell.

van Leeuwen, T. (1995). Representing social action. *Discourse and Society*, 6(1), 81–106.

van Leeuwen, T. (1996). The representation of social actors. In C.R. Caldas-Coulthard & M. Coulthard (Eds.), *Texts and practices: Readings in critical discourse analysis* (pp. 32–71). London: Routledge.

van Leeuwen, T. (2008). *Discourse and practice: New tools for critical discourse analysis.* New York: Oxford University Press.

Verschueren, J. (1999). *Understanding pragmatics.* New York: Arnold.

Walsh, N.D. (2005). *What God wants: A compelling answer to humanity's biggest question.* New York: Atria.

Walsh, N.D. (2013). *What God said: The 25 core messages of conversations with God that will change your life and the world.* New York: Berkley.

Walshaw, M. (2007). *Working with Foucault in education.* Rotterdam: Sense Publishers.

Watts, A.W. (1951). *The wisdom of insecurity.* New York: Pantheon.

Wodak, R. (1999). Critical discourse analysis at the end of the 20th century. *Research on Language and Social Interaction*, 32(1&2), 185–193.

Wodak, R. (2001). The discourse-historical approach. In R. Wodak & M. Meyer (Eds.), *Methods of critical discourse analysis* (pp. 63–95). London: Sage.

Wong. A. (2000). Keynote address by Dr Aline Wong, Senior Minister of State for Education, Ministry of Education, Singapore, at the International Baccalaureate (IB) Asia-Pacific 16th annual regional conference on curriculum, assessment and cultural equity to be held on Friday, 24 November 2000, at 9.15 am at the Raffles City Convention Centre: Education in a multicultural setting – the Singapore experience. Retrieved from www.moe.gov.sg/media/speeches/2000/sp24112000.htm

Young, M.D. (1958). *The rise of meritocracy*. London: Thames and Hudson.

Zelizer, V.A. (1979). *Morals and markets: The development of life insurance in the United States*. New York: Columbia University Press.

Index

Page numbers in **bold** refer to tables.

Made in the USA
Las Vegas, NV
29 October 2024

a2fd17b7-3bc4-4914-9923-897f95ceb57aR01